Beyond
the
Flower of Life

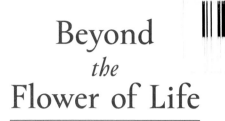

"*Beyond the Flower of Life* gives Maureen St. Germain's unique Practical Mystic perspective on a number of wonders of the new age. She shares the wisdom and joys that she and her students experienced by doing the spiritual work outlined in this book. This new release is updated for a new generation of seekers."

DANNION BRINKLEY, NEW YORK TIMES BESTSELLING AUTHOR OF
SAVED BY THE LIGHT AND COAUTHOR OF *AT PEACE IN THE LIGHT*

"Maureen, with the council of the Archangel Michael, has your highest good in mind in offering this new and updated edition for a new generation. Her goal is to assist you to jump start your own spiritual renaissance. Maureen provides an easy and accurate way to connect with your Higher Self and improve your connection to the Divine. At a challenging time in our evolution, we need this counsel more than ever."

SHARLYN HIDALGO, AUTHOR OF *CELTIC TREE RITUALS*,
THE HEALING POWER OF TREES, CELTIC TREE ORACLE,
AND *NAZMY—LOVE IS MY RELIGION*

"*Beyond the Flower of Life* will open your mind and experiences."

BERNIE SIEGEL, M.D., AUTHOR OF *NO ENDINGS,*
ONLY BEGINNINGS AND *THREE MEN SIX LIVES*

"Maureen's love, skill, and experiences in her spirituality have led her to travel this planet and touch the lives of thousands of students. Her approach to integrating a spiritual life with the physical world has provided many tools to uplift consciousness while grounding practical principles of spirituality in the here and now. Maureen's dedication, adventure, and enthusiasm fill *Beyond the Flower of Life.*"

RONALD L. HOLT, COFOUNDER OF SEED OF LIFE INSTITUTE
AND CREATOR OF QUANTUM NAVIGATION

"I highly recommend this book to anyone at any level."

LYNN ANDREWS, NEW YORK TIMES BESTSELLING
AUTHOR OF THE MEDICINE WOMAN SERIES

"This special edition of *Beyond the Flower of Life* has been revised and updated to bring this classic to a new generation and clarify many questions. Whether you are a MerKaBa meditator, curious about the MerKaBa, or are just looking to improve your spiritual practices, you will benefit from this book."

BOB FRISSELL, AUTHOR OF THE 25TH ANNIVERSARY EDITION OF *NOTHING IN THIS BOOK IS TRUE, BUT IT'S EXACTLY HOW THINGS ARE*

"*Beyond the Flower of Life* is a road map to the new enlightenments that are and will be defining the next human evolutionary trajectory that is happening at this very moment! Maureen J. St. Germain has pre-paved the future into the only place of real power—the NOW—and clearly shows us the layering of invisible energies. Take a ride into the worlds of immeasurable connections and unnamable infinity and truly open up the bridge between human information, factual knowledge, and the amazing intimacy of the eternal cosmos NOW!"

HARRISON KLEIN, AWARD-WINNING PERSONAL GROWTH TRANSFORMATIONALIST AND WEALTH AND BUSINESS GROWTH CONSULTANT

"Maureen St. Germain has done it again! Complete with exercises to help you advance your spiritual practices, I encourage you to read this updated edition. The information is very timely, and you'll likely deepen your practices, further advance your soul, and maintain an open heart."

MARGARET M. (PEG) DONAHUE, FOUNDER OF FENG SHUI CONNECTIONS AND COAUTHOR OF *MONEY IS AN ENERGY GAME*

"Maureen has hit it out of the park once again! The new edition of *Beyond the Flower of Life* assists readers, both novices and adepts alike, to truly grow their meditation practices and have an accurate and clear connection and unification to and with their Higher Selves. This book will also truly assist you to deepen and expand your gifts to humanity, and you will love the tips and practices included! "

LORI ANN SPAGNA, AUTHOR OF *MANIFESTATION MADE EASY*

"Maureen provides many tools that anyone can use to uplift their consciousness while grounding their spirituality in the here and now. Her dedication and enthusiasm is infused throughout this updated edition, meant for a new generation of seekers ready for their next step."

LYSSA ROYAL HOLT, SEMINAR LEADER, CHANNEL, AND AUTHOR OF *GALACTIC HERITAGE CARDS* AND *THE GOLDEN LAKE*

Beyond
the
Flower of Life

Advanced MerKaBa Teachings,
Sacred Geometry,
and the Opening of the Heart

MAUREEN J. ST. GERMAIN

Bear & Company
Rochester, Vermont

Bear & Company
One Park Street
Rochester, Vermont 05767
www.BearandCompanyBooks.com

Text stock is SFI certified

Bear & Company is a division of Inner Traditions International

Cataloging-in-Publication Data for this title is available from the Library of Congress

ISBN 978-1-59143-405-4 (print)
ISBN 978-1-59143-406-1 (ebook)

Printed and bound in the United States by Lake Book Manufacturing, Inc. The text stock is SFI certified. The Sustainable Forestry Initiative® program promotes sustainable forest management.

10 9 8 7 6 5 4 3 2

Text design by Priscilla H. Baker and layout by Virginia Scott Bowman
This book was typeset in Garamond Premier Pro and Gil Sans with Hermann and Museo used as display typefaces

To send correspondence to the author of this book, mail a first-class letter to the author c/o Inner Traditions • Bear & Company, One Park Street, Rochester, VT 05767, and we will forward the communication, or contact the author directly at **maureenstgermain.com**.

✳

This book is dedicated to Archangel Michael. Without his presence in my life as a guide and helper, I would not have written this book. I believe he is the original sponsor of the Flower of Life in this reality. He continually appears in our midst and speaks to many of us personally, including some who are mentioned in this dedication. When I picked up the pen to write this dedication I originally intended to start somewhere else, but Lord Michael came through with this very sincere message of his sponsorship. Thank you, Archangel Michael!

As I prepared to update this classic for its twelfth-year anniversary edition, I realized I had dressed wearing the beautiful royal blue we associate with Archangel Michael. Without a doubt his presence is found throughout this update as well.

The dedication in the original 2009 edition included Flower of Life (FOL) facilitators and the FOL research organization who are still my heroes. They created the network of amazing individuals who brought the original Flower of Life material to life, including, of course, Drunvalo Melchizedek. However they are no longer the only wellspring of this body of knowledge, which now further focuses on Michael. As my understanding has evolved over time, I have come to know this body of knowledge to be a meditator's guide to higher awareness.

Special thanks to my editor, Meghan MacLean, at Inner Traditions who understood what I hope to communicate, and thanks also to their wonderful team.

Last but not least, this book is also dedicated to all the readers who wish to grow their meditation practices and finally have an accurate and clear connection to their Higher Selves. Thank you all. You each have played a significant part in spreading this gift around the world.

Contents

Prologue

This book is intended for use as a supplement to your inner work (i.e., meditation practices) along with the Flower of Life MerKaBa Meditation, or geometric symbol of creation and unity, and with all of sacred geometry. (The term *Flower of Life* has often been interchanged for the actual MerKaBa Meditation as well as the geometric shape.)

If you have been working with any sacred geometry books, including MerKaBa knowledge, you may find this book a wonderful follow-up, but nothing will replace a MerKaBa Classic Workshop (the Original 17-Breath Meditation). The MerKaBa Meditation I teach, as given through Drunvalo Melchizedek, is one of the simplest available versions of the MerKaBa. You can find it in a fully digitized format online at www.MaureenStGermain.com/MerKaBa. Give yourself this gift; you will thank me later!

I have coded the book with guidance information so that you can access my knowledge base intuitively and spontaneously, without knowing why you understand it perfectly. This is a gift of Spirit and I am honored to be the conduit. This information comes from a reservoir of knowledge collected over years of teaching, meditating, and communing with Spirit.

Please ask your Higher Self to step in and personally guide you through this process. You may also ask for a direct connection to my Higher Self for the purpose of clearly understanding the teaching being given through this book. It is my desire that you have the tools to maximize your effort, and that it be for your highest good and my highest good. I already feel so much love for you. Thank you for joining me on this incredible adventure!

The great theologian Thomas Aquinas used the writings of the notable Muslim philosopher Averroes to justify the clear separation of faith and reason, a Muslim ideal that formed the basis of modern scientific inquiry and led to the European Renaissance. May this knowledge inspire you to begin your own Renaissance!

Author's Note

Terms denoted with a ◈ have been explained in detail in the glossary at the back of the book.

History of the MerKaBa and Important Notes for Your Practice

What You Will Learn in This Chapter

- My personal history with the MerKaBa
- History of the MerKaBa
- Little-understood details about aspects of the MerKaBa
- Why you will want to learn the MerKaBa

My MerKaBa Story

My initial encounter with the MerKaBa was through my first spiritual teacher, Charlotte Alexander.* When I asked her about the MerKaBa she explained this unfamiliar concept as a kind of spaceship around the body. Back in 1982 we were not studying much about that in a spiritual context, but it seemed important so I made note of it and set it aside.

Then in 1994 I was at a t'ai chi class when I saw a notice on the bulletin board for an introductory class on the MerKaBa. Wow! I was immediately interested. Unfortunately, my personal life was falling

---

*My first spiritual teacher—an amazing, brilliant, loving woman who inspired and taught me patiently and generously—passed on December 19, 2008. Thank you, Charlotte. May your family of light continue to honor you and your memory.

apart and I was preoccupied, so I promptly forgot it. Then I saw the same notice in a magazine and again later at a store. Enough! I immediately agreed (with Spirit) to attend the class.

At the intro class I was stunned to find that everything I had ever been interested in and studied in my whole life was all rolled into one package. I had aced geometry in high school (and this was sacred geometry), and in college I had a perfect score on my final oral exam in astronomy. During the introductory evening, with the blessing of Jeff, the host facilitator, I was permitted to answer questions on these subjects that the host was not able to provide. (I think I had some help from the unseen helpers.)

When someone asked what it would take to become a facilitator, his answer was, "We are not training anyone now; we want to make sure there are enough students for the teachers that have already been trained." He also noted that the teacher training with Drunvalo required taking the course a second time to complete certification.

After I completed my first MerKaBa series in December 1994, I immediately signed up for the class a second time. Jeff asked, "Why are you taking it again? Did you not get it?" Of course I had, so I gave some nondescript reason, not really wanting to listen to the same objections I had heard earlier, but he persisted with the question so I told him: "It is my intent to become a facilitator and I know that the course must be taken twice." Again he said, "We are not training any more teachers." And my immediate response was, "That is your reality; I choose another." Six months later I was trained and certified by Drunvalo himself! This was the last training Drunvalo personally taught on the 17-Breath Original MerKaBa.

The magic did not stop there. Drunvalo asked each of us to make a commitment at our certification ceremony. I promised at my graduation that I would reach millions of people with the MerKaBa. Initially I had no idea why I said that or how it would be accomplished. I never thought I would eventually give up my full-time, well-paid corporate job to be a full-time spiritual teacher.

I had the good fortune of having a job with a very generous three-week vacation schedule. I used all my vacation time one day at a time to teach the MerKaBa workshops in cities all over the country, traveling on Fridays to destinations, returning Sunday nights or early Monday mornings. This enabled me to step into my passion job, teaching the MerKaBa.

My corporate job was as a fundraiser for a small, local charity; my title was Development Director. I used the MerKaBa to help me build the donor base (see chapter 6, "Programming Your MerKaBa"), and in four years I had increased the donor list by more than one hundred times its original size. A year after I left, the new development director came to me and asked if I could explain why donor numbers fell by *half* after I departed. I did not give him a clear answer because I have a policy about sacred information: unless you are in a class or training session with me, I require that you ask me twice before I release any spiritual knowledge. Usually the first time someone asks it's based on noticing you are different, but the person may not be ready to hear the answer. The second time shows there is serious interest. The first query is based on mental curiosity, but if there's a second, it indicates an open heart.

After I left my position I used the MerKaBa to help me get a job where I would be loved as much as I loved my employer. I was hired by a trade association as their manager of regulatory affairs, and that job fulfilled that desire of mine. I openly shared with them about my weekend seminar business and I was able to continue both jobs, yet I soon discovered I loved my seminars even more than the dream job. After about a year I realized I was being called to do the MerKaBa work full time, and I was able to leave my full-time job with severance pay and their blessing. Since then I've spent more than twenty-five years traveling and teaching.

I had already recorded the MerKaBa CD while still employed and had committed to a national advertising campaign with the *Sedona Journal of Emergence*. I remember that very first directive from my Higher Self—to spend $250 a month to promote the workshops in the *Sedona Journal*. At the time it seemed a fortune.

That first year I filled every weekend with workshops. I was so worried about making it financially that I thought if I had a workshop every weekend, that would ensure sufficient income. It did not always work out that way, and I have had a lot of support from family and friends to stay solvent.

When I learned the MerKaBa Meditation back in 1994 we were not taught how to do the last three breaths that would activate the MerKaBa. We were told, "Wait until you have permission from your Higher Self." However, there was no advice or training on what the Higher Self information would look like! In chapters 4 and 5 of this book you will find detailed instructions on how to develop a Higher Self connection that is accurate and reliable.

My friend John Ammond, who took the class at the same time, called me once to ask if I'd gotten permission from my Higher Self to activate the MerKaBa. "Yes," I answered, because I was pretty sure I had permission. "Did you activate?" he asked. I replied, "No." "Why not?" he demanded. I was pretty sure I had permission. I thought my Higher Self had said, "Yes," but I was not 100 percent sure. I did activate my MerKaBa shortly after that.

This was the aha moment and became one of my goals. How could I know for sure? What could I do to help myself know the Higher Self connection? What did it look like? What did it feel like? I am not a very visual person and was the last, in our class of seventeen persons, to get the "color" exercises we did at the first MerKaBa course.

Later, as a teacher of this knowledge, I asked for and received direct guidance from Source on how to develop this connection, and spent seven years perfecting the process. My goal was to build a library of tools for my students to help them identify and know with absolute certainty that their Higher Self direction was real, provable, and authentic. In the pages of this book I will share these tools and give you specific examples and exercises to get you to a place of accuracy. What a relief to know you can do this!

I was so mental in my own way that I felt there were many professionals like me who wanted proofs for sacred geometry, the special codes we used to activate the MerKaBa, and more. The pages of this book contain those proofs.

I am so grateful to be able to share this information with you! It has come through years of study and from thousands of students' feedback. Every one of them taught me something. In facilitating so many individuals, the knowledge just poured into my being. You, dear reader, will benefit from all those who have gone before you, and I appreciate them all.

When I was growing up we had to spend hours at the library for school research. There was a catalog card for each book. We spent hours sorting through thousands of cards in huge trays to get the same information you can now print out from the Internet in about three seconds. Research reports from then and now could be the same, but you will not have to work as hard as I did to gather information. This book will give you that same type of light-speed leap. With the tools and practices in this book, you will not have to work as hard as those who have gone before you. So let's get going!

What Is the History of MerKaBa and What Are Its Origins?

This is a big question. I offer what I have learned in the years of immersing myself in the MerKaBa as an instructor and practitioner.

Translated literally from the Hebrew, the noun *merkavah* means "chariot to ride in" and relates to the throne-chariot of God in prophetic visions. A likeness of a man drives the chariot.

The MerKaBa as we mean it here is a Body of Light or Light Body. It is activated from a geometric field that exists around the body. Everyone has this field around them, as do planets, solar systems, and other living entities. This means learning it is a *remembering* experience for humans. Once you have remembered the MerKaBa, you choose to activate it daily until it becomes permanent. Do not worry; it will.

The spinning of counter-rotating fields is found throughout the cosmos. This spinning is an accurate reflection of nature. In the Zohar, the mystical commentary on the Judaic Torah, there is a reference to the MerKaBa and the four wheels spinning "without turning," so I believe the information we have today is both ancient and accurate, and was already known at some level long before the MerKaBa became available to all of humanity.

The MerKaBa is mentioned in the Old Testament in Ezekiel 1:10. The actual throne on its chariot goes back to the first chapter of Ezekiel and his vision of a throne of glory that is a source of centuries-old mystical and visionary traditions. Some versions do not use the word *merkavah* when referring to the vehicle seen by Ezekiel, but it most certainly was this chariot that Ezekiel saw.

According to a later tradition found in the Zohar, written by the Spanish Kabbalist Moses de Léon, the vision of Ezekiel was a flying vehicle. Personally I have always interpreted the MerKaBa as a flying vehicle that you build by yourself for yourself. I believe that all who have had knowledge of this either knew or assumed that it was meant for humanity at some point. In the verse noted above, Ezekiel is commanded to ingest part of it.

I now know it to be a **fifth-dimensional**◈ garment that we remember and activate. It is not necessary to acquire it, since it is already there. It is from the future of a more advanced version of us. This, combined with the Christ Consciousness Grid around the earth, ensures our **Ascension**◈. For simplicity's sake, let us understand that our Ascension is becoming a perfected human, or in spiritual terms, the Ascended Master you.* This could be compared with purchasing an annuity for your child's college tuition. You then teach him good study habits and pay his way in advance so that if he is a diligent student, his ability to graduate is assured.

All versions of the merkavah in the sacred literature contain references to Angels. (Modern usage of this word is simply *MerKaBa*.) This is important for a number of reasons. Drunvalo always referred to the two Angels who taught it to him and how to implement it. Throughout my life Archangel Michael has always been with me, especially as an instructor of the MerKaBa. He clearly came through during the writing of this book and identified himself as the original sponsor of the MerKaBa in the dedication.

The Jewish Gnostics' first known document, the *Sefer Yetzirah* (Book

---

*Ascension has many meanings; see my book *Waking Up in 5D* for a clear, and deeper, explanation of the Ascension I refer to here.

of Creation), lists the MerKaBa as one of the *elements* (others being virtues, or *sefirot,* the ten emanations in Kaballah) and notes its relation to the letters of the Hebrew alphabet and the cosmogonies and anthropogonies—theories of the origin of the Universe and human origins.

What are these elements? I think of an element as being a construction piece of a set used for the construction of the Universe. I believe the MerKaBa being listed as one of the elements means it is part of the basic set of construction materials of the Universe. It also means the MerKaBa is the basic structure found around everything! This is why it is so significant. It is why remembering and activating it changes lives and improves every other spiritual practice you may follow.

According to Spanish mystics the entire vision, including the orbits of the planets and the entire solar system, is properly called the merkavah, or chariot of God. This resonates with the photograph of the Sombrero Galaxy, 30 million light years distant, as the popular depiction of the MerKaBa. In addition, one of the sections of the Kabbalah, which deals with the arts and sciences of those planes under the heavens, is also called the merkavah.

Ultimately the MerKaBa is related to the Book of Revelation, the final book of the New Testament. It is a vehicle supported and drawn by cherubim, which is also the throne *and* that "still small voice" with which God manifested himself to Elijah. Perhaps this is the Higher Self of today's language.

Confusing? Yes, this is why Drunvalo said it is a vehicle, yet it could be anything! For sure it is a manifestation field, because it truly is a fifth-dimensional garment that, when remembered and activated, enables the wearer to accomplish that which was not previously possible.

Historical Data

As I understand it, this throne/chariot was a central subject of meditation in both ancient and medieval Jewish esotericism and mysticism, but the guardians of rabbinic orthodoxy tended to discourage such speculation and study.

In the Mishnah, which embodies the oral tradition of Jewish law, it is even suggested that no wise man share the knowledge of the merkavah with someone less knowledgeable.* This may be why there is very little written. I share this constraint as I, too, have come to understand how very powerful it is. Proceed with caution and reverence! This book will not teach the MerKaBa that you must learn from other sources, such as my video seminar. This is for supplemental work.

I do know that it is a remarkable system to activate. I can attest to the differences it can produce for you and within you. I have worked with it personally since 1994 and know for certain it is a valid way to connect with the entire reality as well as one's Divine Self. It is remarkable beyond anything I have ever encountered. It does not interfere with any other spiritual practice; rather, it elevates everything else you may do.

In the Dead Sea Scrolls we find a text that adds significance to what has been handed down through history. I have included it in its entirety below:

> The ministers of the Glorious Face in the abode of the gods of knowledge fall down before him, and the cherubim utter blessings. And as they rise up, there is a divine small voice and a loud praise; there is a divine small voice as they fold their wings.
>
> The cherubim bless the image of the Throne-Chariot [merkavah] above the firmament, and they praise the majesty of the fiery firmament beneath the seat of his glory. And between the turning wheels, Angels of holiness come and go, as it were a fiery vision of most holy spirits; and about them flow seeming rivulets of fire, like gleaming bronze, a radiance of many gorgeous colors, of marvelous pigment magnificently mingled.
>
> The Spirits of the Living God move perpetually with the glory of the wonderful Chariot. The small voice of blessing accompanies the tumult as they depart, and on the part of their return they worship the Holy One, Ascending they rise marvelously; settling, they stay still. The sound of joyful praise is silenced and there is a small voice of blessing in all the camp of God.

*As related in Willis Barnstone's *The Other Bible* (New York: HarperCollins, 1984), 705.

And a voice of praise resounds from the midsts of all their divisions in worship. And each one in his place, all their numbered ones sing hymns of praise.[1]

Why Was a Combination of Methods Chosen from Hindu, Egyptian, Hebrew, Tibetan, and Other Traditions for the Original 17-Breath Meditation?

Some mistakenly believe that each religion's tradition is unique. I believe this concept is a myth. Here is why: the more we know about world religions and the evolution of spiritual thought, the more we see the previous cosmologies emerging from the existing ones, producing common threads appearing everywhere.

Most religions draw from elements of their predecessors. An example in our known traditions includes Christianity. Research shows Christianity borrowed from the Hebrew tradition (and interpreted it) as well as the ancient religion of Mithraism. Many elements of the Hebrew tradition borrow their cosmologies from earlier traditions.

Much of the Hebrew tradition is identical to ancient Egyptian tradition. For example, some sections of the Book of Solomon were copied verbatim from an ancient text written by the Egyptian sage Amenemope.

Research into Amenemope shows that he borrowed from a far older work called the *Wisdom of P'Tahhotep,* which dates some 2,000 years before the time of King Solomon.[2]

Out of the Hundreds of Mudras, How and Why Were These Chosen?

There are mudras, or meditative hand gestures, to accompany each of the seventeen breaths:

Part I, the First Six Breaths: The mudras for the first six breaths are related to the meridians in the body that move through the fingers. There are six meridians; one is not on the fingers and is a redundant one. Also, the number six is directly related to the six external points of the **star-tetrahedron◈**, or Divine Light Body. There are actually eight points of the MerKaBa as you work your way around the star-tetrahedrons, but two reside in the axis points and get cleared each time you pulse. It is possible to repeat the same mudras and breaths up to eight if you wish, but those numbered one through six are all that is necessary.

Part II, Breaths 7–13: For breaths seven through fourteen, the mudra of your thumb and first two fingers is a balance of male/female and neutral (see figure 1.1). One of the goals of those breaths is to bring you into full balance. This includes every aspect of you coming into balance with YOURSELF and *within* yourself.

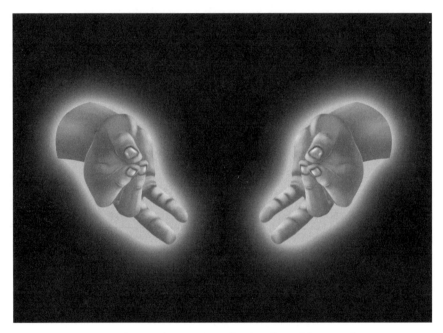

Figure 1.1. This mudra connects the thumb and first two fingers
to balance male/female and neutral.

Part III, Breath 14: The last mudra, used from Breath 14 onward, balances either male or female, depending on what is needed for the individual (see figure 1.2). Each person selects one or the other position. This mudra places the right hand on top or the left hand on top. Most men have the left hand on top and most women have the right hand on top, but yours could be the reverse. The right hand on top adds male energy to the field; the left hand on top adds female energy. Women usually need more male energy and vice versa. When one does not identify with their gonads, it could be reversed.

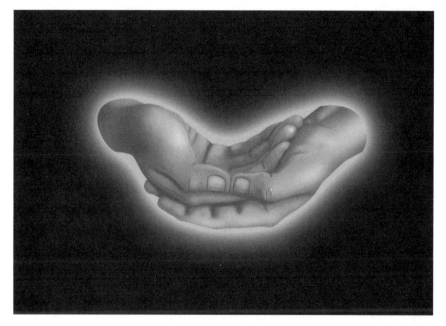

Figure 1.2. The mudra for Breath 14 balances
male and female as needed.

The Alternate Mudra for Breath 14

This mudra is formed by placing the fingertips of one hand inside the spaces between the other hand's fingers (see figure 1.3 on page 12). You'll need to remove any rings from your fingers in order to do it properly. The way to know if you are doing it correctly is to stand at a sink, with your fingers touching the skin between each finger (not sticking out either toward the palms or back of the hands), and see if you can carry water. No leaks means you have done it correctly. The mudra allows for both male and female energy at the same time. Using this mudra, if you can carry water without dripping, you've got it right.

Figure 1.3. The alternate mudra for Breath 14 allows for
both male and female energy at the same time.

A good place to contact your Higher Self is after Breath 14. You
can find steps for developing your Higher Self contact on page 115.

This mudra was given to me by my Higher Self. I seriously questioned why I would be shown something that did not comply with what Drunvalo had taught me. When we were all together in a facilitator gathering in 2001, I showed Drunvalo this alternate mudra. He instantly turned to the whole group and said, "Hey gang, from now on you can do this as an alternate mudra for Breath 14 and beyond."

The MerKaBa Is Like a Car

The MerKaBa is a vehicle so it may be thought of like a car. In phase one, the first six breaths, you are taking the car in for detailing. The phase two set of breaths, from Breath 7 to Breath 13, is like your car's 75,000-mile tune-up. Phase three, Breath 14, is putting gas in your car. Breath 15, in phase four, is turning on the ignition. Breath 16 is putting your car in gear, and Breath 17 is stepping on the gas.

The Last Three Breaths

In my travels to teach the MerKaBa I was invited to Ithaca by a particle beam accelerator operator employed by Cornell University. A particle beam accelerator is a complex machine that uses electromagnetic fields to propel charged particles at near light speed, while containing them in confined beams. This gentleman took me on a tour of the lab, and what I learned there put a capstone on the MerKaBa information for me. I found proofs at that particle beam accelerator lab.

The job of a particle beam accelerator is to accelerate and amplify the energy of a beam of particles. I learned during my lab tour that when an electron "strays" from its home rotational field, its speed is one-third the speed of light. Likewise, when you turn on the MerKaBa at Breath 15, you do not yet have a "complete" system, which is why the rotational speed is one-third the speed of light, the same speed as an electron that is temporarily "homeless."

Breath 15 is the activation of the star-tetrahedrons (two nested tetrahedrons) around you that move in opposite directions at equal speed. Remember, these three star-tetrahedrons are part of the bigger system that is put in place in the earlier parts of the meditation. How much does the speed increase? The rotation automatically jumps to one-third the speed of light. Your intention to "start the motor" increases the speed to one-third of light speed.

At Breath 16 you are activating the ratio 34/21. Drunvalo says that this specific ratio reflects the exact location or overtone on the third dimension where we reside. DNA is measured in angstroms. An angstrom is one ten-billionth of a meter, so small that you cannot see it with the naked eye.

What we now know from DNA photography is that there are certain DNA strands that measure 34 angstroms between the long grooves and 21 angstroms between the short grooves. Even something as miniscule as the measurement of DNA gives us this exact proportion. Can it be an accident that this occurs? Hardly. This is why I'm always appalled at anyone who suggests we change the MerKaBa activation codes or has already attempted to do so. These activation codes are directly related to the physical body and our evolution process, and they are reconfirmed by science. Anyone attempting to create a MerKaBa with Kabbalistic numbers or master numbers (energetic numerology-based numbers) totally misses this point.

Although those number sets (master numbers or Kabbalistic numbers) may be sacred, they are not directly related to the body and will not work. In some cases they may cause great damage. Do not change the MerKaBa activation codes to some other numbers. You could become physically or mentally ill, or worse.

Breath 17 activates the relationship to nine-tenths the speed of light. The mental body star-tetrahedron is the only one spinning at nine-tenths (the speed of light). The emotional body star-tetrahedron is spinning at nine-tenths the speed of light (c) divided by 34/21 (1.61904761904 . . .). That means the emotional body star-tetrahedron is spinning at 0.760857 the speed of light (that is, slower.) That ratio, nine-tenths the speed of light, is the exact same speed that electrons move around the nucleus of an atom.

Why is this important? It shows that the relationship you are creating is sacred and found in *all* of nature. At what velocity are the physicists accelerating the particles in their accelerator lab in Ithaca? You guessed it, 0.9 the speed of light. Why would they choose that speed? I believe it is because they are looking for information that helps define the differences found at the quantum level (subatomic) and the physical matter reality of the world in which we live. That is one of the biggest questions of quantum mechanics: How is it possible that the real visible world appears to be so vastly different than the quantum (subatomic) level?

How Will You Know If Your MerKaBa Is Permanent?

Answer: Ask your Higher Self.

Any other method to determine this answer is inferior. No amount of research or feedback will be able to verify that your MerKaBa is permanent. Some have said, "I will feel it when it is there all the time." Yes, well, what if you are one of those individuals who do not consciously feel the MerKaBa? "Well, I will feel it if it goes inactive" is a common reply. My response is that not everyone has the ability to sense the

MerKaBa this way. All sensing is inferior to knowing. Knowing comes from the Higher Self, as it requires no proof.

In chapters 4 and 5 you will learn a precise protocol on how to connect to your Higher Self with 100 percent accuracy. Activating your MerKaBa on a daily basis will go a long way toward achieving a permanent MerKaBa.

Purple Cones Coming Off the MerKaBa

If you watch the old Drunvalo MerKaBa videos as many times as I have (I estimate more than 600 times), you start to see things nobody else has seen. So many insights and so much information has come to me while watching them. Much of the content of this book is based on my being in incredible alpha to theta states while watching. One thing he points out—yet never explains—is the purple cones that appear in the emulating software that he wrote and used in his workshop videos. One day those purple cones spoke to me and showed me where they originated.

Begin by extending a line from the edges of each of the tetrahedrons into the air. The easiest way to see this is to tape skewer sticks to the edge of a cardboard MerKaBa* and then spin it—imagining that there is one spinning around you to the right (emotional body star-tetrahedron) and one to the left (mental body star-tetrahedron) around a stationary one. At once you will see the very same cones that Drunvalo's software emulated! It produced cones that appear to be slightly off-center. Upon closer examination you will see that they are secondary rotational fields created from the edge of the star-tetrahedron field.

A car's four-cylinder engine will create a secondary counter-rotating field within the engine's cradle, called the engine's harmonics. Anyone who has worked on an older car uses a strobe timing light to balance this and keep it in harmonic resonance. In the same way, the MerKaBa's secondary field is creating harmonic resonance that stabilizes and harmonizes everything within it.

---

*For instructions on how to build a cardboard MerKaBa, visit the MerKaBa page on Maureen's website.

My Request to You

Everything in this book is offered to you with specific steps in mind, in a specific sequence. Since 1995 I have worked to develop, understand, and teach these recommended steps. These instructions are not to be taken lightly.

Many of you are so hungry for this knowledge you may be tempted to skip ahead and find what you think is "the good stuff," and think you will achieve the results you desire. Just like a body builder knows well that you cannot fake it, nor can you race it or reduce the effort it takes to achieve results, please know that only your authentic effort will enable you to achieve the results you seek.

If you are sincere and truly desire to build a MerKaBa that will enable you to know what you need to know, see what you need to see, or be where you need to be, then follow the practice offered in this book and you will amaze even yourself. You will discover incredible results while building an authentic connection to your Higher Self that will steer you in times of chaos, and much, much, more.

The MerKaBa is a marvelous manifestation tool. I have been studying the art of manifestation since the 1970s. I have absolute conviction that the use of the MerKaBa as an aid to manifestation, to advancing humanity toward its Ascension, is greater than anything I have ever encountered.

Without it, I would not have been able to achieve all the things I have accomplished since 1994, when I started working with it. I am greatly indebted to those who have gone before me, worked with the knowledge, and made it available to the masses. It is my pleasure to support your practice with new knowledge that will enhance what you have already unraveled. Everything you need to be fully connected to our reality is in this book.

When Drunvalo first brought forth the MerKaBa teaching, he thought everyone would intuitively understand what to do next with the MerKaBa. I think there is a reason for this, and I believe part of the reason is hidden within the mission of the Christ Consciousness Grid. The Christ Consciousness Grid is covered extensively in chapter 13 of this book.

Breath 18

To those of you who think you found the eighteenth breath and have attempted to use it, I wish you well. It is an elusive matter. The more you chase it, the more hidden it is. Seek instead to achieve Ascension by following the steps of this process. Some of you will master the steps faster than others. That is okay. Skipping the steps is not a good idea. The eighteenth breath will find you when you are ready.

Step-by-Step

Steps to knowing your Higher Self can be found on page 115. Remember that the MerKaBa is alive. You will learn how to create your own programs that are in harmony with the Universe.

It is not enough to know how to program your MerKaBa. You must know what you wish to accomplish, and you must learn and understand that miscreations can happen. It is your responsibility to do everything in your power to maximize your understanding to prevent unnecessary miscreations. One way to ensure you are in harmony is to carefully follow the instructions contained in this book. First and foremost, develop your Higher Self connection to 100 percent accuracy. Then whenever you wish to create something (as taught later in this book) you will ask your Higher Self, *Is it in my highest and best good? Is it in the highest and best good of those who would be affected by my actions?* In this way you will avoid miscreations.

The purpose of this material is the elevation of humanity. I believe that sharing this knowledge will help many more individuals. I have had countless experiences working with the MerKaBa and workshop participants. I have discovered the ensuing group consciousness brings in new information.

I have kept meticulous journals for years, and hope to share with you a small sampling of what can occur, what has already occurred, and how you can capitalize on the experiences of those who have gone before you.

Drugs and Other Stimulants—
Some Very Important Information

The sacred gifts from Mother Earth are forbidden without the use of an elder shaman who is initiating you. It is never appropriate to do any type of earthly mind-altering drugs even if they are from Mother Earth.

The knowledge of these mind-altering drugs came to us through the shamans and must never be self-administered. The shamans who work with these are trained for years, and they prepare for years to lead and perform hours and hours of cleansing ceremony to maintain a sacred space around them and the people with whom they are working at the time.

When they do this work they are able to anchor in a sacred space for themselves and those with whom they are working. They are creating space around you and your group, and very often pray and hold ceremony for hours in advance.

You, individually, have no authority, no permission from Mother Earth or right to use these mind/body/health-altering substances without the specific permission that must be gained from an elder or council of elders who can initiate you and hold the space for you.

These substances would never be used for recreational purposes, and never, never, never used on a regular basis. Even when they are administered, it is always as initiatory experiences to jump-start your connection with the Divine.

These substances alter who you are. Used sparingly, within the Mayan, African, or Native American traditions, they may hold some merit. If you are taking these earthly substances you are largely flirting with danger and I urge you to find a way to let go of your addiction and stop using. Even if you do not think you have an addiction, if you cannot stop, you know.

The MerKaBa is from the future and is far more advanced than the present time. Because it is from the future (a future version of a greatly evolved you), and an appropriate vehicle of Ascension, its use is not only approved but recommended.

Some have attempted to compare the MerKaBa to a drug, in as far as its ability to assist you with your Ascension is irrational. There is no comparison! They are not even in the same league.

One student commented, referring to these mind-altering substances, "They can bring one into a heightened level of awareness and will even bring you to the heavens we could only dream about. It lets you experience these beautiful things. . . . And now I wonder why you are suggesting we are not permitted to use them? It is almost like by denying Mother Earth's gifts, we are denying ourselves of our true potential."

These tools from Mother Earth were never meant to be a crutch to take away your willingness, desire, passion, and persistence to earn the ability to achieve this heightened awareness on your own, without this crutch.

If you play a game of cards and find that with an ace or two up your sleeve you can always win, do you think it appropriate or acceptable to continue to use it so that you can always win? Is your goal to learn to play cards well or to win at any cost? Is your goal to achieve your Ascension or to go for an Ascension-like ride that may or may not crash and burn?

Changing the MerKaBa Meditation

I am continually amazed at the people who have arbitrarily changed the MerKaBa Meditation. There are dozens of stories about individuals who have taken the teaching that Drunvalo brought forth and amended it to suit their purposes. You may have heard of them. Please practice discernment if someone tells you that another version of the MerKaBa is better or more correct. There is a 5-D MerKaBa, as taught in my book *Waking Up in 5D*,[3] but this is intended to supplement the activated original 17-Breath MerKaBa.

I know of MerKaBa teachers (none certified by FOL) who have changed certain elements of the MerKaBa. In every instance, no one has been able to demonstrate that these amendments have improved the original MerKaBa. Nor have they helped individuals with their Ascension work. Furthermore, as previously discussed, the formula for an activated MerKaBa is validated by what we know about nature found in scientific fact. If you have a question that relates to this, I strongly urge you to reach out to me; perhaps I can assist. Because of the extensive number of individuals wishing to amend the MerKaBa, I will not attempt to rebut them all. I will, however, address specific questions. You can email me at info@maureenstgermain.com.

Make no mistake: the MerKaBa has evolved since it was first presented by Drunvalo. This is discussed at length later in this book. However, these changes were directly related to the simplification of the meditation as it became a more tangible part of our reality.

What about the Violet Flame?

In one instance a woman wrote that the **Violet Flame**◈ of the legendary spiritual master St. Germain was necessary to clear the energy of the earth. At around the same time a number of individuals picked up this thought form telling me that they had decided to change the meditation and not send the energy through the point of the earth tetrahedron. It was as if someone were projecting the thought that the clearing work in the first part of the MerKaBa was dangerous to the earth. Nothing could be further from the truth!

The Violet Flame is a marvelous tool and may be useful to augment the MerKaBa, but it is not part of the MerKaBa. The Violet Flame is a dispensation from St. Germain and the Great White Brotherhood* for mankind, to give humanity a lift and an edge to get past our karmic situations. The MerKaBa is also a gift—an advanced fifth-dimensional tool—but its nature is different from the Violet Flame.

The more capable we are of connecting with unconditional love, the easier it is for Mother Earth to feel our love. To that end the Violet Flame is extremely useful. It is entirely appropriate to gown yourself, your family, and friends with the Violet Flame. It will help you to transmute your fear and judgment, enabling you to be a happier, holier you. I have invoked the Violet Flame daily since the 1980s with incredible results and wonderful stories to tell about it.

---

*The Great White Brotherhood is the body of ascended men and women, regardless of race, whose sole purpose is to assist humankind and move creation toward the light.

Assuming you need it to amend the MerKaBa implies that Mother Earth is not capable of resolving your clearing. Please do not judge the energies you are releasing into the earth. Mother Earth may be using and recycling what we send to her. There is a South American tradition that explains that our garbage sent directly to Mother Earth is fuel for her. In a modern adaptation of this idea, in the classic film *Back to the Future* garbage was used for fuel in the DeLorean auto. Our discarded energy is recycled by Mother Earth and used appropriately.

The Violet Flame transmutes human suffering and expression so that we can feel our connection with God, but you do not need to imbue the MerKaBa with the Violet Flame. The MerKaBa is about God identity, so it is already fully connected to God. The Violet Flame is also for the transmutation of karma. It is a wonderful tool to assist us in getting to the fifth dimension, but the MerKaBa is already a fifth-dimensional vehicle.

Using the Violet Flame to "fix" the MerKaBa just does not make sense. It does not need "improvement." Mother Earth and Father Sky are healed by our love and not our judgment.

Can You Travel in the MerKaBa?

Traveling with the MerKaBa does not mean moving from one planet to another, but much more. It is moving within a global energy field that does not belong to time and space but works as a kind of geometric reference for outer manifestation. Once understood, it allows complete freedom to move about in consciousness.

This means the MerKaBa puts you perfectly in touch with the third-dimensional and fifth-dimensional reality in such a way that you always know what you need to know when you need to know it. And it supports you to manifest easily.

A New Source of Information and a Guide Appears

In 2004, I was given a message by my guides to contact an astrologer, Marilyn, for a message. Marilyn is not in the business of "messages," so she was surprised she was being asked to serve as messenger. She checked in with her guides to receive a surprising message: *Maureen is being given access to a dimension that had been closed to humanity for millions of years. . . . She is being given a permanent guide who will be with Maureen for the rest of her life.*

The remainder of the message was for my personal guidance and so is not shared here, as much of it was personal in nature. In addition it led me to the understanding that it is my job to work with knowledge and my privilege to be the conduit. I thank you from the bottom of my heart for your interest, because without that, there is no message.

Who Should Teach the MerKaBa?

At one time it was said that even though you could find the meditation on the Internet and in Drunvalo's books, he believed that learning the MerKaBa correctly on your own was nearly impossible. Initially he thought his instructions were enough, and that people would follow them. Later he realized that people misunderstood instructions and decided to pull back a little, asking students to work with facilitators. Today learning it is much easier since it is in human consciousness, and there are now enough people doing this meditation correctly that it will self-correct. I am continually amazed at the number of people who communicate with me to tell me that a friend of theirs taught them the MerKaBa Meditation or that they learned it from Drunvalo's book.

The true nature of a mystery school is to study something until you have integrated the knowledge. This way you can impart the information you received after you have moved from the initiate phase. The ancient teachings are based on an oral tradition that requires an initiate to absorb, repeat, and relay the teachings hundreds or more times while the teacher observes and makes sure the understanding is clear. This tradition also ascertains that the student can express those teachings in a clear and concise manner.

In your own mind you may believe you clearly understand what you have learned, but there is no way of confirming this knowledge without your extensive investment of time and effort. Further, on your own you have no way to know if you have the ability to translate that knowledge into words that are understandable to the listener, whoever that might be.

The Mantle of the Teacher

Wearing the mantle of the teacher is a powerful and significant responsibility. It is only bestowed upon persons who have gone through many initiations to prove their worth and their willingness to be students of Source.

Here is a question I received regarding this issue:

"I practice MerKaBa daily with your CD. I have come to understand why we cannot teach somebody else. The person has to be ready for this big jump to next consciousness and they are only ready if they pay for it. Am I wrong?"

Answer: You are wrong. It is not about money; it is about commitment. A person who does not pay (with light/money) is not committed. There are ways a person can demonstrate commitment, one of which is money. It is not the only way.

This book contains advanced material. Students who are called to study with me are a gift to me, as are the students who follow after them. You are enabling me to bring forth material of a highly evolved nature. Your presence enables me to transmit the material and work with individuals at an advanced level. Those who choose to learn from my words are present because they are ready and able to receive material of an advanced nature. The entire planet is getting ready to receive this, and many already have. Without this knowledge base that acts as a Source Code, information could be imparted in a way that could cause misunderstanding and misinformation. Let the reader be aware.

Why Participate in the MerKaBa Training?

Since there are no more facilitators actively teaching the MerKaBa in a Flower of Life workshop, your way to learn the meditation is from a recording made of a live workshop. You will understand this complex meditation and activate your MerKaBa in a video that is a total of four hours for the condensed version, or about fifteen hours if you opt for the full version. You may choose to meet with like-minded people, create a community event, learn heart-opening exercises, and practice the MerKaBa until you get it right.

Even though the trainings are not live or in person, it is preferrable to watch a video rather than simply learning the MerKaBa from a book. The written instructions have often been misunderstood, so it is recommended that you try to watch the videos available.

Here is one example of the perils of teaching yourself: A brilliant, gifted, and well-educated healer working in the medical field as a nurse practitioner had taught herself the MerKaBa through Drunvalo's book, but was doing it incorrectly.

Her boyfriend, I will call him Richard, had the ability to see interdimensionally. Richard could see that something was drastically wrong with her field, and knew intuitively that it could be dangerous. Even though he had no personal interest in attending a Flower of Life workshop himself, he begged her to stop doing this practice and learn it correctly from a licensed facilitator in a proper workshop. Fortunately, I learned of this experience when the nurse practitioner attended a class with me. She told me her story, found her mistake, and corrected it.

In another example, a self-taught person who signed up for an Akashic Records reading from me asked her Akashic Records guides in her session why she had not seen any progress, even though she had been doing the MerKaBa for more than a year. It turns out that she also was doing it completely incorrectly. She was fortunate that she did not do any damage to herself.

New Tools for Learning and Practicing Unconditional Love

What You Will Learn in This Chapter

- Getting into your heart
- How to get help from the Hathors
- Rewriting the script of past hurts
- How to move from forgiveness to gratitude
- Specific tools for opening to self-love and replacing the judgment in your heart
- Dealing with a blow to the heart

Unconditional love is changing the planet. You and I are part of the massive change occurring everywhere. This section is probably the most important element of the MerKaBa practice. Everyone knows how important it is, and we are learning to pay attention to how we can become unconditionally loving. Our governments will catch up.

Mother Earth is healed by your love, not your tears!

Daily Practice and Opening Your Heart

Drunvalo says without the heart connection your MerKaBa will not go anywhere or even be effective. However, I have really good news for you. In spite of everything, if *all* you do is the MerKaBa, your heart will open. You cannot continue to activate your MerKaBa daily, getting all the elements of yourself in perfect balance, without opening your heart. In other words, activating your MerKaBa will result in opening your heart.

What this means is that you could close this book right now. I know you won't do that, and I would like to tell you a very poignant story related to this. A number of years ago I started receiving phone calls from the wives of men who studied with me in various Flower of Life classes. It was usually about three to six months later.

Each wife would identify who she was and then invite me to come to teach the class in their home. It happened so frequently I knew I was being shown something. The conversation was always the same: "My husband has changed so much since taking the course from you; I want what he got."

The daily practice of the scientifically geared, logical practice of MerKaBa will open your heart, regardless of what else you do. It is amazingly profound to know this. It makes me think of working with a personal trainer who promises to help you make your body perfect if you give her five minutes a day. What could be easier?

Learning the meditation takes four focused hours in a MerKaBa workshop. Practicing it takes no more than five minutes daily. This is not a big investment for the results you will achieve that will be with you for the rest of your life. I know you are eager to make progress and take your MerKaBa practice to the next level, so if you've already learned the MerKaBa and quit before it became permanent, it is never too late to start anew. Begin today by adding it to your daily practice.

The most important element of the MerKaBa is unconditional love. Unconditional love is the rocket fuel. The level of unconditional love you have is directly related to your performance. Can you imagine making an investment on a great sports car and not being able to get gas?

This will power your meditation the way high octane gasoline improves a car's performance.

The benefits of developing your connection to your heart and unconditional love are enormous. Take a stroll with me through the toning section and the exercises that will support your advanced MerKaBa practice. You'll be very glad you did.

> Accessing the unconditional love energy of the Hathors is an instant solution to hardness of heart, anger, resentment, or any other thing that stands in the way of an open heart.

Working with the Hathors

The Hathors are interdimensional galactic beings already anchored in this dimension by virtue of their fifth-dimensional presence on Venus. It is not just one whole race; they are a species. The Hathors are the most intelligent, most advanced race of enlightened beings in our solar system, more advanced than the dolphins. They represent only peace and love, and communicate through singing or toning, not spoken words.

Not all Egyptians could see the Hathors, but the artists who depicted the Hathors were able to experience them and create the beautiful sculptures we still see today. Many were defaced by early Christians, so finding an undamaged statue is a challenge, but it doesn't seem to matter.

Tom Kenyon and Virginia Essene have written extensively about the Hathors in their book *The Hathor Material*.

How the Hathors Work with Us

The Hathors work with the **ankh**◈, the hieroglyphic symbol of life, using uninterrupted circular breathing and toning. Three separate but continuous tones can take someone directly through Ascension. Toning with the Hathors and others worldwide has given us an enormous body of knowledge. They have worked through me giving initiations and assisting others with their Hathor communication. They are willing

Figure 2.1. The ancient Egyptian goddess Hathor, Venusian goddess of unconditional love, crossed boundaries between worlds. It is widely believed that Sanat Kumara, Ancient of Days who came to Earth to help bring Earth out of her darkest hour, invited the Hathors, who also resided on Venus. (CC BY-SA)

and able to assist you with your heart opening, but remember, we are in a free-will zone, so it is up to you to ask for their help. Expecting them to help you will not bring their help; you must seek it!

In toning we find that individuals experience more than one voice coming through their vocal cords. There are often additional sounds similar to what can be heard in recordings of Tibetan monks performing overtone singing. Joining the Hathors in toning is quite the experience, as you will learn.

One place you can hear their toning is on my *MerKaBa II* CD. It was recorded with Hathor toning in the background, to elevate your MerKaBa experience and support you in opening your heart to the level of the Hathors.

When you are feeling particularly unloving, as most of us do from time to time, simply ask the Hathors to send their "electronic presence" to overshadow you. For example, when you must deal with someone toward whom you do not feel loving, the Hathors can help you. Their mastery will provide you with the perfect template of unconditional love.

Stay Open to the Energy

Stay open to the way the Hathors manifest their energy to you. My first experience with them was as feline energy. However, when I conversed with a woman who had lived in Egypt for ten years she corrected me, telling me they were bovine! I could not understand why I felt so strongly that they were feline. I felt stupid, but could not shake the feeling I had when I first experienced them. I decided it was a simple mistake and not to worry about it.

On September 11, 2001, I was given a direct message from the Hathors. In meditation, I kept asking, *What is going on? What is the meaning of all this?* I was told, *Sekhmet.* I had never heard this word before and wondered if it was a word at all!

I found a local church service that I could join with in praying for the families of the 9/11 disaster. We prayed. Then each of us felt the need to tell our stories. I waited. Finally, no one had anything else to say, and I shared the information I had received. One woman knew about the Egyptian gods and goddesses and told our assembled group that Sekhmet was the goddess of war and of healing. I then searched through all the books I could find to learn about Sekhmet.

Sekhmet's legend, found in the tomb of Tutankhamun, tells us that Sekhmet emerged out of the eye of Ra, the sun god, whom some consider the one true god. Sekhmet was sent by Ra to straighten out an errant mankind, and got carried away. Thoth was called in to put a spell on her and turned her into Bastet, the cat goddess, goddess of war and healing, so feline energy made perfect sense. I was vindicated!

I believe many of us experience the Hathor energy as feline. If you have trouble experiencing the Hathors as bovine, which is one way the goddess is depicted, you are not alone. It is okay to experience them the way they feel to you.

What to Ask

Remember that the Hathors hold the flame of absolute love and live on the planet Venus. They can be present on Earth at our behest. Their primary communication is through singing. If you ever hear your name being sung to you as if the sound is coming through water, you are hearing the sounds of the Hathors. There is a warble and waver in the sound, and it may be audible only to you.

Their tones can also be found in the warble of your own voice when they overshadow your toning. You can make a practice of toning to develop their presence. Practice your toning and ask them to join you, lead you, embrace you, and love you.

Ask for their vibration of love to embrace you and all with whom you interact. Ask them to become one with your heart. Ask them to overshadow you while you are dealing with a difficult situation. It is their joy to serve in this way.

Learn more about the Hathors in the next chapter on toning.

✸ THE "I LOVE YOU" EXERCISE
✸ A Writing and Speaking Exercise to Open Your Heart

Some of us are so left-brained that we struggle mightily to get past our logical thinking and into our hearts with sound. The following exercise will allow you to get past your internal gatekeeper. It will assist you in retraining your subconscious mind to discover who you really are, allow you to accept your divine origins and perfection, and assist you in becoming truly open in your heart.

As this occurs you will experience a changed self-view. It will empower you to love yourself and, as a result, become at one with your heart. Your whole being—body, mind, and spirit—will quite literally start to resonate at the heart. You will learn to trust your heart and yourself, and to trust others and open your heart to them. As in the game of dominoes, in changing only one thing you change the world.

Begin by writing statements you have heard from those closest to you, such as mother, father, siblings, life partner(s), or children, then moving on to friends and coworkers. Write a full page (minimum) of all the wonderful things that have been said to you by people who have cherished you.

For some people a beloved friend, even one who is not a part of your present life, may have said the most complimentary things. If this is the case you might prefer to start there. Another option would be to begin with your current beloved or treasured memory of a significant other, parent, best friend, son, daughter, or grandchild.

You may want to simply start with the most recent loving statement that you remember.

Give yourself permission to look at yourself from the other person's perspective. If you are able, you might connect at the soul level with each person (or at least some of them), and then you may be able to hear them telling you exactly how they love you. Write these statements in the present tense, even if the friend or family member is no longer in your life. It will look like this: "(Your name), you are so loveable."

Keep moving in an outward circle to the various people and energies in your life and see them experiencing you with a joyous heart, expressing their gratitude for knowing you and for the gifts you bring to the relationship, family, friendship, and world. Make sure you include Mother Earth and Father Sky. You might hear Mother Earth express her gratitude to you for helping to keep the earth clean, for example.

Listen to Mother Earth speaking to you with gratitude for all you do for her. Hear Father Sky giving you compliments for who you are and the joy you bring to the earth, the care you take to assist with the environment, and other things you do to support the ecosystem.

Now think about improvements. How can you become a better person? If you are lacking in something (and every one of us is), then allow the voice of one loving person who is observing you to speak to you with kindness, to remind you that you are growing in that area, and to support you in becoming the perfect you. Then name something, whatever you choose, to no longer be an obstacle in your world. You might write something like, "Every day I am surrounded by people who help me to perfect me in the most loving and joyous way. When I need a reminder to be patient, it allows me to appreciate someone else's presence in my world and it helps me to grow and learn."

Another example might be, "When I forget important details, it gives others the opportunity to see *how important they are* in interacting with me. When I graciously receive their reminders, they feel important, loved, and appreciated by me. This, in turn, teaches me to be more attentive to details, for which I am grateful."

I have found that my willingness to learn, adjust, and laugh at myself makes it possible for me to evolve. Let yourself feel gratitude to the Universe for the abundance of people in your world who help you with that aspect.

✸ Clearing the Residue of an Abusive, Unloving Parent

You are about to learn a very specific technique for clearing your subconscious of all the old programming of anything less than unconditional love. I developed this tool based on years of sales experience when I needed to counter objections by potential buyers. It occurred to me that a person could answer and clear inner objections in the same way. This is a technique that will slip by your internal gatekeeper and allow the new statement to be seeded into your subconscious.

Begin with a typical but milder version of a hurtful or critical statement that was spoken to you. What did that person say to you? Then follow it with "but now" and write a new script for that same critical statement. For example, if your mother always criticized the way you dressed you would write the following script:

"(Your name), I used to criticize the way you dressed and questioned your taste in clothes, but now I see you have beautiful taste and are always well put together, and I am so proud of you."

If you experienced a hypercritical parent who thought you could do nothing right you might write: "(Your name), when you were younger I always said you could not do anything, but now I see clearly that you can do anything you put your mind to, and I am so proud of you!"

Each time you will rewrite the script in a very precise way. If you could put words in the critic's mouth, what would you like to hear from that person? As you rewrite the script of the people you *wished* had loved you unconditionally, make sure you examine the statements so that they contain the following elements:

- A clear reference to *before* (I used to think or say . . .)
- Followed by the derogatory statement (may be a milder version)
- Followed by "*but now* I can see . . . "
- Ending with a statement that is completely unconditional and supportive

This is to be scripted whether the person might say it or not, and whether or not the person is still living. You are the scriptwriter and have authority to put words in this person's mouth. You are claiming your right to rewrite your past programming into a pattern that reflects who you really are.

Remember, before you begin writing this part you must understand and follow a specific method to ensure the clearing of the old criticisms. Start with the people you really care about who have not treated you the way you'd like, and go from there.

Make sure you write it in the following way, "Michelle, when you were a child I was always critical and mean, but now I can see that as an adult you are super-talented, hard-working, and loving. I love you. I am so proud of the woman you are."

Always write the first part of the statement in the past tense. Use phrases like, "When you were . . ." or "I used to think that . . ." followed by "but now" and then the reframe. This is a technique that will slip by your internal gatekeeper and allow the new statement to be seeded in your subconscious.

If you are unsure of your statements, please ask a trusted friend to examine them. Some of you may have been so strongly programmed in early childhood that your reframes might be conditional. You do not want to accidentally replace those old statements with new ones that are still unloving and conditional.

> The original statement is typical of the way that person spoke to you, which will enable your statement to navigate beyond your subconscious gatekeeper. The "but now" erases it from your subconscious, replacing it with a seed thought that creates unlimited possibilities and is free of all self-hatred. This works on your subconscious in a very subtle way that allows you to feel truly **loved and loveable**.

You do not need to write *why* the person said those painful words. In fact, it is counterproductive to write the *why* because it takes you back into a place of judgment and rationalization. None of that matters. When you are completing a fifth-dimensional "reframe" like this, polarity doesn't matter. You do not care why the person did it. Knowing the real reason will not make any sense to you anyway. At some point you might even be in a place where you will no longer need to forgive anyone for anything.

If you find this exercise difficult, it means you need it. Ask for help from a trusted friend who can help you see how special you are and how much you are appreciated, and can help you rewrite statements from your childhood that were hurtful. Sometimes it takes an objective loving friend to see your statements in a light that will expose the misuse of the spoken word, help you reframe the statements, and catch something you are blind to due to your experience with a less-than-loving parent. Review your statements and make sure that after each "but now," everything that follows is loving and positive.

✴ Record Your "I Love You"
Statements

Once you have written the exercise, recording it should be easy. It is important that you record this right away after writing it, so have your recording device at the ready. Do not delay. If you don't have a recorder you probably have a cell phone or answering machine. Use that. No excuses. If you have no other option, you can always call yourself leaving a message on your voicemail.

This one exercise will so transform your inner you that you will become a magical being, far more loving than you ever knew was possible. Trust me, this is amazing.

When you record yourself, imagine you are your Higher Self, the loving being who sees you from all vantage points and knows your true, beloved essence. This is God in you, speaking to you, in your voice, loving you. Pick a quiet spot, preferably with a comfortable chair and light. Test your equipment. Play some nice background music. Remember, you are loved and are loveable.

Practice reading it once or twice without recording it. Get familiar with the words you've written. Let yourself feel the love others have for you. Think of someone you love. That will help you open your heart. As you are speaking from the aspect of the Higher Self, you are addressing yourself as the child, but also the adult. Speak to yourself the way you would like others to speak to you. Speak with gentleness and softness, clarity, and great love. Speak with *joy.*

You are now ready to record. Speak the words of "I love you" addressing you. Record it in its entirety, both the positive feedback and the reframe statements.

Revisit your recording in a few days to consider making some changes:

- You may want to consider rewriting and rerecording it.
- You may remember more people who have said loving statements you can include.
- You may want to change or reword what you wrote.
- You may want to add or change background music.

Then play it back to yourself every day and night for forty-five days. You may repeat again anytime and as often as needed. Write in today's date: _____. Write the date you will be completed with this exercise the first time (forty-five days from when you start it): _____. This targets your completion date, when you know you will be transformed. You will become one with your heart. You will become one with the love you wish to send out to the world. Remember, before you can completely love anyone else unconditionally, you must learn to love yourself unconditionally. This single exercise will do more to help you transform your past than any other thing you can do for yourself. Please do not procrastinate. You will be able to move mountains from this practice.

None of what I will give you in this book as information will be as personally powerful as the exercise of playing the "I love you" recording to yourself for forty-five or more days. You will find it extremely useful when you've had a particularly bad day, where you may be yelling at someone or feeling very judgmental. In my personal experience as a single parent with four sons, sometimes I was pushed to the max. On the occasions that I felt my tone was too harsh, or whenever I experienced a particularly frustrating day, I discovered playing this self-made recording allowed me to find my heart center. It helped me to stop hating myself for not being a perfect parent, and to become more openhearted with not just my children but everyone I encountered.

All my students relate that they have radically changed after doing this practice for a month. I know you're hungry for the knowledge and that you really want to know more, but please believe me when I say this exercise and the one following will advance your Ascension work significantly.

✺ SELF-FORGIVENESS

This next exercise is deceptively easy. Doing this exercise immediately following the previous exercise should be spectacular.

The first time you do this, stand in front of a mirror. Hug yourself. Look at yourself with love. You might imagine that you are looking at yourself as a child, your child, for indeed, your body is your creation. Just for a moment forget your flaws in loving acceptance.

Say, "I forgive you for all the times you let me down. I know we agreed beforehand to experience all these things together in order to learn. Thank you for your willingness and courage. I love and appreciate you for all that you are."

Say, "I accept the love from God as it flows through my entire body, into every organ, nerve, bone, and cell. I let this high-frequency energy nurture me from the inside out, replacing dense resistance with joy and light."

Take some time. Relax and enjoy it. Feel the sureness of renewed energy and well-being. Know that this inner peace is a gift you can give yourself at any time. By doing this exercise you will gain a powerful ally in your Ascension.

✹ FORGIVENESS EXERCISE

This amazing exercise has been around for a long time. My sister Chris told me about it originally. I've used this process many times, and I have some amazing things to report about it.

Starting today and every day for forty-five days, write out the names of everyone you need to forgive. Set your goal completion date forty-five days from now on your calendar, to make it easier to remember.

List the names of individuals you need to forgive. Then write one of the following statements, or something similar that feels right to you:

- I forgive anyone I think has harmed me in this or any lifetime, anywhere, on any plane.
- I forgive all debts and erase all karma.
- I choose light for myself and for all my selves.

You do not need full names for these people, just a way to identify them. For example, "the woman who cut me off in traffic yesterday" is sufficient. Nor do you need to write why you think the person did what she did. Just as in the previous exercise, it would be counterproductive because you would be reverting to a place of judgment and rationalization. None of that matters. When you are completing a fifth-dimensional reframe like this, polarity does not matter. You and I do not care why they did it. Knowing the real reason will not make any sense to you anyway. Even the Course in Miracles says forgiveness is unnecessary.

If you forget to do this written exercise one day and remember that you forgot, just pick up where you stopped. **If you forget that you forgot,** you are done.

After you have completed this exercise, the following statement will make so much sense to you. This was written by a participant just a week or so after learning the MerKaBa:

I am on day 4 of the forgiveness exercise. I am listing not only people but events and actions. I find that 90 percent of all the stuff I need to forgive has to do with only myself. Most of my list is a version of "I forgive myself for . . ." What I am realizing is that most if not all of my 'stuff' around 'being wronged' has everything to do with my filters, perceptions, and journey, and nothing to do with others or what I perceived they had done to me according to my reality at the time. I believe that this clarity is due to the work.

✵ ANCESTRAL CLEARING

It doesn't matter whether or not you believe your ancestors have anything to do with you and your current experience. Most of us can readily recognize that our culture is the result of the expressions of previous generations and their evolution to the present. Why not consider, then, that your ancestors may be influencing who you are today?

In his book *Karma and Reincarnation,* Dr. Hiroshi Motoyama, then-head priest of the Shinto-derived religion *Tamamitsu Jinja,* made this profound statement:

The parent/child connection manifests as one link in a long chain of ancestral karma that stretches back through time. Your link to your family allows you to be born into that specific line. It is a link that needs to be understood and respected. In this modern scientific age it is very difficult for people to accept the fact that they are responsible to their ancestors, that they are actually liable for the actions of their ancestors if the resulting karma has not yet been dissolved. Many find it absurd to think that the actions of an unknown ancestor could possibly have anything to do with what is happening to them today. But time and time again when investigating someone's issues, I find problems that stretch back generations. Their spirit is not just an individual entity, it is also part of the family spirit that births and nurtures it.[1]

The next exercise comes to us from a wonderful teacher, Tony Stubbs, who encourages us to take this step for ourselves. It is called an ancestral clearing and it is a powerful tool.

Speak this aloud to yourself:

I now rescind any and all vows that I have taken to experience the illusion of unconsciousness.

As Lightbearer of my genetic lineage, I break these vows for myself and for all of my ancestors.

I declare these vows null and void in this incarnation, and all of our incarnations across time and space, parallel realities, parallel universes, alternate realities, alternate universes, all planetary systems, all Source systems, and all dimensions.

I ask for release of all crystals, devices, thought forms, emotions, matrices, veils, cellular memory, pictures of reality, genetic limitation, and death—NOW!

Under the Law of Grace and by the Decree of Victory! By the Decree of Victory! By the Decree of Victory!

As Spirit wills, I ask for Awakening. As Spirit wills, we are awake!

In the beginning, I AM THAT I AM! B'ray-sheet, Eh-yah esher Eh-yah![2]

Remember that all the exercises and clearing we do enable us to more easily and fully open our hearts to unconditional love.

The Phoenix Cards

One of the most effective exercises I recommend uses a deck of cards and book called *The Phoenix Cards*.[3] It is a powerful deck and anthropological study that is quite remarkable.

Susan Sheppard, author of *The Phoenix Cards,* tells us that at death our brain cells die and memory is wiped out, causing our memory to need to be rejuvenated in a subsequent lifetime. Why don't we remember our past lives? I believe we deliberately forget so that we can believe we can do better. The brain is merely a tool that accesses our memory and displays it to us, and there are many ways to access this memory. Once we develop a skill in one life, we may be able to recall it in some later life. Although you may hear from some teachers that the Akashic Records are in your DNA, that is only the local part of the Akashic Records. The record keepers tell us to imagine a public library. The main branch is where the Akashic Records reside (in the eleventh dimension). Though you may also find what you are looking for in a local branch.*

Everyone who uses the Phoenix Cards during my classes experiences a powerful shift. They will provide you with a past-life reading of yourself. Understanding your past lives from an anthropological point of view will enrich your self-understanding. It can make such a remarkable validation for you about three things: who you are now, who you have been in the past, and who you *authentically* are. You can instantly let go of old patterns that you did not realize were not your true self! If you have the resources, please find this book and deck and work with them.

Expect a Blow to the Heart

As you move into mastery, expect a blow to the heart. What is a blow to the heart? It is an emotional experience that will occur as a result

---

*The Akashic Records are the library of all human existence located in the eleventh dimension outside of the earth. For more on this topic please refer to my book *Opening the Akashic Records.* You may also decide a private session is appropriate for your needs.

of some unexpected behavior. It typically will occur because someone you are in relationship with does something, or fails to do something, yet you feel the person knew the correct action and should have made a different choice. The blow will come from someone you love and will occur around some real issue.

> When you are in relationship with someone who disappoints you over something you think the person should know or understand, it hurts. I call this a blow to the heart. This occurs as a result of your close interaction with your dear friend or beloved. Only someone this close has the ability to give you this transformational upgrade.

In one instance a woman I will call Michelle disappoints her friend Karen by canceling for an event they had planned on attending together. Karen would have driven an hour each way to visit Michelle and attend the event with her, however, Michelle cancelled with the excuse that she is buying a house. However, since Michelle is *shopping* for a house, not closing the sale on a house, Karen thought she certainly could have found a way to fit the two-hour evening into her schedule.

When Michelle cancelled, she didn't offer the tickets to Karen, but announced she had sold them to a third party.

Karen was extremely disappointed at not being able to see her friend and was hurt that Michelle did not offer her the tickets but sold them to someone else without consulting her. When confronted, Michelle couldn't see that she had done anything inappropriate. Nor did she think she had disregarded Karen's feelings.

Karen has just suffered a blow to the heart.

We all have layers and layers of armor around our hearts, and we add new layers every time we get hurt. This is how we survive. This is normal for all of us as we move from childhood to adulthood; we spend the first thirty years of our lives getting settled into our bodies, building up the ego and the armor around the heart.

We spend the remainder of our lives trying to undo this process! Most of the armor-building is done by the ego, which interprets reality and helps us perceive what is safe and not safe. The ego has done a terrific job of keeping us safe so far and believes these protections are necessary, but the ego is not always accurate.

In another instance, a woman's husband totally demolished their family van. When I arrived to meet with them, the wife, I will call her Sally, broke down in tears. She confided that her husband, Harry, had totaled the van. I could see Harry standing a short distance behind her and could not imagine what was worth all the sobbing.

I asked, "Is Harry okay?" She assured me he was fine. "Did you have insurance?" "Oh yes," she said, "the accident is completely covered by insurance." I was puzzled by the degree of emotion and the information I was getting so I checked in with my Higher Self and was told to stay in the moment, without an opinion, and that we were to go inside, hear the rest of the story, and do the MerKaBa Meditation.

The rest of the story is that Harry was texting when he ran the car into a tree. I still didn't understand why his wife was so extremely upset and looking to me for support.

In the larger scheme of things I was aware of specific marital issues they had. Sally had just suffered a blow to the heart. Without any opinion about the situation from me, we began the MerKaBa Meditation. When we reached the heart, at Breath 14, I asked Sally to ask her Higher Self what she should do. She had a well-developed connection to her Higher Self (a skill you will learn in chapters 4 and 5) and thus was able to ask specific questions and get precise answers.

Sally's Higher Self told her, *You could forgive him.* That hadn't occurred to her. She'd been so stuck in her justified anger that she couldn't get beyond it to see that this incident was a tool for opening the heart. When I asked my Higher Self what was going on here, my Higher Self instructed me that it was a blow to the heart. This was the first time I'd heard this term.

Many clients have been told by their record keepers, through me, "this is a blow to the heart." I now understand that we all get these opportunities to break down the layers of armor around the heart. It is faster than just about any process and it forces us to choose: Will I be forgiving and open my heart? Or will I be stubborn and insist I'm wounded? Being right doesn't always serve us. Forgiving him does not mean she ignores hurtful behavior. It means she recognizes this is his problem, not hers. She allows the blow to expand her heart, giving him room to change or exit.

We all know people who have been through tough time after tough time and are now bitter and angry. We also know people who have been through hell and back, yet seem to find a way to keep smiling. How could you refuse a blow to the heart knowing it is going to give you what you really want—an open, clear channel to your Higher Self and an open heart?

I hope you'll remember these stories so that when you experience a blow to the heart you can decide to open your heart even more and become closer and closer with your Higher Self. Remember that this is a tool to advance your spiritual connections quickly. Always ask your Higher Self for help, and ask the Higher Self of the other person to talk, or intervene on your behalf, to help smooth over difficulties between you and to help you stay in your power.

A Blow to the Heart: Ascension Rocket Fuel

The heart is the translator for Higher Self information. The more open your heart is, the clearer the incoming information will be. It is in your best interest to stay open and work through blows to the heart so that you can advance in your understanding of what your Higher Self has in store for you.

Love is the fuel. Your Higher Self needs your open heart's love (fuel) to understand and interpret the information coming in through the MerKaBa and Higher Self. You are capable of higher and higher expressions of unconditional love. Rocket fuel contains higher octane to produce jet propulsion, just as your love quotient increases your ability to move and understand the third-dimension reality we live in.

Love is the basis for the fifth-dimension reality that is our goal. Give yourself the blessing of opening your heart every chance you get.

What you desire is a level of unconditional love that enables clear communication from the fifth-dimension Higher Self.

When you are learning a foreign language you have the opportunity to make a big leap by visiting the country that speaks your new language. When you take a blow to the heart you achieve a similar leap. Your heart breaks off a layer of armor and you get to choose to remain exposed and more loving or close down and become hard-hearted. The choice is yours.

You may not understand this at first, but it has become abundantly clear to me that the opening of the heart is the key. Nothing will give you what you desire more than an open heart. The keys to the kingdom for all of us are hidden within a blow to the heart.

Fortunately, the blows to the heart get easier and easier. The time I had the wrong key to a friend's apartment in the Bronx after a morning jog in early October was easier to accept than I'd like to admit. I was due in Manhattan in two hours, I hadn't showered or brushed my hair or teeth, I was wearing a T-shirt and shorts with a hole in them, and the key didn't work. Imagine my initial response—"I just will not go!"—to finally begging for $2 from a stranger to get a one-way subway fare and going in my worn workout clothes. If you've ever been in class with me you know I take my professional appearance seriously, so it was a very big deal for me to go to teach a class this way.

When I returned to my friend's apartment later that night he was cross with me. At first I thought it was because my returning for my luggage meant he'd had to cancel his plans for an evening of dancing. Then when I checked in with my Higher Self I was reminded, "He is a nice man and it bothered him a lot that he'd let me down this way." The upshot was that after I had dealt with my own feelings, I had to deal with his feelings of failure for giving me the wrong key. The knowledge that it had been a blow to the heart made it possible for me to remain calm and joyous, and to tell myself that it was not at all about inconsiderate behavior, but a chance to open my heart even more.

I hope you'll remember my tale and laugh about me when your Higher Self informs you that the reason for someone else's awful behavior is a blow to the heart. This laughter will help you open your heart, and believe me, you will need that little laugh to help you get through it.

The Other Person Might Not Own Her Part

Remember the story of Karen and Michelle? Michelle didn't believe she had caused any pain or was a party to the blow to her friend's heart. Sometimes the other person can't understand how you feel, and it is okay to confront your friends. However, if she denies her part you must let it go and choose to accept this blow while maintaining your open heart. That means you do not press for an apology. You have let your feelings be known. Let that be enough.

Please don't misunderstand me. I'm not suggesting you accept inappropriate behavior from anyone. You certainly have the right to confront the person who administers this blow, to say you were hurt and ask that this not happen again. However, if the offending person does not seem to have any idea that the wound was extraordinary, the incident may just be an instrument for your heart opening. You can decide to let it go and open your heart. It is a choice.

You should never accept the same inappropriate behavior from someone consistently. If the same friend does the same type of thing more than twice, her status gets downgraded to acquaintance. We let our loved ones and friends help and teach us by administering a blow to the heart, but if it becomes abuse, we need to walk away.

Releasing your attachment to being wronged (by a friend, again I am not referring to a perpetrator here) will assist you greatly here. You know you were wronged; that is useful to know. Next decide that the other person's mission for you has succeeded—that helping you gain a quantum heart opening is accomplished. Allow your feelings to turn to quiet observation and gratitude. You release the other person, which completely changes the energy.

A blow to the heart is a significant tool to advance your Ascension work. Capitalize on it whenever it is offered to you and you will be amazed at the incredible progress you will make.

Bliss after a Blow

You can expect bliss to arrive after a blow to the heart. This is a combination of both joy and peace, and usually feels euphoric. It is temporary and may last a few minutes or hours. My first bliss experience was the result of clearing a huge block, letting go of something I knew I needed to release but had been unable to do. I asked for a million Ascended Master surgeons to work on me to release from me every obstacle that was keeping me locked in that behavior. I went to bed and forgot about the request.

What occurred next was amazing. At about noon the following day I was sitting at my kitchen table and I felt as if a huge weight were being physically lifted off my shoulders. It was the kind of weight you are so used to that you don't even know it is there until it's released. I immediately went into a state of bliss, stayed in this amazing "high" for about three days nonstop, then gradually dipped back into real life, then bliss, then real life, then bliss, until little by little the bliss highs were less and less intense until there was nothing left. It could be visualized as a decreasing sine wave.

Since then I have experienced bliss many times, but usually it is for shorter periods of time than that first one. I have also been able to recreate bliss and bring in a state of bliss with a homeopathic remedy. I first learned of this remedy from naturopath Eileen Nauman, D.H.M., who used it for sinus issues. She later described its use for bliss, which I found to be accurate. More recently, I created the guided meditation "Activating Your Sixth Sense, The Golden Bowl," which actually opens the sinus cavities to higher consciousness. What is the remedy? *Aurum metallicum*; common name, gold. Dosage? That is up to you. Remember, the higher the number on the homeopathic, the more dilute the potency, the stronger it is, and the more subtle it is. A client took a very strong dose and did have an undesirable reaction. Eileen suggests you ask your trained homeopath, and I agree.

At some point you may have declared, "I will do whatever it takes to get me connected with my life purpose. And by the way I want this to happen *now!*" You may have been asking for something that required more unconditional love than you were at that time able to channel through your body. Maybe you had beliefs and attachments that weren't serving you. Your request would have enveloped much of what you would release and gain. Much loss is associated with pain. When a child outgrows his childhood toys, does he cry for them? Only if it is not his idea to let them go. If you move too quickly you may find that your job, spouse, friends, and career all change abruptly, and even though you say you are ready to do whatever it takes, perhaps you're not. Ready or not, a blow to the heart will give you advancement after advancement in your spiritual connection with your own Higher Self and with God. It is worth it.

Why Doesn't MerKaBa Protect Me from a Blow to the Heart?

The MerKaBa provides an opportunity to receive a blow to the heart and keep an open heart. The MerKaBa field is completely impenetrable. Yet those who are close to you can reach your heart through your emotional body. This allows for your heart to be opened in this way. The MerKaBa provides a completely secure environment for the heart opening and staying open, thus allowing for a greater river of unconditional love to flow through you. Painful? Yes. Perfect? For your emergence to fifth dimension from third dimension, yes.

Even when the strike to your heart is so deep and searing that you wail with agony, know that your activated MerKaBa will be the secure environment for your heart to stay open and create a greater pathway of unconditional love to flow through you. Like a volcanic crater that blows open, your heart may feel as if there is a huge wound. Yet with the MerKaBa in place you can heal all of this pain in an instant. How do you do this? When you are ready, acknowledge the other person has done the job well. This acknowledgment need only be in your own thought. Be clear that that person's whole purpose was to help you get to this state of openness. That will release the charge that keeps you and the other person locked, and frees you from your pain.

Other ways to release emotional wounds include AroMandalas-Orion Series essential oil blends and the Intention disc (from Vibranz)—both available through my website.

Choose to keep your heart open after a blow to the heart and watch your unconditional love rise and grow beyond anything you thought possible.

3

Toning, Chants, and Exercises to Open Your Heart

What You Will Learn in This Chapter

- Sound exercises to heal the heart and clear emotional wounds
- Role of the four lower bodies and the elements
- Powerful chants for different functions
- Restoring our connection with nature

Toning

Toning is singing a specific set of sounds, sometimes specific words, and is usually repeated, which produces a certain vibration of resonance. This resonance will enable you to change your thoughts. It happens at a vibration level rather than a thought level. Because the chant's vibrations are repeated waves, their resonance within the body causes the change.

Toning should be part of your regular spiritual practice. Just as you periodically get an oil change for your car and periodically go for body work, finding time to incorporate toning into your spiritual life is good for your evolution, general health and well-being, and spirit. It will assist you in your Ascension work.

Key Factors of Toning

Toning creates the rarified state of instant fulfillment. This means that toning makes us pure simply by vibrating a pure tone through our bodies, which produces instant connection with all that is. Much like the concept of resonance, items that vibrate produce clarity in the vehicle of vibration and cause objects nearby to resonate with them. Imagine listening to an orchestra warming up for a performance. You hear the flute or oboe play A followed by string and wind instruments all playing the same A note, and then playing it again, till it is exactly the same pitch. That tuning is similar to what toning does in your body. It allows your body to tune to the sounds that are being given or sung.

Many healers use toning as a tool to heal and move energy in their patients. A healer may play a toning recording in the background while working on a patient. The patient may be invited to participate or to simply accept the vibration. You may have heard of tuning forks being used for this purpose.

Motivational speaker and author Wayne Dyer, now deceased, tells of the Tibetans who gave him the knowledge of the sound of God. In his book *Getting in the Gap: Making Conscious Contact with God through Meditation,* the book that accompanies his *Manifesting* CD, he tells of chanting the sound of God—AHHH—in the morning for at least twenty minutes. The sound of God—OHHHH—is to be sounded in the evening for at least twenty minutes.[1]

If a note is missing in your energy field, playing it on an instrument or reproducing it through the voice allows your body to replicate the missing vibration for itself. All vibrational healing works with this principle. You can heal emotional traumas through toning, which means your body can heal itself through sounding a tone that is missing. This is one of the primary reasons toning is so important. This is the principle behind the radionics and EMF machines that broadcast the "vibration of a specific body organ" that you may need.

There is no right or wrong way to tone. Be willing to allow your vocal chords to open and sound an open vowel. Use your voice in a way that is different from normal speaking or singing.

✵ TONING EXERCISE

Begin with one of the easiest practices. Get into a comfortable place, such as the bathtub or a favorite chair, and as you settle in, let yourself make sounds. Do not worry about how it sounds or what emerges. Take your breath in through the nostrils and let it out with your mouth, allowing it to run over the vocal chords. It feels perfect in the moment. It allows you to fill in the gap of whatever is needed in the moment. Play with this. Find your bliss. Experiment! If you are timid, start your toning experiments in the shower or bathtub. You might start with the five vowels—sing at any pitch and play with the rhythm. If you have a Tibetan or crystal bowl, play that first, and then make sounds to go with it! After a while it will feel completely natural.

There are other times you will feel the natural urge to sound—when you are singing along with a song or when you are happy! Go for it. If you are not a singer, it is especially important for you to sing louder than you might be accustomed to making sounds. Why? You may have been told or felt your sounds were unacceptable so you have held yourself back from singing. Singing louder gives you more practice so you can make up for lost opportunity and benefit from this.

Hathor Chant: *El Ka Leem Om*

Toning is the language of the Hathors, and the Hathors channeled this chant to me. It turned out to be a powerful Egyptian chant, so I began to include it in my advanced Flower of Life workshop. After I'd worked with this Egyptian chant for more than a year, a student informed me that it was found in a book titled *The Hathor Material*.[2] This was a complete surprise to me. Although I was familiar with Tom Kenyon's work, I had no idea he had written about this in a book he coauthored with Virginia Essene.

Years later I found a recording in Egypt by an Egyptian woman that explains the chant's ancient Egyptian origins. This is not the only Egyptian chant that has been given to me without my prior knowledge or experience. Since I am an open channel, information comes to me not through channeling but through direct knowing.

I decided to write to Tom asking for permission to use this Hathor chant on my recording, since he had published before I did. He was traveling, but I had already begun rehearsals and was about to schedule the recording studio, and the Hathors were adamant that I move forward with the project. Ultimately I followed their guidance to finish the recording. I became a woman with a mission. If I couldn't get his permission, I would make it available for free. All summer I kept working toward completion and emailing Tom's office multiple times.

The master recording was finally done and I sent a copy of the master CD to Tom's office that fall. Both Tom and Judy Sion, his partner, listened to it. At long last he gave his permission and secured Virginia Essene's permission as well.

Even though he doesn't give endorsements, Tom told me that the Hathors told him this CD* would have its own momentum and would not need any additional help from him. He was right. I get many requests for this powerful CD, and it is one of our bestsellers. Here is an excerpt from *The Hathor Material* about the words in this chant:

> In our worlds we have sounds for each of these four sacred elements: *el* is earth, *ka* is fire, *leem* is water, and *om* is space, or air. These four constitute a vibrational continuum. It is possible to chant the sounds of these elements and enter the archetypal reality in which they exist. It is as if these sounds open the door of perception and allow you to move into the resonant field of consciousness where the archetypal reality of the elements is alive. Indeed, entering into that realm and staying there for a while enables you to shift consciousness and perception in such a way that you sense the profundity of the physical world and also its place within the continuum of consciousness.[3]

I asked the Hathors to give me a way to remember the elements in the sequence used in this chant, since it does not match the familiar way we say earth, air, fire, water. They showed me a volcano in Hawaii.

*Mantras for Ascension by Maureen J. St. Germain.

As we approached this mountain-volcano they identified it as *el*. Then we saw the fire coming from the volcano, *ka*. *Leem* was the gentle rain that followed. And *om* was the wind that swept it all away. You may find this visual helpful when chanting El Ka Leem Om. Several years later I learned that legend has it that the Hathors live in a volcano on Venus!

The Four Lower Bodies

The four lower bodies are physical, mental, emotional, and etheric. They exist around the body in layers. Each of the four lower bodies has a specific purpose, and we work with them in such a way as to allow the pathways of information and experience to be open and congruent. When the bodies are lined up, coherent, connected, and communicating with each other, you are in alignment.

It is important to understand the true link between the four lower bodies and the elements of earth, air, fire, and water. As we engage our energies to clear these basic building blocks in creation, it is helpful to accept the stage at which you presently find yourself. This will help you to move your awareness into this chant. If you do your part, the point-of-awareness shift will be handled by the Hathors.

Physical Body

Our physical body gives us permission to *be* in the manifest form. Your physical presence is the result of what you did as an etheric being when you moved into agreement to embody. The physical body is the expression of that agreement to express in matter, where we get to co-create (in matter) by the very distinct experience of being human.

Mental Body

Deepak Chopra, M.D., estimated from his research that the average person experiences 60,000 thoughts a day, yet only 10 percent of those thoughts are about the present moment. How can we create the present if our thoughts are stuck in the past or future?

The mind uses the mental body to go to the future and discover, *Oh, this happened in the past, therefore I must protect myself* or *I will be*

afraid because this may happen again. Here is my potential for the future.
A clear person can feel all of this and then think, *I can incorporate the past and the future and create a new future.*

It is the mind that goes through the machinations, and sometimes it's like a locomotive that cannot stop. This is why clearing out the **pranic tube**◈ and learning to tune to the elements will enable being in the present, the most important event of all.

Etheric Body Shape

You may sense your etheric body shape if you have an out-of-body experience and still observe your body. Your etheric body is home to your chakras and is your link to your Higher Self.

The etheric body resides energetically just outside of the physical body. The etheric body is part of the body not yet in manifest form. It is your first link to your Higher Self and is comprised of energy that is in touch with Source.

Emotional Body

Next going outward around your body is the emotional body, which is the receptor of all your emotions and may access past emotions through memories in the mental body.

Emotions are energy that holds a purpose or feeling. Emotions reside in the fascia, or connective tissue. When the same emotional wound occurs, the fascia retains divots that accumulate more of the same wound. The Orion Series oils lift and dissolve these stuck emotions. The Intention disc reformats the stretched-out fascia like spandex returning from the laundry. Ascension tools make easy work of clearing your emotions.

The emotional body immediately links to the past. It says, *This has happened before.* Then recognition sets in. The core elements of earth, air, fire, and water all manifest through the emotions. Think about how you use these elements when your emotions become escalated.

Originally creation wanted a way to explore these experiences after they had been felt, thus the emotional body was born. Memory is a good thing but the captain's log of emotion became a miasma of feeling that could be accessed all too easily, replacing the present with its counterpart in the past. It also was not understood how deeply humans would feel emotional pain.

Clearing Emotional Wounds Is Essential

Until we clear emotional wounds our Ascension process is limited. The MerKaBa heals the wounds, however the process can be accelerated with additional emotional clearing.

Even Lord Krishna himself, star of the **Bhagavad Gita**◈, promised to deliver us from our emotional scars and hurts.* He promises to help you with any childhood or other experience that is painful and difficult. Devotion to him is easy through singing *mantras* and **bhajans**◈ to him.[4] His request is to visualize him standing over any past wounds or traumas, in this lifetime or any others. Ron Holt, former president and director of Flower of Life (now closed), was visited by Krishna in a meditation during a particularly difficult time of the FOL history. Once you are visited by Krishna you will never forget him. His body is distinctly blue in color. He is usually seen driving his chariot.

Toning to Clear the Pranic Tube

Emotion is energy in motion. It is *chi* or energy that is qualified with a memory. However, it is energy that is caught in a web, tied to time. Emotion must be felt to be cleared. This is why unexpressed emotion is so dangerous. When your pranic tube is completely clear and resonating, the pure elements, emotions, come and go. They can be deep or wide, but they are in motion. This is as it was intended. Be prepared for some interesting things to occur when you do this chant!

Setting the Stage for the Hathor Chant

This chant creates the link from your own awareness into the archetypal reality of the elements, as is practiced by many indigenous peo-

---

*Known as a Divine Being and an incarnation of the one true God, Lord Krishna is a major deity of Hinduism. He is also the hero of the *Bhagavad Gita*, featured in one of the most celebrated epic stories of the *Mahabharata*, which was written between the fifth and second centuries BCE. It is required reading for any yoga instructor.

ples. If you babysit you become aware of the needs of a baby; if you connect with the archetypes of earth, air, fire, and water your vibration will reflect more authentically the needs of the earth. Take this occasion to spend time in nature. Embrace air, sun (fire), water, and earth. Appreciate them. Allow your awareness and consciousness to become attuned to the four sacred elements. I can promise you they will let you know how much you are appreciated.

When singing the chant *a cappella* (unaccompanied by the CD or other music), you can keep track of the count with an outline of hash marks on a paper you have prepared. This way you can focus more fully on the chant. Chant the names of the elements in a state of reverence and discover that an inner world opens far beyond your imagination. Be aware that the Hathors may cause you to feel like you cannot move. Their energy may "freeze" your physical body while they work on you and clear your pranic tube. Don't let this frighten you; instead say, "Thank you."

After completing the chant take an additional ten minutes of complete stillness and silence. This is quite profound. There may be additional "action" from the Hathors during the still time. What happens during the silence is almost as powerful as the chant. It has been a wonderful experience for thousands who have participated. It is quite amazing to do it in a group setting.

As a result of entering this inner world, the archetypal world of the elements, you are even more deeply connected to the natural world around you, and you will experience this world with new comprehension. You will see and clearly understand that the earth itself is a sacred temple and wherever you go—God is. This new comprehension is so profoundly different from our third-dimension experience that attempting to describe it fails to provide you with knowing what to expect. Be prepared to be changed forever and *love* the rest of your life.

The Hathors ask you to chant four times and only in repetitions of four (for example, 4x, 8x, 16x, and so on). The Hathors show up to work with you in groups of four; one in front, one behind, one on your left, and one on your right, which is why they prefer repetitions of four. Ideally you would recite this four to the fourth power, 4^4, which totals

256 repetitions. You'll be happy to know we have done the counting for you, so using the *Mantras for Ascension* CD (first track) allows you to really get into your toning. This takes about twenty-two minutes on the CD. It most likely will take you longer when you do it alone, as the singers on the CD keep the pace going.

Another benefit of 256 repetitions is that it allows human consciousness to settle and move into the archetypes of earth, fire, water, and air. When that occurs your perception of the elements is crystal clear. You feel their aliveness and they feel your humanity.

The Hathors love you to do this chant out of doors where you are interacting directly with the elements. It is also useful to purposefully put your attention on your pranic tube.

With your attention on your pranic tube, the prana (God's white light) moving through it becomes attuned to pure essence and activated by your sound. This then activates the elements of earth, fire, water, and air *in you*.

Uprooting the Unconscious

The Hathors, through Tom Kenyon, clarify points about negative emotional material, as follows:*

> Another thing to understand about this chant is that material from the unconscious very often begins to rise up, because consciousness settles into a very deep and profound state. One can experience every state of consciousness, every state of awareness from absolute boredom and fatigue to high states of ecstasy and bliss, including an awareness of one's own 'demons,' one's own negative emotional material. All of this can be activated as one chants this chant, so it is important to understand that whatever arises while you are chanting is part of the clearing.
>
> By chanting the chant of El Ka Leem Om a person is, in our understanding, acknowledging the sacredness of the elements,

---

*Quoted material reprinted with permission from *The Hathor Material* by Tom Kenyon and Virginia Essene, SEE Publishing, www.tomkenyon.com.

acknowledging the continuum of consciousness from the Source that you may call "God" through its various subtle levels all the way into the earth itself. Rest assured, you are clearing Mother Earth, too. Here in the physical reality, which could be the densest sacred element level, one is affirming and acknowledging the earth as sacred, one's body as sacred, and one's place in the continuum of the consciousness that one may call God as sacred.

It has been said that the body is the temple of God. We agree that your body is a sacred temple for it is the space in which the four consciousnesses of earth, fire, water, and air (space) offer themselves to you in service.[5]

The Hathors have more to say about personal consciousness:

We see earth as a sacred space, an out-picturing of the sacred elements of the archetypal realm of consciousness itself. We see earth as being as close to God as any other reality, for the continuum is whole. Whether one experiences oneself as close to divinity or separated from it has nothing to do with whether one is on earth, embodied or not. One's view is something that is held in personal consciousness. It is possible to be in deep communion with the Divine, to feel completely at home in consciousness, and still be in a body. It is not necessary to leave earth in order to go "home," for home is a state of consciousness, a state of connectedness generated from within yourself.[6]

Create a Link to the Elemental Kingdom

The Hathors have asked us to look at our modern culture and address a problem experienced by many of separation from nature. I make it a habit to be outside in nature every day. Although taking a walk up the street is good, it is not what is meant here. Try to find a natural area, perhaps a park or nature preserve, that has no electrical power lines. Let this special time help you connect with the elements, the **elementals**◈, and more. Let the **elemental kingdom**◈ hear your appreciation for the abundant beauty of our planet.

One of the most important things this chant will do is link you to Mother Earth and Father Sky. I found that after using this chant almost daily for about a year, my connection with animals and the earth elementals made a monumental leap. I could hear and communicate with them. I was given other gifts as well. A daily practice of this chant for an extended period of time will really open you to this. In addition, it actually helps the elemental kingdom harmonize with the human kingdom, as you are literally singing their song.

The chant also links you to the elemental kingdom in other ways. In addition to being connected to the primary elementals of earth, air, fire, and water, there are personality-based elementals. These elementals are commonly known as earth personalities—gnomes, fairies, and elves; water personalities—**undines**◈; fire—salamanders; and air personalities—sylphs. This chant allows them to tune to you, and you to them. This is like having an exchange student or visitor from another culture; you begin to harmonize with each other.

One day I met them in person while fussing at them about the sorry state of my garden. The cultivated garden around my house was full of weeds. I'd been on the road extensively and had come home to find weeds everywhere! I remember complaining, "This garden looks terrible! I thought you were going to help me keep it nice. I really wish I could hear you guys!" Immediately I heard a cacophony of voices all talking at once. They were all talking to me in my garden (the gnomes, fairies, and elves).

I said, "All right, all right, one at a time!" I heard and saw in my mind's eye a gnome who was the leader. He appeared defiant saying, *You never asked us to help you.* I was dumbfounded. How could this be? I mentally retorted, *Yes, I did. Do not you remember the 150 tulips we planted? I carefully put dolomite in with each bulb and called upon you with every single bulb that went into the ground.* He said, *No, you did not. You expected us to help you. You never asked.* I stood there speechless. He was right!

Now I was going to have to eat humble pie, which I did not want to do. I thought I had the right to get their help. I began to realize that a conscientious person with servants speaks lovingly and with kindness to the servants, and does not demand anything. Who did I think I was anyway? I swallowed hard and apologized. Now I ask for their help.

They do communicate with me now. This gift, along with the others mentioned above, is a result of the practice of the Hathor chant. Here's a little hint for communication with the elemental kingdom: Focus your thought on the concept of a picture (like a single frame from a movie) of what you wish to accomplish. Then mentally project this picture to your unseen helpers.

Hathor Chant Hazard

We practice this chant in the group setting of my advanced Flower of Life workshop.

In one workshop one of the participants, who is an attorney-lobbyist, became paralyzed during the chant. He was able to think and breathe and sing, but was physically unable to move his body, which annoyed him very much. I now advise that you can expect your body to become very still, and if it feels as if you've "lost control" and cannot move, do not worry. The Hathors will work with your pranic tube and may have some very specific upgrades to install for you, which is why you need to be perfectly still. This has happened enough times that I know to expect it. You will be better than before after the Hathor upgrades.

Hathor Humor

In another advanced FOL workshop, during the chanting of this mantra the Hathors appeared to one of the men in the class. He asked the Hathors to show him what the fifth dimension is like. One told him to bite his (the Hathor's) toe. He did. They all laughed hysterically. They said, "Do it again." He did, and they all laughed even more!

When he shared his story, this man was laughing with such joy—like a little child—that we all laughed, too. Who could resist this infectious laughter? Just retelling this story makes me laugh and laugh. When the man in class told it, we laughed until we couldn't laugh any more. If someone bites your toe, you yell for them to stop, but the Hathors did the unexpected and laughed. Don't let the laughter fool you into thinking this is silliness or frivolousness; true joy can come simply through laughter. Let this chant open your heart in ways you have never dreamed. This mantra is very powerful.

Remember, you do not need to use the recording to do this chant, although you may find it is far easier to join with a choir that has mastered the pronunciation and count. It is also fun to sing harmony with it, to change the rhythm and pitch. It is easier to continue to chant with the choir and know it will keep going until you have reached precisely 256 repetitions.

Hebrew Chant

Kadosh, Kadosh, Kadosh Adonai Tsebayoth is the most powerful chant in the known world. Although its origins are Hebrew, it has been used by millions of people for centuries so it carries a remarkable, purposeful, imprint of transformation. Found in many places including J. J. Hurtak's *The Book of Knowledge: The Keys of Enoch,*[7] its purpose is to clear everything back to original intent. Unlike *The Book of Knowledge,* we have used the traditional phonetic spelling and pronunciation.

My personal experience with this chant is nothing short of miraculous. When I worked with a linguist who had spent extensive time in the Middle East and knew both Hebrew and ancient Aramaic languages, she translated this chant to reflect a more current concept of "forsaking all but God." This definition resonates with the effect it creates. Its energy can be accurately described to mean "nothing that is not of God" can exist when it is invoked.

My early training included memorizing this as a form of protection of the purest or highest form. It will clear anything untoward; evil, spirits, or entities. It is especially useful while doing out-of-body work. It clears all the fields in the body and bridges us to all other dimensions.

This mantra activates our holy grid bodies, which are more fully discussed in chapter 13. Singing or saying this chant creates a bridge from third dimension to all other dimensions. Immersed in the chant, you will become one heart and completely connected to the love of God. It is extremely powerful.

You may use this chant at any time or place. If you ever are fearful in real life, or see or experience dark energies on your spiritual journeys (asleep or in meditation), simply recite this chant. If the beings or energy are not of God's pure light, they cannot, they *may not*, stay. This is the second chant of the recording titled "Hebrew Chant" on my *Mantras for Ascension* CD or download.

> The Kadosh chant has been used by millions of people for centuries. It carries a remarkable, purposeful imprint of transformation.

The traditional translation is "Holy, Holy, Holy, Lord God of hosts." Our new definition expands this understanding and helps you grasp its fullness: Forsake, forsake, forsake all that is unlike God. It provides you with additional information that enables you to better comprehend your true purpose and maximize its benefit in your world.

A Remarkable Tool for Emotional Pain

The Hebrew chant is enormously effective for clearing emotional pain, any time you are suffering from a broken heart for any reason. When you are connected to God, all resistance about lack—what you do *not* have—ceases, as you are in harmony with God and all of life.

How Does It Work?

This Hebrew chant clears a direct path back to God. Imagine a man with two machetes walking through the rain forest in front of you. Your complicated path is now perfectly clear. This is what it is like to sing this chant. I have found that most of our emotional pain comes from holding thoughts of the past related to circumstances that we cannot change. This leads to stuck emotions. The Hebrew chant is a marvelous tool to help you clear this pain.

Have you ever been really upset and know that you need to emotionally shift, yet lack the will to act or think any different thoughts? It is easier to observe in others. Have you ever been so miserable that you are happy in your misery? This doesn't mean you do not know better; it is just that the pain is so deep, your wound so great, that your ego needs the validation of time. End result: your feelings are stuck. Persons who recite this chant, or play it when they are in a deeply distraught emotional state, find the results miraculous. Sometimes you cannot really do anything to make something better. Playing this chant is one way to shift from your pain. You can repeat it or sing it to yourself. You don't need the recording to use this chant but it does make it easier.

When you hear it sung, it opens you to start feeling the energy of God. When you are feeling the energy of God it is *impossible* to be miserable about anything. Experientially it feels as if the cloud has lifted, and the presence of God is felt through your newfound peace of mind.

Fast track your Ascension process with these two chants and they will clear you completely on the inner and outer realms, throughout all your dimensions of awareness. You can see why I was instructed by my guides to name them *Mantras for Ascension*.

Additional Powerful Chants

There are other chants you can learn to do when you are stuck in traffic or in the quiet of the night and cannot get to sleep. My personal favorite recordings in addition to the above are by Deva Premal. Wayne Dyer and others have released chanting CDs or downloads. Jonathan Goldman and Gregg Braden have released a CD sounding all of the vowels sequentially as the expression of the name of God. Using this method you would chant the names of the five vowels in the English alphabet. Here they are spelled phonetically in the order they arise in the chant so you can sound them out: *uh, ooo, oh, ah, eye, aye, eee*.

These toning recordings are quite profound and act as another tool for elevating consciousness. The advantage of using an external source of these sounds is that you get used to hearing it, which may make it easier for you to experiment on your own, but you do not need any recordings to do this work.

Chanting Is Timeless

The world's religions provide us with other important chants. You can invoke something as simple as *Hallelujah* or more obscure Sanskrit and

Hebrew chants. Some other traditions provide us with their most popular chants.

Om Mani Padme Hum is a Buddhist mantra, which is also used by Grandmaster Lin Yun's Black Sect Feng Shui as one of the three secret reinforcements for the purpose of energizing a cure or an enhancement. This is part of the Feng Shui training I received as a graduate of one of his teachers classes, and when you have a consultation with a graduate of his training they will ask you to do this to reinforce the positive chi you are creating with the Feng Shui. You can chant or sing this mantra, and there are many recordings available worldwide. My favorite is by Philip Glass.

Om Namah Shivaya (I bow to Shiva), a Hindu mantra used to call for peace, is often sung as *kirtan,* a form of chanting the names of God. The words in kirtan chants are the various Sanskrit names of Hindu deities: Krishna, Ram, Sita (Ram's wife), Gopala (baby Krishna), and so on. There are also occasional honorifics, such as *Sri* (Sir), and expressions of praise or victory, such as *jai* or *jaya.*

The format of kirtan is call and response, a musical style that dates back centuries and is a basic element of musical form in many traditions. For this style of singing, a leader (or first group in other traditions) sings a line that is then echoed by another group. Krishna Das is a well-known example of kirtan singers in this style. The purpose of repeating these names in ever-shuffling combinations is a simple one: to merge with the Divine.

My favorite recording, by Robert Gass, has sold more than 250,000 copies. When the World Trade Center was attacked in 2001, many individuals asked me what they could do. I told them to play this chant continuously and join in this chant whenever a moment became available. It is an easy thing that we can do and I believe it can bring peace.

Ritual vocalizing has been practiced for centuries and remains one of the most universal human impulses.

We have no recordings of the earliest humans, but when we encounter indigenous tribes who've had little contact with modern civilization, they all have sacred chants tracing their oral history back to their earliest origins.

And, if you look into creation myths from different cultures, in almost every case, the world is said to come into being through sound, through chant. It is in Hinduism, Christianity, Judaism, and Native American religions. That is evidence of an indigenous nature. The other evidence you can look at is young children: almost all young children make up repetitive songs—they lose themselves in the rapture of singing.[8]

Composer and pianist Philip Glass has led the charge in bringing lesser-known chants to the West. His *Freedom Chants from the Roof of the World,* with the Gyuto monks, Kitaro, and Mickey Hart, was recorded at the Cathedral of St. John the Divine in New York during the first Chinese crackdown on Tibet. The twenty-one monks are from the 500-year-old Gyuto tantric order, chanting for freedom and world peace. Their throat singing is accompanied by intermittent percussion and horns in a series of meditations to Buddhist deities. It's a beautiful and uplifting recording that is a paean to harmony and tolerance.

In an article on kirtan, frequent contributor to *Yoga Journal* Phil Catalfo writes,

Although we can't prove it, chant, or sacred singing, was probably one of the first expressions of human spirituality. "It seems very clear," says singer-songwriter Jennifer Berezan, "that humans have been sounding and chanting as far back as the Paleolithic Age and beyond." Berezan's album *ReTurning,* which blends original and traditional chants from cultures around the globe into a seamless, hour-long opus, was recorded in the subterranean Oracle Chamber of the Hypogeum at Hal Saflieni, a temple on the island of Malta. This chamber, renowned for its special resonance, was created for devotional rituals 6,000 years ago. "It is likely," she adds, "that for thousands of years there were unbroken practices of sound and song, possibly often relating to various life/ritual practices such as birthing, planting, harvesting, death, and shamanistic practices of healing and visioning."[9]

Chanting in the King's Chamber

Another location well-known for its acoustical properties is the King's Chamber inside the Great Pyramid in Egypt. *Sounds from the Great Pyramid* is a 2-CD set that recreates the experience of toning inside the King's Chamber. Recorded by a group of spiritual seekers who had traveled with me on one of my Sacred Journeys to Egypt, the group is chanting *Om* inside the King's Chamber. Much has been written about this room and many healing experiences have been reported.

My favorite experience regarding the King's Chamber involves Hatem, a group manager for spiritual tour operator Quest Travel. Now operated by Marawan Nazmy, Quest has done much to advance opportunities for spiritual teachers. We all owe them a debt of gratitude. Mohamed Nazmy, his late father, was one of the most well-respected ground operators throughout Egypt. He passed away in 2018 and his son Marawan now runs the company.

Figure 3.1. Maureen with
Quest founder Mohamed Nazmy

We had been in the King's Chamber for nearly two hours. It can be pretty intense, and we are usually soaked with sweat from top to bottom in that hot space. Nobody ever complains; we usually are in such an altered state by the time we come back from our time there that we're oblivious.

I was the last one to come down the plank from the King's Chamber as we exited. I like to be last to make sure everyone in our group gets out. Hatem was waiting for me. Standing full face in front of me, Hatem gave me a full-body hug. This was unusual, for Egyptian men don't necessarily touch women, and tour operators do not necessarily hug their clients in this way. I was surprised, but I let it go. Our tour continued to sacred sites throughout Egypt for the next two weeks.

We all left Egypt and I flew to Paris for a week of teaching. My return to the States passed through Cairo so late one evening Hatem picked me up with his driver from my Paris flight and escorted me to my airport hotel for my brief overnight before my flight to New York the following day. He turned to me from the passenger side of the front seat and said, "Maureen, I have something I need to tell you. Do you remember the hug I gave you after you were in the King's Chamber?" "Yes," I smiled, remembering how incredible that group had been. Leaning over the front seat toward me he continued, "I had had a terrible back problem for the last six months. Every healer, doctor, masseuse, or energy worker I met, I asked to work on me. It would help briefly but nothing lasted. I knew that if I was the first person to hug you after your return from the King's Chamber, I would be healed. It has been three weeks! I am cured. Thank you!"

Hatem is not the only person to credit the King's Chamber with a near-miraculous healing. John Reid, a sound scientist and Cymatics researcher, reports that his back was in such bad shape that he had to pay someone to carry his sound equipment into the King's Chamber. However, after lying in the sarcophagus there, he found his back was completely healed and without pain, and he carried his heavy equipment out of the Great Pyramid effortlessly.

Using the *Sounds from the Great Pyramid* CDs will assist you in recreating the original group's experience. Numerous individuals have used these recordings for various applications from meditation and journey work, to healing physical ailments. I was guided to use toning in the King's Chamber, along with the power of *phi* found in the very structure of the Great Pyramid. Using the knowledge of phi as related to sacred geometry and the Great Pyramid, these powerful CDs are focused on the inner-dimensional portal I believe to exist in the King's Chamber. You may discover that the toning and connection with the King's chamber and phi will take you on a journey greater than you could have imagined! A user of this CD wrote:

As I listened I was immediately transported to the King's Chamber. I felt myself being shot out of the top of the point of the pyramid as if being shot out of a cannon. I was being taken up and up through a space of nothingness. As this happened I saw several events in my life from a new perspective. This is awesome! Thanks for giving us such a powerful tool!

Finally, while beta testing this CD, I received a call from Ron Holt, former president and director of Flower of Life research, now closed. I needed to put the phone down for a moment to get something, and the soundtrack for the *Sounds from the Great Pyramid* was playing in the next room. When I came back, Ron asked, "What are you playing? I could feel something really powerful in that sound. . . . What is it?" When I told him it was the toning in the King's Chamber, he said, "Wow, I could really feel the vibration coming right through the phone!" This was from a small boombox with speakers in the next room.

How Does Chanting Affect Your Ascension Work?

Any form of ritual vocalizing or toning and chanting will bypass the brain and go for resonance. This tells us it doesn't require thinking or emotional processing to heal an emotional wound. Emotional healing is essential for Ascension work, because hanging on to your emotional wounds will keep you tied to past pain and trapped in third-dimensional experience. Resonance will tune the entire body, and especially the heart, to the frequency of God.

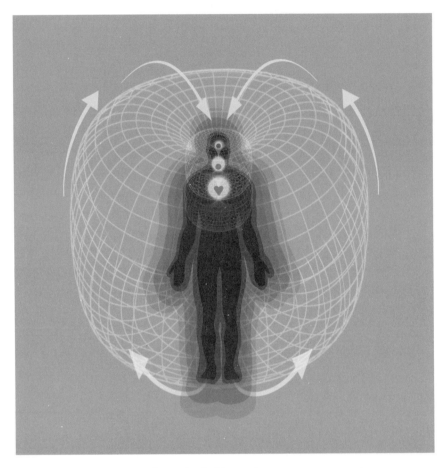

Figure 3.2. This is the field your heart creates around
the body during toning or activating the MerKaBa.

Have you seen the many drawings of the **torus**◈ around the heart
(see figure 3.2)? Toning the names of God in any form, such as kirtan
or vowel sounds, brings you and your awareness closer to the Divine
and aligns you with higher vibrations. Sacred sounds and toning have
been used for centuries by the world's religions with great effect. If
you are having any trouble breaking the barrier to your heart, consider
a toning regimen as a valuable tool to help you bypass the mind.

Opening your heart is essential for the MerKaBa Meditation. The
more your heart is open, the more effective the MerKaBa becomes.

These two elements, the heart opening and the MerKaBa Meditation, will bring you into resonance with the Universe and your fifth-dimensional self (the dimensions are covered in chapter 12). This allows you to tune with the world around you in such a powerful way that you will be able to know what you need to know, when you need to know it.

Initiating Contact
with Your Higher Self

What You Will Learn in This Chapter

- What the Higher Self is and is not
- The first steps to accessing your Higher Self
- How to recognize and use your lower self
- Why you must ask when you wish to receive
- How to establish signals and develop confidence in your Higher-Self connection

---

What Is the Higher Self?

The Higher Self is a version of you that is fully connected to God. It is that part of you that is fully aware of yourself as you *and* as God. Some call the Higher Self the mediator, but even that implies separateness, which is not real. Your first goal is to communicate with your Higher Self. The next goal is to move your Higher Self presence into your physical body. Then you will be a walking ascended being.

Imagine for a moment that your Higher Self is like a circuit board that has unlimited potential. In third-dimensional expression you have a very limited circuit board. If you put too much voltage through the circuit you can burn it out. You can try to go directly to God, but because of your circuit board's limitation, your connection to God is restricted by who you are in the physical body.* Your goal is to use your heart to expand your capacity. As you expand your heart through the many practices offered in this book, you will discover that your capacity to know and express your love of God increases dramatically. Eventually, with an expanded heart you can be a direct channel from Source.

Imagine your cell phone connection in a remote area. Every time you are on your phone, your connection is unstable. Yet, when you have Wi-Fi access, that direct access is easy and fast. You could make an important call from the remote area, but when you know where to get Wi-Fi direct access (i.e., your Higher Self) you would choose that.

The purpose of this section is to help you identify your Higher Self, work with developing your communication, and learn to get direct access to God through your Higher Self.

What Is the Higher Self Connection?

The Higher Self connection is something you build with a specific practice that, if done with diligence, will not fail you in your time of need. Ultimately this is the first step you are seeking. As far as I am concerned, after the opening of the heart in chapter 2, this is the most important part of the book. This is more important than programming your MerKaBa.

Remember, whether you choose to learn the MerKaBa or not, your Higher Self connection is the most important, inner GPS you could ever achieve. It completely eliminates the need or usage of any other form of divination.

> The Higher Self connection is something you build with a specific practice that will not fail you in your time of need. This is more important than programming your MerKaBa.

---

*Some individuals are capable of higher connections due to huge traumas they experienced in childhood that caused them to create "work-around" connections. In my book *Reweaving the Fabric of Your Reality*[1] I explain them as "survival psychics." These connections are a patchwork, evading the heart, not authentic heart connections, and eventually must go through the heart in order to build their God connection authentically. If they do not, they will not be able to achieve full integration of the four lower bodies.

If you attempt to program your MerKaBa without the Higher Self connection, you will fail miserably and can cause considerable damage to yourself and others. Programming the MerKaBa without Higher Self endorsement for each and every program is a form of black magic. After you have established direct communication with your Higher Self, you will be able to integrate more of your Higher Self into your physical form. This is the goal of Ascension. When you do this you are claiming your roots. You are claiming your heritage as a Divine Being.

What's Stopping Me?

When you were born you deliberately placed a barrier between you in your physical body and who you really are, your God-self, in order to move your consciousness into physical matter. Once there, it is very likely that you forgot who you really are. The goal then is to reconnect you to yourself and become an enlightened being. You are not likely to do this instantly.

You are moving through it slowly. You will maintain your awareness in the physical form while bringing in more of your Divine Self. If you brought in all of your divinity at once, you would not be able to maintain your presence in your body; you would pop out of the physical dimension.

As you become more adapted and aware, allowing for integration of more and more of your Higher Self, then becoming the Higher Self is easily accomplished while maintaining your presence in the physical.

Once you have developed your Higher Self connection to this new level, your Higher Self will communicate to you with unsolicited information. This is just like developing a friendship with the shopkeepers at a local shop you frequent. They will anticipate your tastes and interests and offer you things you might like. In a similar fashion, your Higher Self will begin to offer you information that you did not even know you needed. This is just wonderful.

You may remember switching from a regular television to HDTV. You are still receiving the same TV show you were before, only now it's in high definition. The input hasn't changed but your reception has greatly improved. Your ability to perceive the information has changed.

You are a special and powerful being. You know who you are yet at the same time may be afraid to admit it. If you are reading this book, you know that. This doesn't mean you are better than anyone else. You are *not* better. You are equal. Your self-awareness may be larger in any given moment than another's, but this does not mean you are more evolved or better.

What it does mean is that you are self-aware to a different degree. Your role is unique. The color blue vibrates faster than the color red. Does that faster vibration make blue better than red? Hardly!

You could be part of the way-showers who have arrived for the purpose of going ahead and helping others toward their Ascension. If this is true you will be drawn to serve as part of the enlightenment crew. If you are part of this advance crew you may already be an ascended being and are remembering. Keep up the good work and you will be helping many others besides yourself.

Extras Hold the Polarity Reality

Others who are unlike you may very well be placeholders for the polarity reality (third dimension) so that you can totally see what you are choosing to see. Without them you would not be able to see what you see. It may also be that when you no longer need to push toward your evolution and become enlightened, you will no longer need others to hold that polarity for you.* What if all those others you are observing are extras, as they say on a movie set, just holding space for you and there just for your benefit?†

Meriwether Lewis and William Clark‡ were ordinary men, but they were explorers and way-showers. You are one, too. Please believe me when I tell you that those who are reading this page at this point are at the edge of the cosmos of creation. You are at the end of the reality

---

*An enlightened being is someone completely connected to his or her God sense while maintaining a presence in the physical body. Christ, the Buddhas, Muhammad, and others achieved this. So can you.
†An extra in the film industry is a member of the unidentified crowd who has no speaking lines.
‡The Lewis and Clark Expedition sought the (nonexistent) Northwest Passage in the Louisiana Purchase of the United States, 1804–6.

of creation, which means that you may feel as if you are out there all alone or with relatively few others. Remember though, Lewis and Clark had the full support of the United States government behind them. You have the full support of the Great White Brotherhood behind you.

Some would say that an *important* person must lead or go first to deal with all the fears and surprises, which may be difficult. I like to say it is a privilege and honor. Both are correct. Whatever the case, you are up to the challenge. They only send the strong to do this sort of job. If you are reading this, chances are you are one of the strong, volunteer way-showers. You did not come in alone. You have plenty of unseen helpers. You have plenty of support from the Creator. All you need to do is ask for the help you need. Do it daily, since this is a free-will zone and you get a clean slate every day.

Ask for What You Need

A military officer sent to the field does not think twice about requisitioning supplies he may need to get the job done. If you need help and don't ask for it, you are missing the element of humility that allows you to ask for and receive help. Please ask for the help you need. The price is right and believe me when I tell you, the beings of light are here to support you and *need you* to *ask* in order for them to fulfill *their* mission. Remember, we are in a free-will zone.

What is required of you is the ability to be fully present in the reality. That is a form of training. Anyone who is forging new paths—the Wright Brothers, Martin Luther King, Nelson Mandela, and so on—relies on his wits. He also receives plenty of support in terms of getting all the latest information and tools that enable him to perform groundbreaking feats.

He gets all the glory and credit, even though there is a huge body of personnel, research, and science behind him that makes his mission possible. He still must apply his personal ingenuity to complete the job. You must be willing to take the first step, to step up to the plate, as they say in baseball. You must be willing to risk failure to achieve your evolution.

Use this metaphor to know that you can ask for, and are entitled to, all the support required. If you are not getting what you think you need, ask again with clear conviction that you submitted the purchase order and that the system (the Universe) absolutely must fulfill this order.

One thing is certain: just because your friends and family might not provide a whole lot of positive reinforcement, that doesn't mean all of heaven doesn't care. All of heaven is asking you to break through the patterns of your past, your family, your generation, our society, our culture, and so on. Not having support from your physical family forces you to gain conviction about what you believe and what you want. This actually helps you define boundaries and claim your power! Support is likely to be there from the heavenly hosts because you are at the front of the masses. Ask.

How Will You Know You Are on Target?

Your Higher Self will know. You will use your Higher Self connection to validate that what you are being given is on target. You can ask your Higher Self to validate anything you want.

The saints and masters have achieved a full connection, and so can you. The way to a complete awareness of God (enlightenment) is through your Higher Self, and there are many ways to get connected to your Higher Self. Doing the MerKaBa (and using the tools found in this book) is one of them.

Connecting with the Higher Self is a key element to learning the MerKaBa. We all have a Higher Self we can access and use, although many of us are not aware of it. How do you connect with the Higher Self? How is that different from just "tuning in" or asking for guidance?

Before we begin that, allow me to introduce the lower self. The lower self is like the child to your adult ego self and is made up of elements.

The Lower Self

Yes, there is a lower self. When I first learned about a Hawaiian spiritual practice for connecting to the lower self from Drunvalo, I ignored it. After all, I already had a strong connection with my Higher Self. I really did not need to be concerned about a lower self I didn't believe existed. Drunvalo had learned about it from a student in his class who radiated so much light that Drunvalo asked the man what he did.

He was a Hawaiian *kahuna* who taught about both the lower and Higher Self. He said that ancient Hawaiians believed the lower self is like a child, and that you must become like an innocent child to connect through the lower self with the Higher Self.

I believe this same concept is why Drunvalo suggests you become like a child to connect with the Higher Self.

I didn't know anything about the lower self at that time either. Through trial and error I learned why it is so important to understand this concept. In my own experience I became aware that my lower self was not only the little girl in me, but much, much more.

The lower self is dedicated to keeping you safe, teaching you about the ways of the world, and helping you to understand life. In a way it is the simplest part of you. It is a compilation of mostly your ego and your desire body, emotional body, mental body, and physical body. It includes all the elements of you that operate your four lower-body systems (physical, emotional, mental, etheric) that are centered on a physical incarnation. Up until now the lower self has done a good job. After all, it has gotten you this far!

The Lower Self Is Your Friend

The lower self will give you accurate information for the immediate circumstances, especially if it has to do with your physical safety or your emotional body. Lower self feedback can be influenced by individuals who are around you and the environment, however, so the information is accurate but only to a point. The lower self also keeps track of past hurts and wounds to help you avoid similar situations.

The lower self can also jump in and answer your questions without you realizing it is the lower self. To help illustrate this, I will be sharing with you stories about how the lower self can interact with you and you mistakenly could think it was your Higher Self. But first let us learn more about the lower self.

The practice of kinesiology,* or muscle testing to read the body, is lower self information. You can get lower self data from a pendulum as well. I don't recommend the use of a pendulum because you can

---

*Kinesiology is the technique of monitoring a body response to stimulus. Professionals who use this tool will ask for a physical body response such as being able to resist pressure for the "control" and then base further responses on resistance or nonresistance responses.

become dependent on it and because it can be influenced by your environment or the material that it is made from. Ideally you will develop a connection with your Higher Self that makes the use of the pendulum obsolete.

I am not saying using a pendulum is wrong. Remember, your goal is self-mastery and becoming your most evolved expression of you. You must learn to access your most authentic source and in all cases this source is your Higher Self, which is your direct connection to God.

Lower self information is accurate to a point, but its operating system is based on experiences gained from living in a physical body. The lower self is pulling its information from the limited database of your four lower bodies—physical, emotional, mental, and etheric. It may also be pulling information and collecting data from individuals around you and from the environment.

Because the lower self keeps track of past hurts and wounds, it can influence you to stay away from situations. Your lower self might choose to avoid similar painful situations that may be important to you now. You could be influenced inappropriately by your lower self if it is reflecting the data from your physical location or from nearby persons. This is why it may be useful to use kinesiology or a pendulum to determine what vitamins you should take, what therapies you might need, or sensitivities to food. The practice of applied kinesiology* or manual muscle testing to read the body is lower self information. You can get lower self data from a pendulum as well. Your Higher Self is your direct connection to God.

Because the lower self keeps track of past hurts and wounds, it can influence you to stay away from situations. Your lower self might choose to avoid similar painful situations that may be important to you now. The children's story *Peter Pan* by J. M. Barrie gives us a very compelling look at the lower self. It shows Peter Pan giving an accurate display of the lower self making all the decisions and avoiding situations that may be useful to an adult.

---

*Applied kinesiology tests muscles for strength and weakness.

The lower self has your best interests at heart, but it acts like a child in comparison to your Higher Self. This means that it has a limited vision of what you wish for yourself in this reality. It also is not as readily able to cross-reference all of your needs into one composite understanding.

How Do You Distinguish Your Higher Self from Lower Self?

Whenever you ask your Higher Self a question, always begin with, *Higher Self . . .* Do not assume that if you pose a question in your mind the voice answering is your Higher Self. Unless you have specifically addressed your Higher Self by name, it can be anything.

The lower self can jump in and answer your questions without your realizing it is the lower self. There was a woman who asked her Higher Self if she should go on a date with a man she found attractive. She received an affirmative answer. They went out, nothing bad happened, and nothing good happened.

The woman, who also valued her time, came home frustrated and asked her Higher Self, *What was that all about?* Her Higher Self responded, *You never asked your Higher Self when you asked the question.* She was astonished. Her Higher Self continued, *Your lower self jumped in and answered for your Higher Self.* The woman was quite shocked. It had never occurred to her when she asked the question that her lower self could answer for her Higher Self. It was at that point she realized she had not specified *who* should answer the question and presumed it was her Higher Self.

There is also the possibility you may have entities that will answer your questions. They may give you accurate but biased information. Be careful. Remember your Higher Self will answer when called.

The woman who went on the fruitless date with a man who turned out to be of no interest to her was getting accurate information from her lower self. Why? Because her lower self was expressing for the little girl who wanted to be special; the woman in her who wanted to be desirable; and the part of her that wanted companionship. Had she also known there would be no friendship and it would not go anywhere, she would have declined the invitation. Her Higher Self would have known other factors that were more important to her and given her a different answer.

When this decision was put into the context of her busy lifestyle, it was very clear to her that it was a waste of her time. Only her Higher Self would be able to arrive at that conclusion by weighing all of her needs and providing her with a response that would be the perfect solution for her.

The lower self has your personal information close at hand. The Higher Self has access to *all* the information from the four lower bodies, your Divine Self, and other persons involved, and is able to integrate them all to bring balanced responses. You may not know *why* your Higher Self gives you a certain answer and it may seem counter-intuitive. Your Higher Self has access to everything beyond your physical senses as well, along with everything beyond your mental awareness in the recesses of your mind. When you go on a driving road trip and use your GPS or maps app, it tells you all the roadblocks and delays. Using the Higher Self is like using your GPS. This can be compared to the lower self that may be reading a map or looking at a compass, but might not have the latest updates.

The Higher Self along with your activated MerKaBa responds to your current request, taking in all factors, known or unknown to you. Using your Higher Self along with your activated MerKaBa ensures you are fully connected to the reality throughout all time, all dimensions, and all space. Your Higher Self connection is valid whether you are practicing the MerKaBa Meditation or not. Your MerKaBa helps you maintain your fifth-dimensional energy flawlessly. In spite of this, if you could only do one thing, the Higher Self connection will steer you toward love and the highest and best choice for you in the moment. The Higher Self is the central guide, the activated MerKaBa makes living as a 5-Der easier in a 3-D world.

What Is the Difference between
Your Higher Self and Your Lower Self?

- Your Higher Self is proactive; your lower self is reactive.
- Your Higher Self knows and understands your circumstances from a universal perspective and integrates all of your needs, wants, and desires as well as the activity of the physical world around you.
- Your lower self is operating from a limited perspective and is not fully integrated so it cannot weigh conflicting desires the way the Higher Self does. Given the choice, most decisions would benefit from full awareness of the reality.

What about Intuition?

Information received intuitively can be coming from any of the above places. It may or may not include all pertinent data. Your intuitive information could also be coming from external entities, or energies that are not authentically you. Other people's thoughts can enter your head, especially if they are thinking about you and you are thinking about them. Many couples experience this communication phenomenon as normal.

Information coming from your lower self may feel like it is coming from intuition, but it could come from your desires, from external entities, or from the child in you who wants something you have long forgotten. Your information might come from your Angels or guides.

Angels and Guides

What is wrong with getting information from the Angels or guides? Nothing is wrong with that, except it is not authentically you, and your purpose and goal here is to learn and gain access to your Divine Self. Our Angels and guides stand ready to help us at any time, and are probably with you now. The purpose of the Angelic presence on Earth is to help build a personal relationship between Creator and the human race.

They want you to gain this connection and will fully support your getting it. In fact, my Angels have given me a metaphor to explain this. Suppose you are driving a fun sports car on a mountain road. Initially you might be going pretty fast as you enjoy the open air, the sunshine, and the beautiful countryside. Then your lower self kicks in (that part of you that keeps you safe most of the time) and decides maybe you should slow down and take it easy; after all, it is a pretty curvy road. Or maybe it is one of your guides or an Angel telling you to slow down.

Another car approaches from the opposite direction and you manage to stay out of its way, even though the driver has crossed over the center line into your lane, right in front of you! You end up swerving to your side of the road, but still safe. You manage to pull yourself together and think, *Wow, that was a close call! Good thing I slowed down and my reactions were so quick.* Lower self is reactive.

Your Higher Self Is Proactive

Your Higher Self would experience this whole scenario and take a proactive approach. Your Higher Self will be aware of the oncoming car long before you are and send you a message such as, *Why don't you take a break? You've been driving for a while and need to rest. There's a scenic overlook coming up ahead; pull over and enjoy the view.*

When the car from the other direction comes down that road toward you, you are out of harm's way. You might not even know that a reckless driver is coming down the hill. You never notice because your Higher Self directed you to get off the road. You are able to see how your Higher Self influenced your actions proactively and allowed the circumstances to occur around you, while keeping you from being directly involved. Your Higher Self is proactive; your lower self is reactive.

There Is No *No*

Many years ago when I first started working with this information I realized there was only *yes.* Although you can teach your Higher Self *no,* technically there is no *no.* This is why I refer to choice as "God" or "not-God." So if you get a good clear signal for *yes,* and nothing for *no* or *neutral,* you have enough information to operate in the reality. Go with that.

Advance Awareness

One of my longtime students shared what happened to her.

Ginny was very proud of having earned her black belt in karate, a feat she accomplished after she turned fifty! Those who have arrived at this karate milestone know that once you've earned your black belt is when the serious work begins.

Every Monday morning she dutifully drove one hour on an interstate to get to her dojo in the next city. One particular Monday morning she decided she wanted to meet with her teacher. She calculated that if she started out one and a half hours early, it would give her plenty of time to meet with him. She left her home at 7:30 a.m. for her 9 a.m. class. Along the way she received a message from her Higher Self.

On this highway there are three exits going into the destination city. Her Higher Self instructed her to take the first exit. The first exit is convenient and entails the fewest miles, but it takes much more time due to local traffic and rush hour.

The second exit, although longer by miles, is the most direct, routing around city traffic. It generally takes the least amount of time. The third exit is way out of her way. While driving, she was told three times to get off at the first exit. She rationalized each time that it would consume some of her precious extra time for her desired meeting with her instructor.

She drove right past the first highway exit. The second highway exit was closed, because there were men working in it. Taking the only remaining exit she now was required to drive quite a distance out of her way. The instructor did speak to her the moment she arrived. He commanded fifty push-ups since she arrived late to class!

Ginny was able to recognize in hindsight that her Higher Self had been trying to provide her with what she really wanted. She dismissed it because she was accustomed to feeling that her best information would come from using her logic. Three times, while driving, she was told to get off at the first exit. She rationalized each time that it would take too long and chose to follow her ego. Have you ever done that?

Hindsight leads us to a different conclusion, and we understand that fifteen minutes early is better than fifteen minutes late. There is a logical reason for using your Higher Self information and we will get to that shortly.

I have been teaching this aspect of the Higher Self connection since I began offering the MerKaBa Workshop in 1995. On September 11, 2001, I had my own hindsight about how significant this Higher Self connection really is.

Higher Self and 9/11

I had been guided to hold my series of workshops in New York City in September 2001. In New York I did not have a host, and selected dates based on my Higher Self direction. I had been going to the city regularly and had received prompting from my Higher Self to be in New York in September, and the exact dates to be there. Once the workshop dates had been set, I decided I would add an extra day to shop and visit friends while I was there. Back then I did not ask my Higher Self about a vacation day!

This particular trip had me flying home on September 11. However, when I attempted to purchase my airline ticket, I felt my Higher Self directing me to come home immediately after the workshop, on September 10.

People have asked me, what was it like? For me, I had this sinking feeling. Have you ever played the game of Monopoly? Think about how you feel when you pull the card that says, "Go to jail, go directly to jail. Do not pass go, do not collect $200." It was that kind of feeling, and very strong. I asked, *What am I to do then?* I was told, *Go directly home, no playtime this trip.*

At the time a friend asked me, "Why aren't you staying as you planned?" and I told him, "I really do not know. I just know I need to be home. Maybe one of my sons will need me for something." When one becomes accustomed to the voice of the Higher Self, it is easy to listen and to follow the direction given. The Higher Self does not always show up for me as a voice; sometimes it is a feeling. In this instance, I had no idea how significant that would be.

I would not have been on the downed flights of September 11 if I had stayed in New York that extra day, but I would not have gotten home. There were no flights anywhere in the country for a whole week while the government sorted out the next course of action to follow this terrible act. I was very grateful not to be caught in the chaos of being grounded at an airport far from home while a teenage son was at home for a week without Mom.

A student in that class had a job interview that Tuesday morning where she was scheduled to walk through the World Trade Center just about the time of chaos. That morning she was so uncomfortable with the prospect that she called her interviewer asking if she could interview by phone. She understood in hindsight that her feeling of discomfort may have saved her life.

Invocations

In my invocation at the altar at each workshop I ask for a direct connection with my Higher Self and the Higher Self of each person in my class. I specifically ask that their Higher Self be able to communicate directly with mine so that I might serve each person perfectly. I then ask for the same connection with each of us, that we might all serve each other perfectly.

A similar invocation is also part of my daily practice. You are encouraged to do the same. My favorite is an exceptionally helpful tool to receive Higher Self assistance with interpersonal interactions when trying to communicate with someone who may not be hearing what you have to say in third-dimensional reality: *I ask for my Higher Self to work with the Higher Self of (the other person) for the purpose of (fill in the blank) and that this communication be for the highest good of all, creating a win-win circumstance for everyone.*

We all have interacted with bosses, spouses, relatives, or customers who, for whatever reason, are unable to hear what we have to say. I have often advised people who may be facing a difficult meeting or negotiation to ask for the Higher Self connection between all persons so that everyone's needs can be heard, met, and addressed. Following is a true story of a woman who made such an invocation, and how it may have saved her client's life.

Higher Self to Higher Self in the Emergency Room

One of my students, an alternative healer named Juanita, was giving ongoing monthly treatments to a client named Susan, a medical doctor. Prior to their work together, Dr. Susan had landed in the emergency room with a panic attack. The drugs used to treat her turned out to be totally wrong for her, causing her to leave her body and have a near-death experience.

Four years later Dr. Susan had another emergency room visit, with what turned out to be another panic attack. Although she is a medical doctor, some major emotional things had just occurred in her life to trigger this panic. Although the attack was not at all related to the healing work they had been doing together, Juanita knew Susan needed to go to the emergency room and insisted she go.

Because of their ongoing relationship, Susan asked Juanita to work on her remotely while she was in the emergency room. Because Juanita had trained with me and understood the use of the Higher Self connection, she called in the Higher Self of the attending physician and asked for both Susan and the physician to be connected to their Higher Selves, and to each other's Higher Selves. The instruction was that whoever was the emergency room doctor would get his instruction on the appropriate medicine from Susan's Higher Self.

Later Juanita spoke to Susan about this. The healer's prayer occurred at the same time that the attending physician announced with considerable passion that he was going to "go with his gut" and use a specific medication. He selected a less commonly prescribed medication, which turned out to be the exact one able to heal the anxiety attack and help Susan through her crisis without a drug reaction.

Juanita explained to Susan that her Higher Self had directed her to create a link between the two doctors (the emergency room doctor and the patient doctor) at the Higher Self level. The emergency room doctor accepted his strong feelings and let them guide him to an alternate medication. He was in reality getting accurate information from the Higher Self of the patient, Susan, making sure the correct medication would be used this time.

Higher Self and Family Matters

In another example, a young mom wanted to attend a seminar. She and her former husband were alternating weekends with their sons, and the weekend of the workshop was clear for her. But then one of her sons was selected as one of a hundred finalists for a full scholarship. All the candidates and their families were invited for a weekend at the college, where the students would go through a series of interviews and tests. This was, of course, the same weekend as the seminar.

The mom knew it would not be fair to haul all their children for the eight-hour drive to the college. Caught in a dilemma of what to do, she consulted her Higher Self.

The first thing her Higher Self told her was, *This is not your decision. This is your son's decision. Tell him there are three choices and all decisions are equal: he can drive to the college with either parent or fly by himself.* When given the choice, her son didn't hesitate. "In that case, I will go by myself and fly." This mom would never have considered the third alternative, but because it came from her Higher Self, she was confident it was a good decision for all involved. This enabled her to take care of her son and also attend her seminar.

What Is a Signal from the Higher Self? How Do I Know I'm Getting a Real Signal?

A signal or symbol from the Higher Self can take any form. For those of you who are kinesthetic, you may experience a feeling; others have a sense or knowing. If you already have this sense or feeling, you will understand it more confidently with practice.

Others get colors, shapes, or other visual experiences; some will hear something; still others will notice a scent.

I have included examples in the table on pages 90–91 from a few of my students to show you what some other people have experienced.

What If I Don't Get *Yes* and *No* Symbols or Signals?

If you have been doing MerKaBa Meditation for a while, asked your Higher Self for symbols or signals, and you come up with nothing, it is time for you to select symbols you can understand and teach them to your Higher Self. You will need to pick something to communicate this knowledge of what you want for the signals or symbols signifying yes, no, and neutral.

How Do I Teach the Higher Self My Signals?

What if I do not get a clear signal in meditation? Now what do I do? When my oldest son was a two-year-old, he taught us the word for cheese; it was *ga.* He could not say *cheese,* so every time he saw cheese, a favorite of his at the time, he named it for us. We learned that if he wanted cheese he would say *ga.* If your Higher Self doesn't give you clear signals, then you will assign values that you can recognize in this same way.

To set the matrix for these signals, select something you can easily replicate in your mind's eye. Make it something simple that you will accept. For example, if you see colors easily, green could stand for yes, red for no; or thumbs up for yes, thumbs down for no.

If you find it easier to experience energy in your body, or a feeling, you might decide that a simple energy "whoosh" on the right side could stand for yes, on the left for no, and in the middle for neutral.

Many people experience geometric shapes as one of their signals. Whatever it is, choose something that will work for you. But *pick something* and let it stand. Do not question it.

If you decide that a red car should be your signal for yes, and you close your eyes and cannot imagine a red car, that is not a good signal for you. You must select something you can replicate in your mind's eye, and then your Higher Self can communicate it to you to experience it.

Then practice with something you already know the answer to so that you can get the feel of it. An example is, *Do I have a son?* You already know the answer. Let the correct symbol or signal present itself.

Continue practicing with mundane questions such as, *Higher Self, is it in my highest and best good to wear this shirt today?* If the answer is *no,* move to the next shirt and repeat the question. You can ask, *Higher Self, is this route my highest and best good?* Keep asking the same way. Looking at a menu ask, *Higher Self, is it in my highest and best good to get the soup?* If the response is *neutral* ask, *Higher Self, is it in my highest and best good to get the salad?* If the response is *neutral* ask, *Both?* The response may be *yes.* Remember to phrase them as yes or no questions, always addressing the Higher Self by name. Notice the tendency to ask, *Should I?* has been replaced with, *Higher Self, is it in my highest and best good?*

What about Neutral?

There are five possible reasons for a neutral response. They will be discussed in the next chapter. Please note that neutral is *not* maybe. Many people get this confused! Neutral means neither yes nor no. You might want to ask more questions after the neutral response to get clarity. Once you understand the five possible reasons for the neutral response, it will make more sense.

Examples of Symbols or Signals

Brian's *yes* symbol is a smiley face. When he went walking on the beach right after the meditation where that information came in, he found a shell with a smiley face worn into it by Mother Nature. The synchronicity of finding that shell was the Higher Self providing clarity and reinforcing his signal.

Kelly first experienced her Higher Self through the Michelangelo painting of the hand of God reaching for the hand of man as her symbol of the Higher Self. Her *yes* signal was a thumb pointing up and thumbs down for *no.* Dennis's Higher Self has a sense of humor; his signals are a Mickey Mouse white-gloved hand with the thumb up or down.

A man in the class was the "drag-along" partner of a woman who was very into this work. He decided to attend on a whim. He had never really done any meditation before and he asked me, in a whispered voice,

"Can your Higher Self have a sense of humor?" When the Higher Self connection was made, his Higher Self showed him a red beating heart for *yes* and green M&Ms for *no*. That same man was given a vision of his Higher Self the following day. He whispered in my ear, "Can my Higher Self be a woman?" Coincidentally, that same man shares the same first name with another male student from a few years back. Both men's Higher Selves appear as a woman.

In one class there was a lot of crystal energy expressed in the location, and the store hosting me had hundreds of crystals. Many participants in this class experienced their signals in the form of crystals. In another class a man, Tom, was a former military guy. His signals reflected him as a paratrooper getting ready to jump from a plane. His *neutral* signal was at the open door of the plane (and he never jumps). His *no* signal is the jump and his parachute does not open. *Yes* is him jumping and the 'chute opens! Another man in that same class sees his Higher Self represented by lightning. Jagged means *yes* and has a direct feeling. Spiral lightning is *no* with a dancing-type feeling, and *neutral* shows up as a flat line of lightning.

The signal for neutral frequently tends to come up as a flat line or some variation thereof, such as a horizon, the sea, or a minus sign. The table on pages 90–91 contains some of the information from students coming through the meditation where I introduce the Higher Self and ask for the Higher Self signals.

Help! I'm Not Getting Anything!

If you do not get a symbol or signal, don't despair! You are not alone, and I will be providing tools to help you communicate with your Higher Self. If you do not get a signal it just means you are not visual or auditory. It may mean that you are so mental or cerebral that you have not allowed those signals to appear for you.

Allow yourself to see or feel any kind of response, and with practice, you will find the Higher Self connection.

In the next chapter you will receive instructions and techniques to help you develop and strengthen your Higher Self connection. Practice is critical.

SAMPLE SIGNALS FROM THE HIGHER SELF

IDENTIFICATION AND EXPERIENCE OF THE HIGHER SELF	YES SYMBOL OR SIGNAL	NO SYMBOL OR SIGNAL	NEUTRAL SYMBOL OR SIGNAL	AS PART OF THE INSTRUCTION, WE ASKED FOR A MESSAGE FOR THE INDIVIDUAL, CLASS, OR WORLD
Flood of light warmth	Openness	Tightness	Wobbly spin	Flood of color, Dragon—strength—power
Vast—deep blue to light blue to white connectedness	Door closed	Door open	Door unable to move	Funny to have open door for no! I am one with the Universe.
Male (significant because this was a woman) dog ears	Golden sphere	Tetrahedron point in front	Purple color	Purple is a common color for Higher Self.
Tingle throughout the body	Constriction at bottom of throat	Constriction at top of throat	Absence of any feeling	Love yourself.
Intimate conversational connection	Sphere brightness	Sphere darkness	Sphere neither light nor dark	Flow freely.
Multicolored	Strong energy solid, solar	Standing in heart energy	Horizontal movement from left to right	Middle point, water dancing, freedom, laughter, cherished
Pervasive warmth	Spoon with three bands at joint	Walnut	Circle with a dot	Pay attention, communication with elementals, especially Higher Self.
Light warmth tingling awareness, also eye of Horus	Eye of Horus closed (Funny again, closed is yes!)	Eye of Horus open	Eye of Horus winking!	The more we connect with all of the parts of being, the more one can create harmony, laughter, joy!

SAMPLE SIGNALS FROM THE HIGHER SELF

IDENTIFICATION AND EXPERIENCE OF THE HIGHER SELF	YES SYMBOL OR SIGNAL	NO SYMBOL OR SIGNAL	NEUTRAL SYMBOL OR SIGNAL	AS PART OF THE INSTRUCTION, WE ASKED FOR A MESSAGE FOR THE INDIVIDUAL, CLASS, OR WORLD
Shown from outside her as a holographic projection of self "I told you if you were really here the Earth would not be able to hold your love."	Geometric shaped letter Y	Geometric shaped letter N	Visual of a line of words—"flat line"	Empower yourself!
Streams, trees, huge crystal energy, geometry shapes, purple-orange-blue—all colors, metaphysical masters—Jesus, Quan Yin, and Akashic Records 180 times—do you want to do this anymore? Multi-Universes—home let us go home	Yes	No	Silence	Went directly to Source. Is this my Higher Self? This is everyone's Higher Self—Everything, everyone.
String pulled tight	Head nodding yes	Head nodding no	Pivot around an axis	Is this dumb? Man on a one-person sailboat—three sails—small trapeze . . . sense of freedom and power!
Way more than words—joy, peace, compassion. Heard Archangel Michael talking to her.	Thumbs up	Thumbs down	First and little finger up, the rest down, waving hand	Butterflies, giant crystal, illumination, Earth beyond beautiful mosaic of love. Lay your feet upon me, know we are one—go deep—illuminate, embrace, merge, remember. Beacons to transcend and transform.

When Do I Ask My Higher Self These Questions?

Initially you will ask your Higher Self questions while you are in meditation. If you are doing the MerKaBa it is between Breaths 14 and 15. Many of us take a little pause there and it is a perfect time to connect with your Higher Self. This is because you are anchored into your heart starting from Breath 14. I always invite my Higher Self to join me in my heart. You will also find this instruction in my version of the MerKaBa Meditation in the CD audio *MerKaBa II.*

Remember that the ideal meeting ground for you and your Higher Self is in your heart, because it is the one place you both have in common. It is much preferable to check in with your Higher Self while in your meditation. Just as on a cell phone, it is far easier to receive clear communication if you are in a place with good reception. If your cell phone keeps cutting out on you, you are likely to limit your conversation until you have clear reception. Remember that the best reception between you and your Higher Self is while you are in your heart. You may even wish to go back to chapter 2 to review some of the heart-opening exercises.

How Do I Actually Do This?

Upon completing Breath 14, while you are still in meditation doing the MerKaBa, you simply think or ask the following:*

1. Higher Self, I am choosing to be in my heart. Please join me in my heart.
2. Higher Self, I am making a commitment to build a new level of communication between me and my Higher Self.
3. Because of this, I am asking my Higher Self for a signal or symbol for *yes,* I am asking my Higher Self for a signal or symbol for *no.* I am asking my Higher Self for a signal or symbol for *neutral.* (Wait for the signal or symbol to appear.)
4. I thank you, Higher Self, for working with me.

MerKaBa II, Guided Meditation CD, contains these statements after Breath 14.

Even if you think you already have a good connection with your Higher Self you can always improve it. No matter what level you are at with your communication there is always room for improvement. If you disagree, then you do not need this book.

A woman observed in a class that everyone around her was getting guidance from Higher Self, yet she was not. Someone said, "Have you asked?" Asking your Higher Self to work with you more closely will bring the Higher Self in more closely. You are also making a clear commitment to start to interact with your Higher Self. It is an important act of will. Make sure you ask!

Fuzzy Information

Occasionally as your Higher Self connection becomes richer, you will discover something will not feel "quite right." Perhaps the information will be muddy or seem strange compared to your usual feelings when checking in with your Higher Self. Pursuing this suspicion will help you recognize to reframe your question or ask, *What is going on?* Lack of clarity is significant and requires further investigation. Ask, *Is this my Higher Self?* Only your Higher Self may respond with a *yes.*

Getting to know your Higher Self communication leads to all kinds of information you did not expect. Find a way to unhook from your *need to know,* or any other need. Be open and consciously work at non-judgmental review and reaction to your Higher Self information. Choose to step away from the habit of interpreting everything from a polarity vantage point. Instead of saying, "I am not getting anything"—especially if you usually do—consider that vagueness has its own message.

What Is Going On?

You will learn more about the higher dimensions in chapter 12. Ultimately I concluded that there is only one question to ask your Higher Self. That question is non-pejorative, nonjudgmental, and very open-ended. It is, *Higher Self, what is going on?*

Now, the opening of your heart is the key to understanding the information you are getting. Think of your heart opening as if it were a translator. The more open and receptive to giving and receiving unconditional love, the more you will be able to comprehend the incoming data. The more experienced your heart is in practicing unconditional love, the more incoming information will be meaningful to you. There is a direct relationship between your heart and your understanding. If it is knowledge you seek, then open your heart to get the answer.

To learn the maximum amount of understandable information, we simply ask the question with no bias. The question that reflects no bias is, *Higher Self, what is going on?* I suggest you use this formula every time something happens that defies the rules of reality.

It Is about Free Will

Until you have an open heart and establish a connection, your Higher Self does not care about you or interact with you. In fact, it is against cosmic law for your Higher Self to intervene. Higher Self is not permitted to interact with you (unless by prior-to-incarnation agreement or other special circumstance) until you decide you want to communicate with it.

If your Higher Self initiated an interaction with you before you asked for it, then your Higher Self would be violating your free will. That, for your Higher Self, is not possible. Higher Self communication into third-dimension reality must be initiated by you.

What about the people who spontaneously start getting information? This is generally by contract, and you may have preexisting agreements with your Higher Self for something significant to open you to the Higher Self communication. Even those of you reading this may be able to pinpoint an event that started you in this direction.

Communication in Both Directions

If you are studying with a piano teacher, she might decide you are ready for a difficult piece and purchase the music on your behalf to help you with it. If your teacher saw some music that she thought you would like, she might suggest that you explore it and offer guidance on playing it.

When your communication with your Higher Self is reliable and consistent, the communication will begin to travel in both directions. Your Higher Self will begin to give you information that you may need and desire that perhaps you did not specifically ask for in the moment. The free flow of information occurs as you grow your connection to your Higher Self with your practice and devotion.

In the next chapter we will develop this newfound knowledge. If you are serious about developing a connection with your Higher Self that is virtually foolproof, you will choose to practice. You will choose to practice with questions that have no consequence to you. We will explore that and your commitment next.

Keeping Your
Higher Self Connection

What You Will Learn in This Chapter

- Next steps in talking and listening to your Higher Self
- How to practice your Higher Self connection to support living a fearless life
- Once your reach a certain level of mastery, the only question to ever ask your Higher Self

Commitment Time

If you already have a great Higher Self connection, a six-week review and practice will still improve your connection from where it is today. Many successful actors and dancers continue to take classes long after achieving prominence. How will you know if you really need to practice?

If you do not follow your inner guidance/Higher Self 100 percent of the time, you do not really trust it. You decide, here and now, that you will keep a practice period, like a trial period. Your trial period is a segment of time that you choose for yourself. It can be any length of time. It should be at least forty-five days.* It could be longer. Make sure you make

---

*It takes forty-five days to process a decision before new genetics kick in, according to Donald Epstein, D.C., founder of Network Spinal Analysis® chiropractic system and author of *The 12 Stages of Healing.*

this decision at the ego level. This is to ensure that the decision is being made in a way that you are completely happy with your choice. I will refer to the practice period as being six weeks for the sake of discussion. Your practice period is forty-five days or more; the exact length of time is for you to decide.

Once you have established or received your signals or symbols from the Higher Self, it is time to make a commitment to continue to work with your Higher Self for a period of time.

You are learning the language of the Higher Self and you need to get really good at it. If you were learning a foreign language the first thing you might learn is yes and no, but you do not stop there.

I am asking you to make a commitment of time to work with your Higher Self and practice. I want you to perfect your practice. Your Higher Self connection will be with you for the rest of your life. In the overall scheme of things, six weeks is a small investment. Choose your practice because it pleases you and you are willing to commit to the time. After you select a timeframe, please assign a future date to it. This means that if today is the fifteenth of the month, and your practice period is for six weeks, you will name the first of the month two months hence. Specifically if today is July 15, your practice period will end on September 1.

If you breezed by the methods for connecting to the higher self in the previous chapter, this would be a good time to go back and review them before continuing.

What Kinds of Questions
Will You Ask during Your Practice Period?

This is one of the most critical sections on how to work with your Higher Self. You will choose questions that have no value to you and are of no consequence to you. These questions will be about things that you really do not care which way you do it.

The reason you ask about insignificant things is because you do not want your ego to participate. Your ego has done a terrific job of getting you where you are today and it will not be able to resist participating on issues that matter to you. So give yourself a break from the ego, and select questions that do not concern the ego.

For example, you might ask, *Higher Self, is it in my highest and best good to wear the red shirt or the blue shirt?* If you are meeting your best friend who always compliments how you look when wearing red, you probably would want to wear the red shirt, so it is not a good practice question.

Ask Questions about Actions
You Are Willing to Complete

Make sure your practice period is loaded with questions you are willing to ask and follow through with, no matter what your Higher Self tells you! If you are unwilling to follow through with the Higher Self's answer, don't ask it.

If you love chocolate chip cookies, don't ask your Higher Self about having one, because the temptation to eat one will be too great. You might decide to eat one and then later tell yourself, *Well, the no really was not a clear signal, and I really could not tell.* You do not want to sabotage yourself, so do not ask Higher Self questions if you already prefer a certain outcome.

If you ask your Higher Self a question and then decide not to follow through on the answer, you will be sabotaging your practice. During the practice period, please remember that if you ask your Higher Self, *you must follow through.* If you do not, you will interfere with your communication and defeat the purpose of your practice period, which is to develop this spectacular connection.

Why Is My Ego Eliminated
in This Equation?

Your ego does not need you asking your Higher Self for things it is accustomed to handling for you, and will not easily relinquish the job of running your life. You are very likely getting great information from your guides and Higher Self already, but then your ego, which has managed all of this input for you in the past, gets in the middle and you begin to doubt and second guess.

In fact, your ego may have been instrumental in influencing your buying and reading this book that led you to this point. Your ego wants you to be happy. Your ego wants you to get what you have determined is important (that is, information, knowledge, understanding, and more). Your ego collects its information from your lower self and the world around you.

Imagine for a moment that your ego is a really good administrative assistant, or admin. Your admin does a wonderful job of making appointments, purchasing, organizing, setting up your business meetings, and managing your day. Your ego is like that. Next imagine the reaction you would get if you told your admin you were going to handle all the appointments, purchasing, business meetings, and organizing and didn't need her anymore. The admin might ask, "Is there a problem with my performance? I have done a great job for you so far. Are you trying to eliminate me?"

If, however, you told your admin you would start taking out the trash, she would reply, "Great! Take the one under my desk first since it gets filled the fastest." If you tell her you will start washing the windows, she will tell you that the ones in reception need it the most and to do those first. Why? She does not want those jobs anyway. Your ego will not resist your Higher Self communication by selecting things that don't matter to you (or your ego)! This is an easy way to learn the language of the Higher Self. If you are a control freak and need to decide everything then you will have to pay extra attention to this.

For example, some people know exactly what they want to wear, exactly what they are going to eat, and manage even the most mundane details of their life with great precision. If this is you, decide now what you are willing to negotiate. Find out what you are willing to ask your Higher Self and then use that short list every day. *Higher Self, is it in my highest and best good to take this route to work?* Avoid using "should I" and always use the formal. *Higher Self, is it in my highest and best good to use the Stairmaster now? Higher Self, is it in my highest and best good to prepare green beans? Higher Self, is it in my highest and best good to make spinach for dinner?* Then sit back and watch the magic.

Maybe you prefer to use the treadmill in the gym but you get a *yes* when you ask about the StairMaster. You get on the StairMaster machine and watch someone else get on the treadmill. Your envy turns into appreciation when you see that the treadmill is not working. It was the same machine you would have used! Little by little the seeds of faith and knowing get planted. Within the practice period you've established, you will have enough synchronicity to know with great certainty the very real and tangible benefit of your Higher Self communication.

At some point your ego is looking at all of these wonderful synchronicities and starts to see that you will get everything (happiness, knowledge, understanding, and so on) if you ask your Higher Self to decide.

Full Integration of the Higher Self

In reality you are integrating the ego into your Higher Self so that your Higher Self is expressing God's will. It is a powerful place to be—to be so fully connected to your Higher Self that you are always operating from your fifth-dimensional self, or 5-D. (We will explain 5-D in chapter 12 of this book.) Ultimately what you are doing is weaving the Higher Self and the ego together so that your ego wants what your Higher Self offers you, because the benefit is clear. Your practice period gives your ego the proof.

I am not one of the teachers who believe the ego must be subdued. Instead I believe the ego can be integrated into the Higher Self and vice versa, creating one will—God's Will.

Later, after your practice period is complete and your Higher Self connection is crystal clear, it is okay to not do what your Higher Self tells you. I am laughing as I write this, because when you test this out a few months from now, you will realize that once your Higher Self tells you any answer, you will regret not following it. You will probably choose not to follow your Higher Self only once! I only did this once and will write about what happened later in the book. I was sorry, too. Furthermore, in all cases that I know of, the Higher Self connection will always *insist and persist* if it is critical, so no worries there.

Remember, if you do not think you can go either way regarding something your Higher Self tells you to do, then do not ask. This is a perfect indication that you have an attachment to the outcome and that it is not a good Higher Self question for you during your practice time.

Belief

Asking why serves the ego. Belief involves *understanding,* which still relies on the ego. Beingness relies on knowingness. Trust will follow after you have blindly followed your Higher Self signals for six weeks. Your practice will develop confidence and that will lead to trust. It is about knowing that your Higher Self makes it possible for you to be *in the moment.*

In the case of Higher Self questions, you choose to rely on the feedback you receive. This means you do not worry about whether you get *immediate* feedback about the choice and whether it was the perfect one or not. You will wait for some lovely synchronicity to give you feedback that shows the accuracy of your communication.

For example, when you call a friend for lunch and he agrees to meet, you might ask where he wants to go. He does not care and offers, "You pick, I chose last time." So you ask your Higher Self, which is in my highest and best good? Chinese? Pizza? You ask your Higher Self for each one, yes or no. Both answers should validate each other. Your Higher Self picks pizza, and while you are there you run into someone you had been trying to connect with for months. Here the Universe is giving you the synchronicity and reinforcement that lets you know you are getting good information from your Higher Self.

Remember, you must agree to follow whatever your Higher Self gives you during your practice period. If, during your practice period, you ask your Higher Self a question and then you decide not to follow it, you will sabotage your language skills.

Forget Keeping Score

One man I worked with told me he was still having trouble with the Higher Self answers. I asked what kinds of questions he was asking and he said that he would ask his Higher Self if the traffic light in front of him would turn green before he got to it. I remember laughing and saying, "You still care about the answer!" and he replied, "No, I really do not care if the light is red or green." And I replied, "Yes, but you are looking for immediate feedback that proves that you are right!" He said, "No, I really do not care whether I get home five minutes later."

As an engineer he felt it was his responsibility to track his Higher Self's accuracy. What he is doing is keeping score. He thinks it is necessary in order to make sure the Higher Self is responding. He is an engineer and of course believes that he has to collect this data. While it is true you are to collect data, you must not seek immediate feedback. Instead, wait for synchronicity to provide the data to prove your Higher Self connection.

If you practice basketball you might stand in front of the basketball hoop, aiming and shooting dozens of times. At each opportunity you would adjust your aim based upon the feedback of where the ball goes. If you look for this kind of immediate feedback with Higher Self practice you are likely to dismiss the correct answers as lucky guesses, and the wrong ones with, "See, it doesn't work."

If you keep looking for feedback to get the evidence that your Higher Self was right, you have not totally detached from the practice questions. The purpose of this exercise is to learn to allow your Higher Self to communicate, so that your ego will observe and conclude that this is a good thing. Ultimately your goal is to incorporate your ego with your Higher Self so perfectly that the two become integrated into one will, God's Will.

Asking unimportant questions means you are not tracking the results. It is the very "not tracking" that produces the "not caring" attitude so very necessary to your success. As you let go of the need to evaluate or be right, your Higher Self will be able to give you enough evidence via the fifty or more daily questions that the results will be irrefutable. Instead of scorekeeping, let the synchronicities produce the score.

Remember, it's important to choose questions for which you have no attachment to the outcome. Any sort of predictive question meant that the engineer would know instantly if his Higher Self was right or wrong. When he was right he would compare it to all the wrong answers and conclude this whole Higher Self thing wasn't working. Again, scorekeeping isn't allowed during your practice period. Instead let the synchronicities produce the score!

I Ask My Higher Self a Question but I Never Get an Answer

If you do not get an answer to the question *Is this my Higher Self telling me something?* consider the possibility that your Higher Self did not advise you like you think it did. Perhaps it is other forces within you. Be specific and confirm that it was your Higher Self giving you the answer.

As a parent, have you ever heard a child answer to "Who ate the last cookie in the cookie jar?" Of course not, no one will answer that question!

The point is, if there is an entity in you urging you to take some action, or your lower self is wishing for some preferred outcome, you may think it is your Higher Self when it is not. When you ask the question, *Is this my Higher Self telling me to (fill in the blank)?* and you do not get your well-practiced *yes* signal, *that is* the answer. This lack of an affirmative signal is proof it is *not* your Higher Self leading you into this action. This is important to remember. The absence of a clear signal means it is *not* your Higher Self that was advising you in that moment.

The only way to know for sure, especially when you are in a dilemma and really wondering, is to ask, *Is this my Higher Self telling me to do this?* Only your Higher Self is permitted to answer. This is cosmic law. If you are having trouble with this, try rebalancing your energy by asking your Higher Self to show you your *yes* signal, your *no* signal, and your *neutral* signal. This will neutralize the field. Then ask the question again.

Please be very careful. Your Higher Self will never tell you to do something that is dishonest or immoral. Your Higher Self will never justify any action that would hurt another. If you are suspicious of an answer from your Higher Self, ask again. When in doubt, do without.

How Do You Achieve Proficiency?

Promise yourself that you will keep this commitment to ask your Higher Self as many mundane, ordinary, unimportant, or insignificant questions you can think of each day during your six-week trial. I suggest you ask practice questions fifty times or more each day. Your

Higher Self will not mind. It is an investment in your future!

What kinds of questions are considered mundane? Anything to which you do not have an attachment.

What kinds of questions will you ask?

Is It in My Highest and Best Good to:

- Wear the red shirt or the blue one?
- Follow this route or that one to work?
- Skip dinner?
- Call someone now?
- Go to the gym today? Now?
- Take a break now or later?
- Prepare carrots or cucumbers for dinner?

If your dinner guest loves carrots, you may already have decided on cooking carrots to please your guest. Just cook the carrots and do not ask during your six-week trial.

On the other hand, if you don't have a plan for dinner guests and you ask this question, and the response is to cook carrots, then do it. Then when the doorbell rings and the surprise visitor who ends up staying for dinner happens to love carrots, you can thank your Higher Self for knowing this before you started cooking.

No Exceptions

During this practice period please refrain from asking your Higher Self questions that are exceptionally important. This is to make sure you are not jeopardizing your practice period with issues to which you are attached! If you need to make an important decision that is time sensitive and you need to use your Higher Self, please do. But this should be a rare exception. Kindly postpone every significant question you possibly can until your practice period has been completed.

Learning the Language of Non-Judgment

How do you learn this language? Ask your Higher Self to work with you in achieving this awareness. Although it is not natural by normal standards of mass consciousness, you can acquire it with practice. Approach it like any change of habits. Perhaps when you were younger you used slang words and now you don't because they do not give you the results you now want. It is a bit like that.

If you have been in a class with me you know we practice reframing judgmental statements. For example, if you ask your daughter to stop being mean to your house guests, you are actually locking her into that behavior by asking her *not* to do that. Instead you might ask her to be kind to everyone who visits because, "That is how we do things in our house." Notice that this statement does not state your daughter's behavior is good or bad, yet clearly conveys a different behavior is required.

Neutral Response

In the beginning of this Higher Self connection I asked you to also ask your Higher Self for a signal for neutral. What does neutral mean? How can you use neutral?

One of the easiest ways to reframe your judgmental statements is to begin to recognize polarity words that everyone uses and decide to stop using them in this way. It is easy to see polarity in the five reasons for neutral.

Five Reasons for Neutral

When your Higher Self gives you the neutral response to a yes or no question, you can use it to get more information. Neutral can mean one of five possibilities:

1. *There is no difference.* Either answer will produce the same result. For example, you are at a fork in the road and your Higher Self can see that the fork merges before your destination, therefore there truly is no difference.
2. *Ambiguous question.* Perhaps you have asked something like, *Will I marry Henry in September?* What if you will get married to Henry but not in September? Or which September do you have in mind?
3. *It does not serve you to know.* Sometimes you and your Higher Self

know that you will act inappropriately if you know the answer. For example, if you ask if you will make your Ascension in this lifetime, perhaps you will become overconfident and miss opportunities. This is called Divine Timing.

4. *It does not serve you to know now.* This is also about Divine Timing and is similar to number 3 above; sometimes it just does not need to be known *now.* For example, when you ask, *Will I pass the test tomorrow?* and you might use that information to go out and party instead of studying, your Higher Self will give you the neutral response. Perhaps after you have studied and are ready for bed, the answer, when the question is asked again, will be *yes.*

5. *It is not in your stewardship.* This means you do not have the right to know this information. You do not have the password. If you ask, *Is my neighbor pregnant?* and get *neutral,* it is really not your affair. In polarity-based 3-D we would say, "It is none of your business." There is a very strong charge on this statement and it should help you begin to see the difference between polarity-based thinking and word choices versus unity-thinking and non-polarity word choices.

> Knowing the five reasons for neutral will accelerate your understanding of the neutral response and your ability to discern your Higher Self information.

What Is Next After a Neutral Response?

You can follow your neutral Higher Self response with a second question. *Is it useful to pursue this further?* If the answer is *yes,* you can begin to see one of two possibilities: either there is no difference or your question is ambiguous and needs clarity. You may now proceed to know more. If your answer to the question *Is it useful to pursue this?* is *no,* then you should drop the whole line of questioning.

It is very important to understand that your Higher Self is not giving permission. When you ask your Higher Self a question you are developing a relationship with the version of *you* that is fully connected to God. This is akin to asking about what will put you in alignment with who you are at your highest level of evolution. Your Higher Self knows this and will always answer with this in mind. Your Higher Self never corrects you or tells you that you are wrong. Being wrong is completely impossible in the fifth dimension. In fifth dimension the only choice is a God-centered choice, and the not-God choice does not exist. So in 5-D your response to any situation is always a good one.

As you become more and more your fifth-dimensional self, this type of polarity thinking does not occur to you. You have full awareness of your God connection, which makes choices that align with that God connection.

Open-Ended Questions
Are for *After* Your Practice Period

Open-ended questions are questions that could have any answer. Typically, they are the opposite of yes/no questions. You can ask your Higher Self any open-ended question. *Who did that? When will my son understand? Why is such and such happening?* One time I asked my Higher Self why my van was making a certain noise and surprised even myself with the precise answer that I had no reason to know or understand.

Developing Mastery with
Certain Kinds of Questions

I discourage you from asking your Higher Self questions so you can make a decision about something. This is because you are using your mind to draw information from your Higher Self, whereas your Higher Self might actually have information that you failed to ask, to reach a different conclusion. It is the last question you ask. It is more appropriate to ask your Higher Self what you should do in a situation. For example, instead of asking your Higher Self if someone you do not care to see is going to be at a party so you can decide whether or not to attend, you could ask if it is in your highest and best good to be at that party. It is never advisable to ask your Higher Self about a situation and then make a decision. That action is ego driven.

At a certain level your Higher Self will start giving you unsolicited information. This is the ultimate. If you develop a rapport with an expert who lives near you, at some point in the friendship that person will offer information you have not requested. Why? Because the friendship and connection imply your interest in his advice. Actively soliciting your Higher Self many times during your practice period will open the gate and keep it wide open for information to flow freely in both directions.

The Logical Reason for Following Your Higher Self

I always followed my Higher Self, knowing it is worthwhile, however I desired to provide proof for those who were new to this arena. *Knowing* vs. trusting the Higher Self could make a huge difference in deciding to *always* follow your Higher Self.

For months I meditated on this question. I was obsessed with finding a logical reason to follow Higher Self unwaveringly. I understood this question would be useful to type-A personalities. I knew many individuals would benefit from a logical reason for always following your Higher Self.

One morning the answer arrived as I was coming out of the dreamtime. I was seeing a local weather report as it interrupted a movie on TV. Why do we listen to this interruption? Logic tells us that when a weather report interrupts local programming there is an impending change in the weather. It tells us this situation that *appears* normal is about to change drastically. It is a warning to "take action now." If hail is suddenly expected, you may want to put your car in the garage.

Once your Higher Self communication is strong and flowing easily in both directions, the logical reason to always follow your Higher Self is that your Higher Self will communicate with you in advance of when you need to know or do something. Having this advance notice system that is always turned on and communicating with you allows you to quell the voice of logic that may be telling you something different. This is because your Higher Self is providing you with an interruption of "local normal" with an update to inform you that things are not normal as they appear. Once you commit to always follow your Higher Self it will be second nature for you to follow through.

Learning the Difference between Third Dimension and Fifth Dimension

Certain kinds of open-ended questions elicit more information than others. Open-ended questions may still hold expectations that would translate to their being third-dimensional questions. These questions ultimately are still polarity based. Why? This is because they are based on limited thinking instead of possibility thinking. They are looking for an answer so you can take an action or understand something. Third-dimensional thinking seeks understanding so that the ego can act. Fifth-dimensional is not thinking; it is knowing.

Where did my stuff go? is looking for a place to go to retrieve it. *When will my husband understand me?* asks how long I have to wait. *Who is responsible?* helps me know who to blame. *Why did that happen?* helps me to understand or change the situation so it will not happen again. In all cases these questions use the Higher Self in a *limited* way because we then take an ego-based action after we get the polarity-based information.

Missing Objects

Save yourself hundreds of hours of effort by understanding this simple principle. Over the years I asked more and more questions of my Higher Self. I paid close attention to things that happened that defied the rules we believe are supposed to govern our everyday activities. I began to notice that objects would disappear. Occasionally they would reappear. In my frustration, I would complain, *Where did my stuff go?* The answer was always the same, *It is in the higher dimension.*

This happened frequently enough to make me begin teaching participants in my workshops how to handle this if it was happening to them. They all reported it was, so I taught them what I had learned. I discovered I could ask for my object to return from the higher dimension. I would state, *If my object is in the fourth dimension, I would like it back. Thank you very much.* You can, too. Your belongings didn't move to another location, they were there all the time, yet you couldn't see them in your third-dimensional state.

One day in Asheville, North Carolina, I had a class where a builder who owned his own contracting business complained that his wife had lost her cell phone. He said she'd lost it four months prior and was sure she'd lost it in his truck. They took everything out—seats, carpet, and tools—looking for that missing phone.

In the end he gave her his cell phone and purchased a new one. He asked, "What do you say to get something to come back?" I gave him the exact words: *If my wife's cell phone is in a higher dimension, I would like it back now. Thank you.* He repeated this after me and added with emphasis, "I'm driving to take us to lunch today!" At the lunch break he opened the driver's side door of his cab. I opened the passenger side just as quickly. We both wanted to see what would happen. He reached in under the seat and pulled out his wife's missing cell phone. He looked at me as he said, "If this hadn't happened to me personally, I would not have believed you."

Start Asking Your Higher Self How Much You Are Loved

This is so powerful and so significant that I recommend you ask this of your Higher Self every single day: *Higher Self, show me how much I am loved.* It is especially important when you are working at the pioneering level clearing out painful emotional issues, no matter what the subject or venue. I put these "heart instructions" on my *MerKaBa II* CD.* This along with the Hathor toning gives you a leg up on doing the meditation by yourself. Add this to your daily practice and watch your heart heal in ways you did not even know were needed. This request is to help you grow your self-love and develop trust with your Higher Self. It is not typically answered with words that invite you to take action, thus it is not breaking the forty-five-day rule.

In my advanced workshops we have had many examples of what

---

*The *MerKaBa II* CD is available in stores or at the Source Books & Sacred Spaces website.

happens to individuals when they ask this question, and I would like to share a few.

A doctor who asked her Higher Self to tell her how much she was loved saw a beautiful pink rose, then several roses, and then hundreds of roses, and the colors kept increasing, finally representing the entire spectrum of the rainbow. In the spaces between roses the light began to glow, gradually getting brighter and brighter. The whole thing gave her a feeling of soft, nurturing support.

Peter, an engineer, wrote to me saying:

I think I have my Higher Self answers for yes, no, and maybe, but I do not know what good it does me since the responses are unpredictable and unreliable— at least with the testing I am doing. That is why I have not done more along these lines; unpredictability and unreliability force me to put it on a shelf to troubleshoot some time when life allows.

The testing I am doing is picking questions that are not consequential and to which I do not know the answer, but I can verify. The only type I can think of now are of a predictive nature. For example, "Will that streetlight be green when I arrive?" or "Will I have a message on my phone when I get back to it?" The problem with other types of questions such as, "Should I have chocolate or vanilla?" is verification. For example, how would anyone check if one is the "right" answer? Do you have suggestions on the testing and development of a Higher Self dialogue such as we discussed?

My answer signals were ideas that came to me during some afternoon pondering rather than in the moment of meditation. Of course, I checked out the answers in meditation and they seemed to be confirmed but I always have so much uncertainty about these kinds of things. That is why my attitude about such spiritual matters has developed to where I say let it make itself known unmistakably. If it takes a burning bush then that is the way it is and I make no apologies or excuses for that, I have made approaches the best way that I know. Then with a definite, obvious answer I do not always have to drift with all this constant uncertainty. I am sorry about the tone of this note and if I missed some advice you may have given me. If you have any suggestions, I would be very grateful to hear them.

Please note that his answer signals were ideas that came to him after the afternoon of pondering and *not* during his meditation. It can often happen that way when you are trying too hard. When you are determined to make your Higher Self connection clear, the answers will find their way into your awareness, but not necessarily during the actual meditation. This same person goes on to say that he checked out the answers in meditation and they seemed to be confirmed. The important thing is to not *try* to make these concepts work. Be gentle with yourself and find your way.

My answer:

Your questions are insightful. Your experience of yes and no signals is also clear. It is always perfectly okay to assign values for the yes and no signals. The Higher Self will work with whatever you wish as long as you are consistent.

Your intent to get communication from the Higher Self must be built on your intention to practice without polarity-judgment or keeping score. If you ask only questions that are verifiable, you are still attached to the outcome and ultimately not trusting.

What is happening is the ego is still attached to "how things work out" instead of unquestioningly accepting the incoming information. By forcing yourself to ask only questions you can verify later, you still have judgment and attachment and are seriously limiting your practice.

Some information will be verifiable, like what restaurant do we go to tonight? While in the restaurant you discover they have your favorite food that you did not know was on the menu. Other kinds of verification will pleasantly surprise you after the fact. Some will not show up at all; they will just be practice and blind faith, not caring, just practicing.

If you ask what shirt to wear and you really do not care, but you could have worn a favorite white shirt that might have gotten ketchup all over it that day, you may see in hindsight the merit of asking your Higher Self. And you saved your favorite white shirt by asking your Higher Self.

Your Higher Self is fifth-dimensional where there is no polarity. Your Higher Self is nonjudgmental. Therefore when you judge the answers you are placing a third-dimensional interpretation on your Higher Self by placing limitation on information that is coming from your Higher Self. Stop seeing it through the lens of judgment or the lens of the ego and instead allow *your experiences to teach you or show you during your practice period all the way through to non-judgment.*

You must begin to ask questions that are truly nonjudgmental. You do not care if you can verify at the ego level or any other level. The verification will percolate up from within the environment—from sources inside and outside you. I call them synchronicities.

Just as the marksman continues to increase the range of difficulty, you can now increase the level of difficulty in your nonattached questions to include nonattachment as to how they are verified.

Notice that when he was trying to get Higher Self signals it did not work for him, yet later when he was not working on it so intensely, in they came. His clear intent allowed that to occur. If you are like this engineer, Peter, and have a very logical way of thinking and adapting to change, you will need to allow yourself the space and let go of data collection first.

This means you must allow your Higher Self to communicate with you—without your usual record keeping. You must lighten up your scientific thinking into a more playful approach. This is one of the reasons the kahuna tradition says you must be like a child. It will give you the breathing room necessary for your Higher Self to shine. As your practice develops you will notice the value of the Higher Self connection. Challenge your desire to evaluate this before your forty-five days of practice, and let the evidence weigh in at the end of the experiment. This specific practice, as detailed here, will enable you to achieve 100 percent accuracy with your Higher Self.

Advanced Questions after Your Practice Period Is Complete

These questions are for after forty-five days from your start date.

What if I ask my Higher Self about something and then decide I don't want to do it? Your Higher Self will not correct you or save you from your mistakes. Your Higher Self does not sit in judgment of your activities or decide you were wrong or bad because you asked a Higher Self question and then did not respond. Do you remember the story about Ginny, the woman with a black belt in martial arts who decided not to take the first exit? As she discovered, if you do not follow your Higher Self, you will regret it.

One time I did not follow my Higher Self and regretted it later. While teaching in New York I proposed getting together with some dear friends who lived there. The only night I had available they had already made plans to see a movie. I checked in to see if I was supposed to see the movie. Nope. I really wanted to see my friends, so against the answer my Higher Self had given me, I went to the movie anyway, just so I could be with my friends. The movie was so bad I wanted to walk out. They thought the same thing! None of us wanted to be there, but all of us suffered through that awful movie out of concern for hurting the others' feelings. What a waste! Now I know better.

I can promise you that if you ask your Higher Self, you will get the best answer that will please every aspect of you, even the ones you don't usually consider. Your ego might not think so in the moment, but hindsight is a great teacher. Your Higher Self has all your priorities and aspects in full view and is giving you an *informed* answer. The answer is the exact answer you would give yourself if you knew everything, and your Higher Self does.

Become the humble servant. Become the fool to Spirit. Give yourself permission to hear what is going on. Once you have learned to step out of judgment, you will be open to the messages of the Universe all the time. The daily practice of the MerKaBa will clear your judgments, wounds, and fears. Get in the habit of asking in this nonjudgmental way, *What is going on?* You will be amazed at the answers that will start coming. The Universe rearranges itself to accommodate your picture of reality. What fascinates you? This is what the Universe works on. The goal then becomes being a Master of Divine Expression. It means no limitation! We are not locked into physical reality. We are becoming Light from within. We are no longer looking to an outside authority.

Remember, what do you do when something happens that defies explanation? Ask your Higher Self, *What is going on?* After your practice period, you may start asking this and other open-ended questions.

Steps for Initiating and Keeping
Your Higher Self Connection

Step 1: Establish Clear Communication

Do it this way: Invite Your Higher Self

While in meditation at Breath 14 say: *Higher Self, I am choosing to be in my heart. Please join me in my heart. I am making a commitment to be in my heart, and I am asking that you assist me with my communication with you. Please clarify or give me a signal for yes.* (Wait for the response.) *Please give me a signal for no.* (Wait for the response.) *Please give me a signal for neutral.* (Wait for the response.)

Step 2: Continue the
Practice for a Minimum of Six Weeks

Do it this way: Three Agreements with Your Higher Self for Your Practice Period

Do your practice period for a minimum of forty-five days.

1. *Ask questions.* Ask *only* yes or no questions. No open-ended questions. Ask unimportant, insignificant questions throughout the day as often as thirty to fifty times. Do not ask predictive questions that invite your ego to track your progress. If you are tracking your progress, you still care about the outcome. Also, do not ask important questions. If you absolutely cannot defer asking a specific question until after your practice period, then make a rare exception.

2. *Take action.* Always follow through on your answer from your Higher Self. No exceptions.

3. *Avoid other divination tools.* Do not use any forms of divination during your practice period, such as kinesiology, muscle testing, finger testing, cards, or pendulums. You are only asking your Higher Self during this practice period.

Your job during the practice period is to keep your ego out of the action and use passive positive feedback to reinforce your signals.

Step 3: Make a Commitment to Your Practice Period

When you are ready to commit to your Higher Self, during your next MerKaBa Meditation, you will tell your Higher Self you are making a commitment to work with your Higher Self, and you are asking your Higher Self to work with you in return. You name the length of time and the date (such as June 1) your practice period will end. You thank your Higher Self for working with you.

Step 4: Feel Higher Self Love for You!

At each subsequent meditation, during the pause between Breaths 14 and 15, ask your Higher Self to show you how much you are loved.

6

Programming
Your MerKaBa

What You Will Learn in This Chapter

- Beginning programming—Programming 101
- Programming your MerKaBa
- House rules for writing programs for your MerKaBa
- Basic programs to put in your MerKaBa
- Daily programs
- The MerKaBa is not used for protection

Those of us with a midwestern accent think everyone else has an accent—not us! I made a similar assumption about programming and integrity/polarity issues. In the early years I thought everyone experienced the MerKaBa the way that I did. What I discovered is that people experience the MerKaBa through their own templates of polarity. What I knew instinctively as appropriate behavior with the MerKaBa was not easily translated. Even Drunvalo assumed all the facilitators would understand the MerKaBa at a certain level and take it to the next level. I found people would make mistakes and assumptions based upon our unique worldview, which is predicated on our own beliefs and childhood environment. This chapter is devoted to programming based on years and years of practice.

Programming Your MerKaBa

Your Light Body and MerKaBa are interchangeable terms. Many do not realize your MerKaBa is alive. When I first studied the MerKaBa I saw it as mechanistic, like Sir Isaac Newton's machine model of the time, moving like a clock. Scientists now believe this is not the only model. One day my MerKaBa started dancing in the middle of the meditation! I suddenly realized it was alive and responding to me. I called my facilitator and said, "Jeffrey, my MerKaBa is alive!" "Maureen," he said, "some people just do not get it—'til they get it. We talked about that in class. Don't you remember?"

Somehow my own bias for geometry being "just shapes" overrode this all-important fact. I love geometry, as any of my students will tell you. My own overlay of geometry being about static shapes blocked out my ability to "hear" that the MerKaBa was alive at that first workshop. I now know better!

In fact, your MerKaBa is consciously aware of everything going on in the entire Universe. This includes other dimensions along with everything that is important to you here in third dimension, or wherever you reside. What does a seeing-eye dog do for a blind person? It gives a form of sight to the owner. Similarly, the MerKaBa gives "sight" to other parts of reality that we do not see, hear, or notice.

As I emphasized in chapter 2, experiencing unconditional love is the doorway to take you places you have never before experienced. Unconditional love will clear your emotional baggage and blockages. It is not the only way to do this clearing, but it is one way that works. Your sense of this grows as your heart connection opens. Your Light Body becomes more alive and its awareness more accessible as your love for life grows.

All of the exercises in this book leading up to this point are designed to help you let go and forgive those who have harmed you. Being able to observe your (so-called) enemies and releasing them from that role (as enemy) so both of you can move beyond it to the perfection of each moment produces ecstatic states. These states allow your MerKaBa to function on higher and higher levels. Learning the MerKaBa allows you to start in the middle of the Ascension process and then move up very quickly. Everything that you learn from this material is centered on unconditional love. Love is the key.

The MerKaBa Is Alive

Because your MerKaBa is alive and connected to you it can respond to you and your desires. With an active Higher Self connection you can give crystal clear fifth-dimensional directions to help you achieve your heart's desire. Those who dream can build greater and greater things. Our world was built by dreamers who had visions of a better life.

Your dreams can be converted to a set of instructions that can be compared to writing programs for a computer. Your Higher Self can help you develop "code" that is perfect for you. Your code or programs can run in your MerKaBa, maximizing you to your fullest potential.

It is widely known by Native Peoples that crystals carry messages. Marcel Vogel, a pioneer in the exploration of psychic energy, proved that a crystal will accept programs (thoughts, feelings, emotions) and will continue to send these programs forever with great precision, until someone or something erases the program.

Ever wonder why Vogel crystals have so many facets? Vogel found that crystals can carry as many different programs as there are facets on the crystal. Fortunately there are unlimited numbers of programs that can be run in your MerKaBa.

The reason programs are so powerful is because you are telling the Universe, while you continue to live in third dimension, that you no longer abide by the rules of the game that mass consciousness is playing. You are choosing an alternate version of the reality as defined by you.

Careful Now!

Inappropriate programming caused the demise of Atlantis. Programming is not to be taken lightly. The fail-safe solution is always asking your Higher Self to review your programs. In this way you are using your fifth-dimensional self to sign off on any programs that your third-dimensional self may dream and create.

Basic Rules for Writing Programs for Your MerKaBa

1. Always ask: *Higher Self, is this program appropriate? Does this program align with my highest purposes or the highest purposes of those who may be affected by my actions?*

2. You can create a program at any time and in any place; however, seriously consider only creating programs during your meditation. This is to ensure you are checking in with your Higher Self and that your communication with your Higher Self is the clearest possible.

3. If you are suspicious of any information you receive in response to your question, you can ask again, *Is this my Higher Self telling me (fill in the blank)?* Only your Higher Self will be permitted to answer yes.

4. Take all programs down every New Year's Day or other anniversary date you choose to use for this purpose. This is because you may have programs running that you forgot about and need to clear out of your field. This is just good housekeeping. Think of your spring cleaning or periodically defragmenting your computer's hard disk. You must remove all programs to keep your systems running optimally.

Can the MerKaBa Be Used for Protection?

The MerKaBa is a fifth-dimensional tool that's been made available to give us a jump start into mastery of the perfected human. The MerKaBa cannot be used for protection because the energy of the MerKaBa is fifth-dimensional, which is completely neutral, thus not polarized. While wearing your activated MerKaBa you do not *need* protection, because you do not have anything you need to be protected from harming you. Needing protection would bounce you out of fifth dimension because your fifth-dimensional self does not need protection.

The MerKaBa is a proactive tool. Being proactive puts you where you need to be in any given moment, so again, no protection is needed.

> The MerKaBa is a proactive tool. You are where
> you need to be and know what you are supposed
> to do in any given moment.

Finally, the belief in a need for protection creates a "state of polarity" in the manifestation zone of the MerKaBa. Therefore using it for protection produces a *need* for protection, as a manifestation field produces what is seeded in it.

Remember the story I told in chapter 4 about driving the curvy mountain road, where you were learning about connecting with the Higher Self? That story illustrates this point. The activated MerKaBa along with your Higher Self connection will produce such clarity for you that you will always know where you need to be, and you will know what you need to know or do.

Higher Self Is Proactive, Not Protective

I was told to leave New York and go home before the 9/11 disaster. I was pulled out of the action, of being caught in New York like so many travelers who were stranded away from home that week. Your Higher Self is not protecting you from anything by steering you away from a difficult or unsafe situation; it is operating from a sense of being at the ideal place in the ideal time.

From here, looking there, it may seem like protection, but from that vantage point protection has no value. You are connected with all of life and are following your inner direction that puts you exactly where you need to be in any moment. Why do I make this distinction? As we develop fifth-dimensional understanding we change how we look at things. This change is appropriate. I have found that using fifth-dimensional descriptions and language allows thinking and being to shift more quickly.

Imagine you are traveling in a foreign country. If you don't know the language you will need an interpreter to translate the words people are saying. However, once you learn the language you no longer need an interpreter, because you understand what is being said and can read the street signs. Once you are experiencing the language of the Higher Self there is no need for interpretation. You hear and know what is being said as it is being said and know where you need to be. Your Higher Self connection allows you to *be* your Higher Self in the moment, *hear* the thought of the Higher Self, and *know* what the Higher Self knows.

How Is MerKaBa Useful?

Just doing the MerKaBa will help you let go of your judgment about the world and your interaction with it. Just practicing the MerKaBa Meditation realigns your thinking, which will happen automatically. If you are doing the MerKaBa regularly, sooner or later you will understand and, more importantly, integrate this exquisite awareness into your life.

Your activated MerKaBa makes you immune to the effects of mass consciousness programming and mind control. This is another wonderful benefit from an activated MerKaBa.

Programming the MerKaBa

For years there was a raging debate about programming the MerKaBa. After much trial and error I discovered that before we can program the MerKaBa, we need to integrate certain integrity issues. This is because we are third-dimensional beings integrating a fifth-dimensional tool.

If we were fifth-dimensional we would not need to deal with the integrity issues because we would already be so plugged into God that integrity would be a non-issue. At fifth dimension we are so connected with our love of God that certain behaviors will not occur to us. These integrity issues are addressed in the rules for programming your MerKaBa. It bears repeating: Before creating any program in your MerKaBa, always ask your Higher Self, *Is this program appropriate for all involved? Do I have permission from my Higher Self to activate this program?*

Not-God Choice in
the Free-Will Third Dimension

Imagine that I called you to ask if you could host the Dalai Lama or some other well-regarded dignitary that you admire. What is your first response to my request? "Yes!" Next you would ask about other details, such as dates and dietary preferences. Furthermore, if you had a vacation scheduled for that timeframe you would find a way to change it and be available for this important visit.

> This is what being fifth-dimensional is like. You are
> so connected to God that not-God choices
> do not even occur to you.

All of your communication with me would be around yes. The possibility of saying no would not even occur to you. This is what being fifth-dimensional is like. You are so connected to God, so filled with God's love, that not-God choices do not even occur to you. Yet when we are observing ourselves from third-dimensional reality, we do not always recognize when we are out of alignment with integrity. In third dimension we have the choice of not-God or God.

Let me illustrate this. One time, while trying to impress my son with my determination to get him to complete his homework, I took a wire cutter to cut the TV cord. The TV was turned off so I didn't think about the fact that electricity was still coursing through those wires. It never dawned on me that it was live; I was just being passionate about impressing my son. I hope you are laughing at me here, as my friends did when I told them about it. How could I not know it would still have power running through the cord?

Sparks flew everywhere. My sixteen-year-old son started to cry. I got the desired effect, and thankfully the wire cutters were insulated so I didn't get hurt, but it was a dangerous mistake.

What Could Go Wrong?

Those of you who know a little more about electrical appliances than I did know not to do that. Can you see how a novice or naïve person could assume she knew what she was doing? Why would the TV have a power button that *says* "off" if it was live? Mistakes like that can be disastrous. In cutting an electrical cord I could have electrocuted myself or at least received quite a shock.

For similar reasons I have developed rules for programming your MerKaBa, to help you avoid disastrous mistakes. The more I know about the MerKaBa, the more I realize that experience makes me like a trained electrician who understands intuitively what is appropriate for it.

The MerKaBa is a fifth-dimensional tool. If you think of the MerKaBa chariot as a vehicle, you would not give your car keys to a five-year-old. When you finally grant the keys to a sixteen-year-old, you also insist on a learners permit and driver's education classes.

Impact of Your Sexual Partner

Anyone you allow into close proximity, as in a sexual intimacy partner, can accept or alter your programs. Normally this is limited to your sexual partner. Assuming you are not having indiscriminate sex, and that you have high standards and so does your partner, there is no cause for concern. What kind of standards am I speaking of? Illegal drugs and marijuana usage puts holes in your aura. Entities can easily move into your aura and then can be transferred through sexual intimacy. I want you to know that your sexual partner is the only person who can alter your programs, with one very important exception.

When you are carrying fifth-dimensional energies your partner may notice the huge light or energy you carry is different from that of any previous partners. This is especially noticeable after your MerKaBa has become permanent.

Sex is the one arena where boundaries cross and the free-will rules are expanded. Your sexual partner has access to your activated MerKaBa when you are physically intimate. On more than one occasion I have had to clear entities from persons who had sex with someone who was carrying a lot of entities. I have seen many strange experiences where a sexual partner was the source of the problems a person was experiencing. Your sexual partner's extracurricular activities most certainly will affect you and your Ascension process.

If something unusual happens after you have intercourse with your partner, it is a good idea to ask your Higher Self what is going on. You may discover your sexual partner is bringing in stray energies or entities.

The Impact of Drugs

Another thing that can happen is that your auric fields can be opened and torn from using certain drugs such as Ecstasy, entheogens (mushrooms), or heroin. Unfortunately, although marijuana and alcohol are legal, they too will put holes in your aura. The misuse of drugs will have an impact on your auric field, or your partner's auric field, which can then allow holes in your field. There are no checks and balances operating when these holes are created and opened through drug use. Anything nearby can be collected: entities, energies, and God knows what.

Although the MerKaBa can repair this, why would you want to spend all your time in repair mode? Imagine starting to build your dream house, then at night, for recreation, taking a sledgehammer to it.

Start now to repair this problem. Get agreement from your partner that the behavior, whatever it is, will stop and your partner will change or you will stop having sex together. Your MerKaBa will repair damage from drugs, but entities need to be cleared. I have seen hooks, portals, and other strange devices in spiritual beings who had no idea they were being used by dark forces. Once they were cleared of these their behavior changed dramatically or their situation improved significantly.

What about the First Time with a New Sex Partner?

I highly recommend you ask your Higher Self if it is appropriate for you to have sex with the new person. As long as your Higher Self says *yes,* you know it will be all right. Advance planning is helpful! Who wants to ask Higher Self that question when you are already aroused? It is not easy, I know, but I can tell you it is possible, worthwhile, and the only way to live, once you have an activated MerKaBa.

Basic Rules
for Programming

1. Is this program appropriate for all involved?
2. Do I have permission from my Higher Self to activate this program?

Can Programming Be Dangerous?

Programming your MerKaBa could be dangerous if you create something that is out of integrity. This is because your MerKaBa is fifth-dimensional, a realm where there is no polarity, no good or evil. Your MerKaBa can be assigned programs by you that are not appropriate.

Some have said, "If the programming is so dangerous, I don't think I want to use it." Have you ever wondered about someone living in the United States who didn't drive? Except in a few large cities where convenient mass transit exists, such as New York or Boston, anyone without a driver's license is missing a lot of experiences and opportunities. Even though driving a car could be dangerous, we still learn to do it and we learn how to drive safely, including by learning skills from experienced drivers and learning to pay attention.

The famous physicist Albert Einstein said, "The world is dangerous not because of those who do harm, but because of those who look at it without doing anything. . . . Nothing that I can do will change the structure of the Universe. But maybe by raising my voice I can help the greatest of all causes—goodwill among men and peace on earth." He won the Nobel Prize for his work on peace.

The gift of knowing how to program your MerKaBa, along with the ethical understanding of programming the MerKaBa, is the assurance you have that you are maximizing this great gift. In the chapter on surrogate MerKaBas, you will discover some of the mistakes people have made with programming. These mistakes prove beyond any doubt that it is possible to program your MerKaBa inappropriately.

Steps to Programming:
Two Basic Principles Must Be Applied—
Intention and Attention

First, you must ask your Higher Self's approval: *Is this program in alignment with my highest purposes and the highest purposes of those who may be affected by my actions?* If the answer is *no,* you may *not* proceed. Your Higher Self knows for sure if a program you are interested in doing is acceptable for all involved. Now you understand why building an accurate Higher Self connection is so very important.

> Always ask your Higher Self if what you would
> like to do is appropriate for you.

When you get a *yes* answer to your question, you may proceed to the next step. Put your attention on what it is you are working on and place your intention into that area. With your attention focused, *see* the desired outcome.

You may use vague or global words, general instructions, or even pictures. Both have merit. In some cases you will use both. Drunvalo has labeled the various programs as male, female, and child. These labels are simply to help you understand the way a program works: male programming is action oriented, female is receptive, and child is both. The fourth kind—the witness—is not really a program so much as a decision *not* to program. I do not really think it is important to know which one is which, as much as it is important to know they are all acceptable.

Specifically, place your attention on your MerKaBa while you are in meditation (I like to do this on Breath 14, but during any heart-opening meditation will do). Then either speak or think what it is you want from your MerKaBa. Once your MerKaBa knows what it is that you want, it will instantly begin to perform this duty. It will perform this duty forever, or until you stop it or change it, as long as your MerKaBa remains activated.

> All programs have a purpose. The purpose is
> stated in the program.

Stay in Alignment

As you begin to write programs for yourself, after your forty-five-day Higher Self practice, you can double-check yourself by asking, *What is the purpose of this program?* Your purpose is the outcome you are naming for yourself. For example, if your program implies you will be protected, your purpose is protection. You will remember that earlier in this chapter we learned that it is not possible to use the MerKaBa for protection, so this would not be a valid purpose.

In another example, you might ask to be invisible to someone or to groups of people. In this program you would not program them to not see you, even though that might be the outcome. Instead, you program: *I am invisible to everyone who might know me at this location.*

It is a bit like learning how to define what you want, and making sure you do not include changing others. You do not want to interfere with another's free will, so when you make yourself invisible, others may see a person, but they do not notice the individual they are seeing is *you.*

Four Types of Programming

Male: Male programming is detailed, written down, and easily explained to another. It has a repeatable pattern and is usually very logical.

Female: Female programming has a quality of receptiveness and adaptability. It is like your grandma's favorite gravy recipe: "You add a little potato water to the drippings, maybe vegetable broth or chicken broth, some flour . . . " Get the idea? You cannot specifically tell another how to do it, as it will continually change, adapting to the moment.

Child: The child or "both way" is just that. It is sometimes logical, sometimes adaptable, or both simultaneously.

Witness: The neutral or witness way does not take part in the drama of life; it just watches. This is relatively difficult, very fifth-dimensional, and it is now possible. The witness only observes what happens in creation and feels no need to override what is.

Throughout creation the observer makes up the largest part—think the plant and animal kingdoms. Because our prime directive is to create, we will interact with the observers of creation. This is the clear canvas from which we create. All of the observer/witness parts of creation know what is happening and do not care. Remember the reference to "movie extras" who stand in for the nameless crowd? They are literally holding space for creation to occur with the co-creators of the Universe, you and I.

Example: Active (male)
Referring to the negative lines of force, with your intention and attention, say or think:

The negative lines of force are hereby diverted around me.

All harmful electromagnetic fields (EMF) that are being broadcast all over the world have no impact on me.

Example: Adaptive (female)
Referring to the negative lines of force, with your intention and attention, say or think:

Through my intimate connections with God and life everywhere, I program my Light Body to give me whatever I need before I know I need it.

Example: Both (child)
Referring to the negative lines of force, with your intention and attention, say or think:

I program my MerKaBa to provide everything I need, including perfect health.

Example: Witness

Referring to the negative lines of force, with your intention and attention, say or think:

I program my MerKaBa to allow all of creation to move through me effortlessly.

The witness understands that polarity is a means of discernment and nothing more, so it does not see or react to good and evil the way most do. The witness sees good versus evil simply as contrast.

The most import thing that I can tell you about programming is you must *wait* until you have completed your practice period with your Higher Self. This bears repeating. If you do not follow your inner guidance/Higher Self 100 percent of the time you do not really trust it! Look in chapter 5 if you want to review detailed instructions on how to develop your Higher Self connection. This is the key to the kingdom.

Once you have a 100-percent accurate connection with your Higher Self, asking about a program that you wish your Higher Self to run is appropriate. Your Higher Self will provide you with the answers that you need to establish with certainty that your program is appropriate for you and for all who may be affected by your actions.

Everything depends upon your connection to your Higher Self. Not everyone wants to develop a Higher Self connection or needs to, but everyone can benefit from this practice and grow the connection. Enough of us need to develop this level of connection so that we can reach critical mass, to achieve Ascension. You probably wouldn't be reading this if you weren't interested in mastering your Ascension.

General Rules

Always complete your Higher Self practice period (see chapter 5) before attempting to do any programming with your MerKaBa. This is because the only way to know with confidence if the program you are creating is suitable for you is to ask your Higher Self. If your Higher Self connection is not 100-percent reliable, how will you know your programming is appropriate? I insist that you agree to no new programs until you have completed your practice period, so you are certain you are not in violation of some unknown activity.

Then make the following commitment:

I agree to wait to create new programs until I have completed my practice period. (Practice period is fully discussed in chapter 5.)

The Seven Basic Programs

The first step is to ask your Higher Self: *Higher Self, are the seven basic programs from this book appropriate for me?*

If you get *yes* you may proceed. If you get *no* then you may ask individually, before each program. For example, you might say, *Higher Self, is program number 1 appropriate for me at this time?*

If you get *no* now, you may get *yes* later. If you are told *no* on any of these programs, there may be a specific reason for that, but these basic programs are approved for almost everyone. If you do not get approval today you can ask again tomorrow.

I Program My MerKaBa to:

1. Divert all harmful geopathic lines of force, such as ley lines, electromagnetic lines, and black water lines, that exist in and around the earth around me to produce zero impact on me.

2. Divert all harmful EMFs (electromagnetic fields) and other harmful transmissions, such as cell phones, Wi-Fi routers, and so on, around me to produce zero impact on me.

3. Remove and divert all forms of pollution, known or unknown to me, that can adversely affect my physical, mental, emotional, and etheric bodies as gently and as imperceptibly as possible.

4. Be invisible and undetectable to any and all whose purposes are out of alignment with my purposes.

5. Assist me with my own and planetary unresolved issues that may need to be forgiven and released.

6. Remind me to reactivate the MerKaBa before it goes inactive.

7. Place the above programs in my start-up group.

Programs You Forgot About

Darrel, a contractor on Whidbey Island, Washington, had placed a program around the luxury condo building project he had been developing. It made the condos invisible to anyone not involved in the construction project. This proved quite useful, as he did not need to do anything else to limit unwanted visitors. Notice that it is a fifth-dimensional program by virtue of the fact that it is not providing protection. It may seem like protection from this vantage point, but it is truly a proactive program.

I have visited Darrel's home many times to teach. One afternoon he wandered into the class while I was teaching about programming. All of a sudden he tapped his head and left the room. Within a few minutes of his return to the room, his cell phone rang. He had put the condos up for sale about three months earlier and had not received any inquiries, and was really wondering why. When he was listening to my talk he remembered the above program and realized he still had it running! He immediately took it down. Within five minutes a realtor was calling, asking to show the property.

Programs You Can Create

After you have completed your practice period you can add programs on your own. If you already have installed the seven basic programs you may not need anything else.

Even pandemics are addressed by the seven basic programs. You can use these programs as antidotes for anything that may be a threat to you, such as a flu virus or the negative effects of a vaccine. At a certain point these threats no longer have any hold on you because at fifth dimension there is no problem with them. They can only cause problems to someone who accepts what mass consciousness is saying about the reality. Always ask your Higher Self about any programming you are doing.

Programs Work

Programming works because you are operating at a fifth-dimensional level and can create the programs with commands. It may seem that your MerKaBa programs are similar to intentions, although they are far more powerful and effective in third-dimensional reality. MerKaBa programs are absolute. They create from fifth dimension—a place of instant manifestation—into third dimension.

Asking your Higher Self permission is imperative. Without getting permission, there are no checks and balances on your MerKaBa programs. If you are already fifth-dimensional, then of course you would not even think of doing something out of alignment with God. However, you may be a third-dimensional being who is using a "power tool," which is why it is essential to always get Higher Self approval so you do not accidentally cause some ill-intentioned effect. Misusing a fifth-dimensional tool for ego-related purposes is a serious infraction of cosmic law.

What Is a Start-Up Group and How Do You Use It?

A start-up group is a set of programs that run each time you activate your MerKaBa. On a computer a start-up group includes programs that open automatically when you power up your computer. In practical terms, it means that all your basic programs will run automatically when you activate your MerKaBa daily. The start-up group is purposed so that all you need to do is the MerKaBa, and all your basic programs are automatically activated.

How Do You Properly and Fully Take Down a Single Program?

If you have a number of active programs and later decide that one of them is no longer wanted or needed, you will want to remove that program. To take down a single program, you think of or say that program and state with clear intention: *Higher Self, this program is removed and cleared.* You may find it helpful to see it written on a blackboard, and erase it.

How Do You Clear All Programs at Once?

The way to take down all programs is to think or say: *Higher Self, all programs are cancelled and cleared.* You may also use a visual, such as erasing a list on the blackboard. You could also see yourself connecting with all your programs, whether you remember them or not, and pulling the plug on them so they cease to exist. As discussed earlier, it's a good idea to do this once a year.

Is There a Way to Know
What Programs Are Currently Running?

The easiest way to know if your programs are still running is to ask your Higher Self. You may also ask your Higher Self if your MerKaBa is permanent—which will indicate your start-up group is running automatically. You can also ask your Higher Self if you need to keep doing the MerKaBa. Even though the MerKaBa is permanent, you may be asked to keep doing it.

Is There a Way To Know
If a Program Is Running That
You Did Not Initiate?

Again, you can ask your Higher Self if there are any programs running that you did not initiate. This can happen when you are taking an initiation and have given someone else authority over you. Always ask your Higher Self if it is appropriate for you to accept DNA activation or any other outside authority action that will allegedly accelerate your processes. Occasionally accepting such external offerings can be disastrous and can actually throw you back in your progress. Your Higher Self can guide you if you want to accept this sort of boost.

Lessons When Taking an Initiation

An initiation is deliberately choosing to take an advanced expression and integrate it into yourself. Taking an initiation may involve skipping over the natural spiritual evolution that would occur based on real-life experiences and tests. Initiations generally jump-start stalled spiritual processes.

Maybe you have been signing up for some massive initiation work. You may have even said, "I will do whatever it takes to get started on my life path," without realizing it may result in significant changes that could cause a healing crisis.

People are getting DNA activation, **cosmic latticework**◈, and various other kinds of initiation. Sometimes people are getting sick. Why are they getting sick from these initiations? Everyone wants to get on to the next initiation, but your body may not be fully operational due to bad habits, poor diet, lack of exercise, unfinished business from childhood, old wounds, and so on. It is fantastic if you can do this, yet it may be difficult to take on that amount of initiation work.

The Weakest Link

What this means is that you may "blow a circuit" where you have the weakest link. If your lungs tend to be the first part of you that has a problem, when you take an initiation you may get a cold or worse. Knowing this, I suggest you add to your Higher Self request: *I will accept whatever changes in me are necessary. I ask that they occur as gently and as imperceptibly as possible, preferably while I am sleeping. I know they can occur unexpectedly and may be significant.*

I believe problems occur because you are blowing open the weakest link. When a person gets upgraded, either through some sort of initiation or activation, powerful new energy is moving through the energy bodies. Too much too fast will short-circuit and cause you to tear a part of your energy field. This creates a domino effect resulting in an expression of the tear in your physical makeup.

This experience is much like a garden hose that has not been used for a while and develops a weak spot. Then when water comes through with high pressure, it blows right through the weak spot creating a huge hole in the line.

Sometimes we are so eager to keep advancing we proceed recklessly through activation after activation. What can be done to alleviate the effects of this? If you are truly suffering from your latest activation and are in need of some relief, consider this a warning to slow down! Accept that your body may need some integration time. Please also use this awareness to help you listen and accept the advice of a teacher who tells you that you might not be ready for the next step.

Resolve to look for signs of "permission to proceed" from the

Universe. If you ask for a sign that you are ready or are permitted to proceed, your Higher Self will give that to you.

Relief Now!

If you are suffering from the ill effects of too much too fast, there is something you can do about it. To begin with, clear intention is very helpful. With clear intention you can ask for the matrix that existed *before* the initiation or healing took place to be reestablished in your physical, mental, emotional, and etheric bodies.

Allow yourself to temporarily go back in time and space to the place of good health before the initiation, before the shift in energy. This is just a temporary matrix and will not be sustainable, nor do you wish to sustain it. But it could give you enough of a breather to allow your body to readjust to the new energy.

Your sole purpose for creating this alternate reality is to pull a replica of your body elemental from that time period and superimpose it on yourself now. This will serve to retrain or entrain your body to a version that was operating well. Then gradually instruct that matrix to dissolve slowly, at a pace that will allow full integration, as you are ready.

My Favorite Programs

Here's a list of some of my favorite programs that I've written for myself or others. If you would like to use them—that is not enough! You must ask your Higher Self if this program is appropriate for you and for anyone who may feel the impact. Also be sure to add this ending to *all* programs:

I program my MerKaBa to work with my Higher Self and to make all the necessary adjustments and changes as gently and as imperceptibly as possible, preferably during the evening hours while I sleep.

For help with healing big emotional wounds where you have disconnected from your feelings and quite possibly your chakras:

I program my MerKaBa to repair and rebuild my lost or severed connections in my four lower bodies, including connections among all of my chakras. I further instruct my body elemental to connect me with the full-

est and most evolved expression of myself possible in this embodiment, in accord with my Higher Self.

For abuse repair:

I program my MerKaBa to repair and heal all traumas in my four lower bodies—physical, mental, emotional, and etheric—in this and any lifetimes.

For objects disappearing into higher dimensions:

I program my MerKaBa to assist me with the issue of "misplaced" items, understanding multiple realities, and recognizing feelings and answers in order to minimize confusion and frustration and gain efficiency.

For partnerships, including your beloved (especially when both activate this same program):

I _____ (fill in your name) choose to commit 100 percent of my energies to support my relationship with _____ (your partner's name), my beloved. I ask that all of heaven and earth move to assist me with this so I can fulfill my mission with _____ (him or her). I ask all the Beings of Light to assist me in upholding this commitment, learning, growing, and releasing all that is necessary to fulfill our mission.

For your relationship program:

I program my MerKaBa to assist me in balancing, energizing, and healing anything in me that needs healing in order to maximize our physical, mental, emotional, and spiritual union.

For partners who are separated by distance/work:

I program my MerKaBa to assist me and my beloved through this time of separation. I ask that, regardless of our separation, we grow closer together in all ways. I ask my Higher Self and MerKaBa to bring us closer in our four lower bodies: physical, mental, emotional, and etheric. Let it assist us in growing our mutual trust, integrity, kindness, compassion, discernment, faith, forgiveness, truth, love, wisdom, and listening to and hearing each other's needs. Help us to keep romance alive, live in harmony, and develop our soulmate connection to its highest possible expression.

This program will help love grow, but it won't turn someone into your soulmate if they are not your soulmate.

For work (choose what is appropriate for your situation):

I program my MerKaBa to assist me in all ways with (your job).

I program my MerKaBa to locate and teach me all the information that I need to succeed at my job in this project to the highest level. This can include noticing things that need attention, catching exceptions to the rule, understanding special circumstances, and being prepared to handle the unexpected.

I program my MerKaBa to maximize my preparation time so that I will know everything I need to know before I need to know it.

I program my MerKaBa to create connections with all involved in this project so everyone benefits: our company, the staff, contractors and subcontractors, client(s), and customers.

I program my MerKaBa to make each day fun and easy for all involved and create a win-win environment every day for everyone in this project.

Remember to end *all* programs with this:

I program my MerKaBa to work with my Higher Self and to make all the necessary adjustments and changes as gently and as imperceptibly as possible, preferably while I sleep.

7

Black Helicopters

What You Will Learn in This Chapter

- What are these black helicopters?
- Who are they?
- What are they doing?
- Sightings by students
- Time travel and black helicopters

Initially I didn't tell my students about black helicopters. After all, it is a pretty weird experience. I didn't think they really needed to know about it, and I don't enjoy talking about this far-out stuff. I wasn't even sure they would believe me. Then my students started calling to tell me *their* black helicopter stories, along with their fears about what could possibly be happening. I realized I needed to tell them about black helicopters so they would not be afraid. I also realized I could solve the issue by giving them the program for invisibility. This is in the seven basic programs, number four.

This Is Real

At one point several years ago a student in Seattle emailed me about her black helicopter experience and suggested I post it on my website. Her statement was, "The black helicopters are fun!" It did not take long (not even twenty-four hours) until she called me back, begging me to remove that comment. Why? Because they were buzzing her property and wouldn't leave her alone!

A lot of people thought the black helicopter experience would validate the experience of the MerKaBa, but frankly, I do not think you need parlor games to know the MerKaBa is *real*.

I have witnessed first-hand or heard about helicopters in many cities, including Madison, Seattle, Pittsburgh, New York, cities in Europe, cities near airbases, and so on. Even though we call them "black helicopters," they are not always black, as you may discover. I have concluded that wherever the military is set up to observe and monitor an area, there you will find a strong likelihood of their detecting your MerKaBa. Their job is to track "alien" energy, and the MerKaBa appears on their tracking devices as "out of this world."

Who Are They?

I honestly do not know who sent the helicopters. I have seen the helicopters and know they are real.

I've heard enough stories from credible students of mine to know there is a real agency whose purpose is to track the energy anomalies of the planet. Wherever a MerKaBa field shows up they must investigate. There are nonhuman ETs living among us. Most are here with the full authority of the powers that be. Some are not. If you really want to understand all this, I suggest you watch the film *Men in Black*. The movie's premise is 95 percent accurate, and when you watch it again you will begin to understand what is happening. The movie is a comedy but I take this subject very seriously. I trust you will, too.

Once you begin to realize and accept that there are *real* interplanetary aliens among us, working with our government and others, you can begin to appreciate what I will tell you next.

What Are the Black Helicopters Doing?

The job of those in the black helicopters is to "contain" all the aliens in specific areas. Apparently these ET beings are allowed to be located in mostly populated areas where their presence can be tracked. I have confirmation of this from various individuals who are aware of them. A good resource for this information is a book by William Thompkins, *Selected by Extraterrestrials.*

His book details the secret agreements between off-planet aliens and the U.S. government. If you knew that any alien had a MerKaBa field, and that the technology existed to track a MerKaBa field (and it does), you would begin to understand how effortless it would be to locate aliens using this technology. I do not believe this technology is radar. I believe they are using a technology that is beyond our radar but has a similar ability to locate and track energy fields.

They will not do anything to hurt you, but I guarantee, if you have ever been visited by the black helicopters, it is a bit unnerving. They often aim big floodlights at your windows or other areas around your house or place of work. They usually hang out long enough to determine who or what you are, and long enough for you to think, "What are they doing?"

One of my students jokingly suggested that I start sending the black helicopter guys my class lists, since this was becoming pretty commonplace. I have another way to deal with it, which is covered in the next chapter, "Surrogate MerKaBas: Both Useful and Destructive."

I think this discussion itself is humorous; the black helicopter people need to know what *you* are doing. Imagine them detecting a "spacecraft" (your MerKaBa field) and then discovering it is just an ordinary (or extraordinary) citizen (that is, you)! Apparently our MerKaBa looks no different from an ET's MerKaBa, at least on their scanning technology, which is why they send black helicopters to investigate.

The Black Helicopter Phenomenon

The rest of this chapter is going to share more highlights of the black helicopter phenomenon. I have so many of these stories in my files, I feel you must know. Some will find this information entertaining, others will be intrigued, still others will be frightened. If you are frightened, all the more reason to know and understand this phenomenon, because you can do something about it. Refer to my favorite programs and make your MerKaBa invisible to those whose purposes are not the same as yours.

If you have been visited by black helicopters and doubted yourself or never told anyone, now you will be validated. You were not imagining this.

Where Do They Look for MerKaBa Fields?

Not all areas of the world are being monitored. The most monitoring activity occurs in New York and other large cities. Other areas being monitored are near strategic military installations. For example, the population of Boise, Idaho, is only about 204,000. It is not a big city, yet because of its proximity to Mountain Home Air Force Base, Boise is being monitored.

If you don't care about being noticed or "discovered," don't bother making yourself invisible. I have had people tell me they did not care . . . until the black helicopters came. They start to play with them, like the woman who wrote a comment for my website, but within a short time they realize their folly. It's unnerving because you know you are being watched, and you don't know why!

I think you will find that it is not worth the nuisance and that it is easier to do what you want when you are invisible to the military. After all, it is their job to protect the masses. In my opinion, invisibility is standard equipment for everyone's MerKaBa, so I ask each of you to check in with your Higher Self to determine if you should have the invisibility program. It will be a rare exception to be told *not* to have this program running. I did have one student who was recruited by the CIA right out of college. After about six months he was disillusioned and dropped out of the program. Later he participated in one of my classes. He did not have to tell me since I knew about it from my guides.

When we activated these programs in my class, he was actually told by his Higher Self *not* to run the invisibility program. He came to me after the class asking why I thought he would get that direction from his Higher Self. My guidance was that he was probably being monitored anyway and they knew he was in my class learning the MerKaBa. It was better that they see it, since they knew where he had just been. Later, when he is no longer a security threat (he really was not then, but how would they know?), his Higher Self might tell him to make himself invisible. Invisibility is the most important program for your MerKaBa. It is discussed in chapter 6.

Sightings of Black Helicopters

In the early years of teaching the MerKaBa, around 1995, I didn't tell students about the black helicopters unless it came up as a question. Then my students began sharing more and more of these experiences with me and it became necessary to discuss it further.

The most striking experience in my early years was with a woman from Brooklyn who was doing the MerKaBa twice a day. She was very focused with clearing work and was making huge progress on her own inner world. One day a black helicopter showed up in the middle of the night, shining a floodlight into her bedroom window. Her roommate wasn't very excited about that.

The next day black helicopters showed up in the middle of the day at her work. Since her employer was a large veterans hospital, it was quite unusual to see an unidentified, non-medical helicopter in this hospital zone. Since then her life has been more tranquil and she has gone on to be a successful teacher.

On another occasion a group in Madison activated their MerKaBas and within minutes a black helicopter was spotted flying very low over the house where I was teaching.

In a more recent incident I was awakened at 2 a.m. by my cell phone. I don't always have my phone within hearing range, but this night I did. As it rang I mentally checked in, feeling no significant emergency, and I remember thinking, *This had better be good!* to wake me up from sleep on a seminar weekend.

It was a student from New York who had been having a smoke on his fire escape on a corner of Eighth Avenue in Greenwich Village after a chat with a friend. They'd been discussing time travel, warp speed, intergalactic activity, and so on. His friend had a keen interest in extraterrestrials and my student thought he carried a lot of alien energy. All of a sudden a large white helicopter was headed directly up Eighth Avenue toward him at a very fast pace. It stopped right in front of him! As it hovered in front of him, facing his apartment, this large, out-of-place, white helicopter then moved up slowly revealing scanning and other equipment on its belly. By now my student was sufficiently spooked to go inside. This was at 2 a.m.! What happened? His friend had spontaneously activated his MerKaBa through their discussions and connection.

In another example a piano teacher in her sixties named Shirley had asked me to return and facilitate another workshop in her home. She had quit doing her MerKaBa Meditation but invited me because she enjoyed our friendship and wanted to see me again. As she prepared for her vacation scheduled for the following day, it occurred to her that "Maureen will know I have not been practicing [my meditation]." Indeed, every good piano teacher knows when her students show up for lessons unprepared.

Her husband had gone to bed and she decided to activate her MerKaBa, completely forgetting about the seven basic programs, especially the one to make you invisible. Within minutes she heard the "med flight" helicopter overhead. Normally the hospital's medical helicopter flies over their neighborhood on its way to the hospital when bringing in a patient. This time the helicopter came but seemed to hover.

Shirley and her husband live in a large, solid log cabin in a subdivision on a large hill in Boise. When the sound didn't go away, she finally peeked outside and saw not one but two helicopters! One of them was so close she thought it might land on her house. Pretty soon the whole house was shaking like a moving railroad car. Terrified, she decided to turn off the lights and call it a night.

When they returned from their vacation a week later her daughter, son-in-law, and sixteen-year-old grandson went for pizza. "Grammy," the teenager said, "Did you see those two helicopters over your house the night before you left for vacation? There were two of them! One was so close to your house I thought it was going to land on top of it!"

Time Travel and the Black Helicopters

This next story is so surreal I hesitate to write about it. I was teaching a class in New York City, one of many I taught prior to actually moving there. It was unusual in that there was a very interesting energy that seemed to be directing me in my teaching.

Because I am an open, clear channel, I am in constant communication with my Higher Self and guides. I have found that *checking in* (my shorthand for asking Higher Self a question) is almost like working on the Internet. I am "always on" yet periodically check in to get updates and direction, and reconfirm information. During this particular class the entire "live" instruction I was getting was very specific—that I was not "allowed" to follow my normal procedure.

Instead I was given my entire direction through my physical body. It was different from anything I had ever experienced and I was feeling my way through the class, announcing what was happening instead of my usual "We will do this and this and then take a break" based on direct guidance. Although it was unfamiliar, at the same time I found myself completely calm and connected to my physical body.

I led the entire workshop this way. Everything was on a very tight leash, in that I was given short bursts of instruction and nothing more. I remember hearing clearly in my thought, *You have one hour to do the advanced material, black helicopters, and programming, then activate the MerKaBa (in meditation) one more time putting the programming in place.* So that is what we did.

As soon as I announced this next direction to the students, a nurse sitting right across from me became extremely agitated and upset. I remember looking directly at her and saying in a very clear and deliberate way, "Stay with me, I promise it will be okay." Since I had only one hour, I was not taking questions, and we were then to go on and install the seven basic programs into the MerKaBa and end the course.

After class I approached this woman and said, "You were visited by the black helicopters, weren't you?" She immediately seemed to relax, realizing that I knew. I asked her when they came and she excitedly said, "The night before class started!" That means they came a full day before the class began.

Offering more details she told us there had been several helicopters flying around her apartment building in Manhattan, shining floodlights into her windows. She got up and turned on the TV to see what was happening. She asked, in an even tone, "Do you have any idea how many news stations we have here in New York? When I could not find a single one of them with *any* information, I was absolutely terrified!"

My channel opened and I said, "This is about time travel. The first time you did this workshop you went home without the invisibility programmed into your MerKaBa." Back in those days I did not realize students needed some of this advanced material in the basic Flower of Life course and did not always offer it.

How Did I Know It
Was about Time Travel?

Teaching is usually a mental exercise, and personally for me a channeling exercise, where I open my mind to my guides. My guides came in and reviewed with me my workshop experience, encouraging me to see how it was different. Looking back at the experience of my workshop this time, I remembered I was tracing a thread of information coming through my body compared with my usual use of my mind for teaching. I was shown that I was tracing the exact same version of the reality that had already occurred (parallel realities) in which the nurse had gone home without activating the invisibility program.

In this case it was never a mental exercise. My mind was not involved in the class instruction that weekend. My information track was retracing the first time I taught this same workshop (as in multiple versions of the reality). The second time the entire weekend lined up with another version of this same event. We then *changed the reality* at the end of class when I was given a very short window to *alter* the instructions. How did I alter them? I gave everyone the program to be invisible. By putting invisibility and other programs into the MerKaBa we changed the matrix and became invisible so she could go home without being seen.

In the first part of this incredible story, when she went home and showed up with what was perceived as a spaceship, that is, her activated MerKaBa around her body, it attracted attention and some sort of time travel occurred that allowed them to land in her reality the day *before* the workshop. Wild, I know.

Many of the students had gathered around us by this time and a dozen or so persons from the class said that they were getting huge confirmation on this channeled information.

I have written a template on how to "jump tracks," as I call it. This is an amazing tool that you can use any time you are aware that something terrible is going to happen, or if you see a mass consciousness outcome that seems inevitable and you feel the strong need to change it (with permission from your Higher Self, of course). This template is written about in chapter 13 on gridwork.

8

Surrogate MerKaBas:
Both Useful and Destructive

What You Will Learn in This Chapter

- What is a surrogate MerKaBa?
- A surrogate MerKaBa is created with approval from your Higher Self
- When in doubt, do without
- How to create a surrogate MerKaBa
- When to create a surrogate
- When *not* to create a surrogate

Yes, I am going to spend a whole chapter telling you about surrogates and how to build them, and then tell you *not* to do this unless and until you have a clear Higher Self connection.

Knowing about surrogate MerKaBa is a little like sex education. With enough good education, you know when to be careful. Over the years I discovered that individuals would take the information I was giving them and translate it into action, which made me happy with their inventiveness until I realized they were doing programs that lacked certain understanding. At first, in my naïveté, I didn't realize that people would not know not to do certain things. But hey, all of us need an education in certain areas! I had to learn the hard way not to cut the wires of the TV while it was still plugged in—you may remember from chapter 6 that I almost electrocuted myself. You need to develop your Higher Self connection so that you know it is accurate. Then always ask, *Is this program appropriate for me?*

What Is a Surrogate?

A surrogate MerKaBa is synonymous with an external MerKaBa. A surrogate MerKaBa is a program that replicates your MerKaBa in another specific location. Imagine saying in your mind the phrase *copy—paste*. This works like the copy and paste functions on your computer.

> A surrogate is a program to replicate your MerKaBa somewhere else for a specific purpose.

All MerKaBa programs must have a purpose so you must have a purpose for your surrogate. For example, you might have a surrogate MerKaBa over a prayer circle in the woods with the specific purpose of being seen *only* by persons who would recognize and respect this prayer circle. Replicating your MerKaBa in another location without a purpose would be inappropriate. Understand that it is the prayer circle that you are making invisible with your surrogate MerKaBa. This is a purposeful program so individuals with destructive energies don't tromp all over your sacred circle when you are not there using it.

Usefulness of Surrogates

A "spell" of old is similar to a program in your MerKaBa today and must honor the free will of anyone affected by your actions. This is a reminder that surrogates are powerful fifth-dimensional tools that require you to always take care to exercise respect for others' free will in their use. If you do something that would interfere with free will by your fifth-dimensional programming, you are breaking cosmic law. Understanding this is critical.

At fifth dimension there is no polarity, so there is no judgment. You can do what you do and it will not be perceived as good or bad.

Remember that your MerKaBa is fifth-dimensional. Normally, at fifth dimension, you would not even think of doing something that is against cosmic law. Because you are being given a powerful fifth-dimensional tool to assist you with your Ascension, you, in your third-dimensional way of being might actually come up with an idea that is not in alignment with a fifth-dimensional choice.

The surrogate technology is relatively new. When Drunvalo created his original surrogate experiment it was the first time he had ever considered doing such a thing. It amazed him how well it worked.

Drunvalo wrote about surrogate MerKaBas in volume 2 of *The Ancient Secret of the Flower of Life*. The experiment was prompted by his realization that when he was working with a group of individuals the black helicopters kept appearing. Drunvalo was not bothered by all this extra activity but it was a distraction. He thought about what he might do to get them to stop coming and the idea of creating a secondary or surrogate MerKaBa came to mind. As Drunvalo had permission from his students to work with them on this level, he was free to try this. The very first time he created a surrogate MerKaBa around the location of a prayer circle, they did not come. In previous times when they had activated in that circle outside in nature, helicopters consistently appeared. After he created the surrogate MerKaBa, whose purpose was to make the place invisible to the black helicopters, they did not come. This made Drunvalo realize he was on to something.

From that point on Drunvalo's surrogate MerKaBas worked with the intention that their activities in the prayer circle would be invisible and undetectable. On the last day of the seminar he took his group to the woods a hundred miles from the original location, completely forgetting about the surrogate, and sure enough, as soon as they started their activity the black helicopters were everywhere.

Fifth-Dimensional Privileges

I want you to understand you *are* your fifth-dimensional self while wearing your MerKaBa and are expected to operate in the highest integrity and *act* like a fifth-dimensional being. Remember in a previous chapter where the concept of free will and the not-God choice was presented? A fifth-dimensional being does not need to be reminded about integrity, because when you are fully fifth-dimensional the not-God choice does not occur to you. When you are just learning, the obvious will not be so obvious, which is why it is so important to take the time to learn and comprehend these details.

Wearing your fifth-dimensional uniform (the MerKaBa) gives you fifth-dimensional privileges whether you have earned them or not. The **toroidal**◈ (donut) field that exists around your body and is activated with your MerKaBa is powerful beyond third-dimensional reality.

Research of Dr. Glen Rein shows that this shape around the heart (which is bigger than your whole body) is an energy transducer, meaning it converts one form of energy to another because it generates an infinite number of harmonics and allows a stepdown or demodulation of higher energies. Energy travels through the type of torus that produces these harmonics with no loss of power.

Only when the heart is coherent, as in feelings of love and connectedness, can the energy come through in force. Resonance and coherence in an orderly system are tools allowing for access to the energies from higher realms. With your MerKaBa activated you have stepped up this process. It is real and measurable.

Wisdom and
Magic Must Be Paired

Ancient Egyptians had true magicians, those who could truly call in magic. Om Sety, keeper of the Abydos Temple of Seti I, asked her beloved King Sety in one of his many apparitions to tell her why Heka and Sia always accompanied the solar boat of the sun god Ra. His response: "They are shown together to remind all beholders that those who have Heka must have Sia or else they make use of bad Heka. . . . Heka is true magic and Sia is wisdom; without it magic can be misused."[1] In other words, the effects of the MerKaBa can be miraculous, but it must be handled with wisdom and integrity or it can be destructive.

There are many opportunities to misuse the power of the MerKaBa. This is one of the most important reasons I wrote this book, *Beyond the Flower of Life*. The MerKaBa is a powerful tool to be used wisely. This is why integrity issues are so important in third dimension when you first learn the MerKaBa. You may need help discerning what a not-God choice is. This is why you need to work with your Higher Self until your connection is crystal clear and you are getting accurate information, before you write programs.

When Is a Surrogate Destructive?

I choose to use words that are convergence-based, so you will not read *good* or *bad* into this information about programs. In simple terms, the purpose of any program or surrogate must be aligned with the will of the individuals involved. A surrogate is destructive when it causes a person to fall out of harmony with her or his own Ascension process. Attempting to control another in a free-will zone is also considered stepping out of harmony.

Contrary to what you may believe, your Higher Self is not like a parent who lovingly corrects the actions you may take while creating surrogate programs for your MerKaBa. It is entirely possible to create a surrogate program that is inappropriate and destructive as you will see in the following examples.

A man in a recent Earth/Sky/Heart Workshop of Drunvalo's raised his hand as Drunvalo was discussing programs and surrogates. When called upon, he asked, "Can I program my MerKaBa to get my wife to do what I want her to do?" The entire audience of 165 people burst into laughter. How does a person get this far in his spiritual work and not realize the disconnect in this? Maybe he was joking.

I want you to understand you *are* your fifth-dimensional self while wearing your MerKaBa and are expected to operate in the highest integrity and *act* like a fifth-dimensional being! A fifth-dimensional being does not need to be reminded about integrity, because when you are fully fifth-dimensional the not-God choice doesn't occur to you. When you are just learning, the obvious won't be so obvious, which is why it is so important to take the time to learn and comprehend these details.

It is *never* appropriate to put a surrogate MerKaBa around another living being. Remember, the MerKaBa has a torus field. I have seen this torus field of the living MerKaBa. If you were to mix your MerKaBa field with another's torus field, you would be looping their entire matrix energy through your torus. Energetically this is undesirable and makes no sense whatsoever.

The Rare Exception

In the rare exception of a life-threatening situation you might get permission from your Higher Self, and then the Higher Self of the other person, by asking your Higher Self to ask their Higher Self. You would not leave a surrogate in place around someone for any length of time. I know of one instance where Drunvalo put a surrogate MerKaBa around someone and then stayed with the person for forty-eight hours in the Intensive Care Unit. Before leaving his friend's bedside, he took it down. In such cases you will need to get double Higher Self permission: First you ask your Higher Self for permission, then you ask your Higher Self to ask the other person's Higher Self. It is a two-step process and never done lightly.

Misuse of a Surrogate MerKaBa around a Child

Without fully understanding what she was doing, a MerKaBa student in her mid-forties who was the mother of a child with Attention Deficit Disorder (ADD) placed a surrogate MerKaBa around her child to help settle down hyperactivity issues. Initially she was pleased with the results and called me to share her success. I was dumbfounded. I could not imagine anyone doing such a thing and I asked her to take it down. She refused.

This woman is a capable, spiritual, committed person, knowledgeable in shamanic healing, a light worker, and a genuinely lovely person. She wanted to help her child, but it is unethical to put a surrogate MerKaBa around anyone else, *especially* your own offspring. You are interfering with the child's free will. I explained this to this parent and recommended she remove the surrogate for this reason.

She did not follow my recommendation, but kept it activated for a long time. Eventually she attended a workshop with Drunvalo and told him of her success with the surrogate MerKaBa around her son. What do you think Drunvalo told her? The very thing I had said six months earlier: "Take it down."

After she took the program down she fell ill unexpectedly with an unexplained illness that haunted her for years. It began with a case of the flu and developed into a full-blown experience in which she was unable to walk and had a raft of other serious physical ailments.

She suffered through apparent nerve dysfunction, inexplicable pain, loss of motor control, and more. She went in and out of numerous hospitals and was tested for every possible kind of virus and neuromuscular, physical, and mental disease imaginable, but none of her doctors were ever able to identify what caused this. She consulted specialists in both allopathic and naturopathic medicine, and worked with energy healers and spiritual healers.

This parent has suffered greatly. She was in a wheelchair and has been recovering for close to six years now. Her physical issues did not appear to have a physical cause. She would get a little better and then relapse. The road to recovery has been excruciatingly slow. I believe this person's ailments are directly related to the misuse of the surrogate MerKaBa. My guides tell me the two events are related.

Now I want to make something perfectly clear here: She is not being punished for her surrogate program. There is no karma from her program. It is a simple outcome-based scenario. If you mix red wine with oil and then spill it on your shirt, the longer it sits the more difficult it is to get out the stain. Her physical disability is related to the mix-up of her MerKaBa energy with her child's MerKaBa energy. If you mix your energy with someone else's in this manner, undesirable results can occur.

Another Destructive
Surrogate MerKaBa

Many individuals have mistakenly believed they could put a surrogate MerKaBa around an animal. While this is certainly possible, it is *not* advisable under any circumstances.

An animal communicator student of mine put a surrogate MerKaBa around a horse that was not responding to normal treatments or any of her usual pantheon of healing modalities, including **Seichim Reiki**◈, essential oils, and massage. She promptly forgot about it.

My friend started to develop some strange symptoms, a mysterious illness and general loss of well-being. After five days of suffering she could no longer get out of bed. Deciding that something was seriously wrong, she went into meditation to find the answer. Her primary guide came in and reminded her that she had left a surrogate MerKaBa over the horse.

She argued with her guide, saying, *I did not build that; I asked the Angels to do that*. If that was the case, who commanded the Angels? Where did they get the template of the living MerKaBa field? Her guide showed her that *she* was the creator of the surrogate MerKaBa. Since the horse was now looping through her torus field, she was mixing up its energy and hers! No wonder she got sick. She called me a few days after she took it down and had started to get better. The first words I heard from her that day were, "I know you told me not to do this . . . "

The animal kingdom is *not* being projected onto the screen of life from the same dimension as humans. Therefore the practice of placing a MerKaBa around them would link us to that animal and subject us to their reality as well as our own. Since their job is to serve humanity and Mother Earth, that might cause some serious problems. You would not mix two different kinds of fuel to run an engine. I believe that there is a significant difference in the energy (spiritual energy) that humans use. You do not want an animal vibration looping through your torus field.

A Surrogate MerKaBa
Is Not for Protection

It is never appropriate to put up an external MerKaBa that protects another person. The obvious reason: the MerKaBa is not for protection. The second reason is that creating such a field robs her of her Christhood and her path.

One woman, a shaman, put a surrogate MerKaBa around the people in an apartment building in another country across the ocean. Her friend in that location had had a scare of some kind and was quite frightened. She asked the shaman to do something. Naturally the shaman went on a shamanic journey through the ethers. She created a surrogate MerKaBa around the apartment building thinking she would be offering *protection* for this family and everyone who lived in the building. When she completed this project she asked her power animal if there was anything else she should do. Her power animal told her to email me right away and *tell Maureen what you have done.*

At that very moment I was on an airplane headed back home. I was awakened from sleep by my guides telling me to retrieve my laptop from the overhead bin. I was to write, "Rules for programming your MerKaBa." When I returned home, most of the reply email to her was already written. At this point her surrogate had been running for maybe an hour. Prior to that there were no guidelines or rules for creating surrogate MerKaBas. Hence my guidance to write the rules was to prevent future miscreations and to help the shaman understand the nature of her actions.

The MerKaBa Is Not Like White Light

Using Reiki, white light, or the Angels to offer safety and protection in the third dimension is perfectly reasonable. The MerKaBa, however, is a living organism and operates from the MerKaBa field of its creator. It is not like white light, which offers a benefit to everyone. That means that any surrogate you create is coming from your physical MerKaBa. It is a copy/paste version of your MerKaBa and is physically linked to it. Anything that is happening to the surrogate is happening to you, since you are looping the other person through your field.

I explained to this shaman that while her intentions were quite honorable, my recommendation was that she take down this external MerKaBa and encourage her friends to attend MerKaBa training from a facilitator in their area. As long as she had all those individuals in her external MerKaBa (and it was hers, since she created it), she was responsible for what went on with the new energy she might be feeling.

If you did get permission from your Higher Self to create such a surrogate MerKaBa, you would also have to have permission from the Higher Selves of each of the tenants living in that apartment building. Clearly this well-meaning shaman misunderstood the use of a surrogate and unwittingly mixed her energies (remember a surrogate is a copy of *your* MerKaBa). This is completely different than putting a surrogate MerKaBa around a consenting group, as with Drunvalo's prayer circle.

Do you get the picture? Each of us needs to be responsible for our own MerKaBa. While the danger the person faced may have been real, I doubt that it is ongoing. If it is, then perhaps they would consider activating their own MerKaBa. She wrote me back reporting how she had started to feel very strangely after that shamanic journey.

The external MerKaBa should only be created for purposes that will not interfere with another's free will. The shaman in question put one over a building and its residents that she did not own and where she was only tangentially connected. She created a *big* connection with it by virtue of her actions. Thankfully she took it down within an hour.

Because of her shamanic work, along with her curiosity, she immediately went on another shamanic journey to discover more about what I had explained to her. True to form, the information I provided was validated by her second journey when she received understanding to authenticate my communication to her. She then took the external MerKaBa down.

A surrogate is not shared or created lightly. This could backfire on you in ways you cannot even imagine. This is why there are a number of rules for the use of the surrogate MerKaBa.

Should You
Even Consider Surrogates?

One student, in a desire to prevent possible mishaps, suggested we not learn about surrogates. Once the knowledge that surrogate MerKaBas can be created exists, she reasoned, people will be inclined to think up ways to use them.

My response to her was that our world has an abundance of technology we could use that without proper training could cause serious consequences. However, with training and care, tools enhance our lives and our work. The surrogate MerKaBa should be approached in much the same way.

I have confidence you will ask your Higher Self to approve your surrogates. You can be trusted.

Rules for Creating
a Surrogate MerKaBa

1. Always ask your Higher Self, *Is this program appropriate for all involved?*

2. A surrogate is a *program* in your MerKaBa that instructs your MerKaBa to copy your MerKaBa over a specific location.

3. It is activated in the same way your own MerKaBa is activated.

4. A surrogate always has a purpose. Make sure you are *clear about your purpose* when you ask for your Higher Self's approval.

5. Your surrogates will be located around a particular geographic place, for example a prayer circle in the woods, or over a house or place of business. It's important to note the surrogate is located over the place, not the people in the place.

6. It is powered by your MerKaBa. When your MerKaBa goes inactive, your surrogate will also deactivate.

7. Never create a surrogate program over another individual. When in doubt, ask your Higher Self *and* the Higher Self of the individual involved. You will need two permissions: First you need permission from your Higher Self. Then you need to ask

your Higher Self to get permission from the Higher Self of the other person (peer-to-peer). *It will be a very rare circumstance* for you to get both permissions.

8. Never leave an emergency surrogate MerKaBa unattended around another person. Provided you have permissions, you *must* stay physically close. If, for example, the ambulance team will not let you ride together, take the surrogate down.

9. You might put a program over your office or cubicle but not the entire business, unless you were the owner of the business. Remember that your surrogate program should only address the physical area, objects, or space, not the individual people.

9

MerKaBa Permanence and Paranormal Validation

What You Will Learn in This Chapter

- Paranormal validation of the MerKaBa
- Remembering and repair
- How to make the MerKaBa permanent
- What happens next?

Paranormal External Validation of the MerKaBa

> "Gregg Braden isn't the only one who has time traveled in Egypt! Maureen St. Germain has done it too!"
>
> MOHAMED NAZMY, PRESIDENT OF QUEST TRAVEL, EGYPT

You may have heard about people who are able to get streetlamps to go out when they walk past them. You wonder, *What the heck is going on?* In many cases blinking lights or power surges are the Universe's way of reconfirming what you are talking or thinking about in that exact moment.

Goose bumps on the body are another way of reconfirming information. I now call them "body confirmation."

A TV that is turned off and plugged in still has energy moving through it. If you were to cut the electrical cord, sparks would fly. Yet you are not getting any reception. If you were to put an energy meter on it, the energy fields would show some usage. When the TV is turned on, power is moving through it.

Many of you have had experiences with wristwatches and understand that your energy is so powerful that you break or lose them. Likewise, although I love technology and gadgets, I've quit purchasing cordless headsets because they keep disappearing. I've lost dozens of them and finally accepted I am not supposed to wear them.

Brian and Joanna were in deep discussion regarding concerns over the possibility of dangerous earth changes in their location. Brian felt they should consider moving. Joanna completely surrendered to his suggestion, even though they had just spent thousands of dollars renovating their home. Shortly after this discussion Brian began feeling assurance that they did not need to be protected from this presumed danger of the earth changes. He told Joanna and bingo! Immediately the lights in the house blinked off and back on in quick succession.

While I was teaching a class in the home of an Atlanta chiropractor, I noticed there were a number of ceiling spotlights in her living room where we were meditating. Out of seven lights, four were burned out and only three were on. The vaulted ceiling is so high that my host usually has a handyman come in to change them for her. She mentally wished they would come on. Immediately three more of the seven came on, and stayed on, during the entire meditation. When she got up from the room, those same three lights that had come on during our meditation went off and stayed off for the remainder of the advanced workshop. We all laughed at how she managed to get burned-out lightbulbs to come on at the right moment.

I often have participants stay at my home when I teach the workshop at my home. During one such workshop I realized I didn't have time to get a new bulb for the night-light in the bathroom so that my elderly guest could find her way. I asked the Angels to step in and allow the bulb to work, even though I knew it was a burned-out bulb. The light stayed on the entire three days of the workshop and quit working when my houseguest left.

I think the MerKaBa field impacts lights—perhaps overloads their circuits. As soon as the person moves out of range, the lights come back on. Start watching how far away you are when they go out and you can estimate the range of your MerKaBa field.

Remember and Repair

The reason we say that the MerKaBa is remembered is because we are remembering our future. The MerKaBa shape is always around the body. When you do the meditation you are remembering it, then activating it.

At some point the remembering becomes automatic. A metaphor might be that when you have a pet, you always know you have to go home to feed it. Similarly, being connected to your MerKaBa field feels like you always are connected to it. When it becomes permanent you always remember it is there and it is always "running" in the background.

Although the energetic template of the MerKaBa is always around the body, it can be warped, damaged, and even forgotten. If the MerKaBa is damaged, consciously activating it daily will allow it to self-repair. This is why we pointed out in the beginning of this book that the MerKaBa will repair all kinds of damage. I recommend a daily practice for a number of reasons:

It will self-heal if activated regularly.
Activating it daily will certainly make your life easier.
Sometimes the self-healing factor will lead you to a practitioner or healer who will jump-start your processes.

Seeing a practitioner could go either way: fabulous or disastrous. Always ask your Higher Self if this teacher or practitioner is the best choice for you at this time. Then if you get some major repair work done by a master, you can thank your MerKaBa for finding that master and helping you to know what you needed. Not all methods are always good for everyone. Even for a given practice, you might be told *no* at one time and *yes* at another time by your Higher Self.

Is My MerKaBa Permanent?

For the answer to this question, ask your Higher Self. Only your Higher Self will know if your MerKaBa is permanent. There are other ways to know, but all of them are inferior compared to asking your Higher Self. When you activate your MerKaBa initially, it stays activated for only about forty-eight hours.

In the early years everyone took that statement as fact. We now know it can stay up longer than that. I had a student who could see into the ethers. She did not have a big ego about it and used it to keep herself out of harm's way. Because she could see her MerKaBa after she activated it, she checked on it every day. It stayed up for a month! I checked her story and my guides validated it.

Why did hers stay up longer than so many other people's? I believe her survival skills were so evolved that she had the ability to replicate from her psychic abilities, rather than using the heart connection of the MerKaBa along with the body and mind. I call someone with this skill set a survival psychic (see chapter 10).

What Happens Next?

This is the fun part. This is such an amazing journey that I cannot begin to tell you the fun you will have with it. For example, I was with three people who had been doing the MerKaBa for over a year and had all just repeated the FOL course with me on an adventure in Banff, Canada. We kept checking in, asking the Higher Self if we should go to Moraine Lake (*yes*), Lake Louise (*no*). After we visited Moraine Lake we were told to also go to Lake Louise. Obviously we could have asked which one to visit first.

We were all getting rather hungry when we approached the amazing lodge at Lake Louise. Upon entering, we found a great-looking restaurant that didn't look too busy. Since we were hungry and the menu looked fine, we headed in. Then I said, "Wait! Did anyone ask Higher Self?" The two men in our group were *very* hungry and immediately checked in, asking if this was where we were supposed to eat, and both got a *no* answer. Still hungry, we wandered upstairs to find a marvelous restaurant with three-story windows and a breathtaking view of the lake and glacier. Our Higher Selves approved and the hostess informed us there was only a ten-minute wait. Then she gave us the best seats in the restaurant, because that is what opened up for us.

On another adventure, my host in Japan wanted to take me to a hot springs after a long trek to a shrine. It was late and we both opted to skip dinner in favor of the bathing. We went into one hot spring spa near the railway station that seemed nice, yet my Higher Self said *no*. We wandered into the main town where we could see six or so hotels with hot springs. My host, Naoko, now used to my asking my Higher Self about everything, pointed to each of them while waiting for my Higher Self to give approval of one. We went into the selected spa and the desk clerk told us nobody could be admitted after 3 p.m. Naoko told the host that I was here from America and really wanted to experience this particular hot spring. Immediately the desk clerk let us in, with free towels and a lesser price than the first spa we had considered.

It turned out better than we expected because the hotel included dinner with the guest rooms, so all the guests were at dinner while we had the entire spa to ourselves with two pools. One was outside where we could see the full moon.

Higher Self Solutions and Surprises

When I was doing a workshop in Nashua, New Hampshire, staying at a hotel, I was working out at the hotel gym every morning. I was disappointed that the water cooler in the gym did not have the expected five-gallon jug above it. Instead the top of the water cooler was covered with unimportant things, such as flyers, a box of tissues, and other clutter.

On the third day I walked in when a student was getting water from the cooler. Imagine my surprise to discover it was piped in through a set of filters from the wall. My expectation of that kind of cooler did not match what I saw. My bias that the water had to come from a jug above the cooler made me think there was no water in the exercise room, yet there was. The Higher Self is like this. It shows you solutions, ideas, and concepts that you haven't thought of because it has no bias or expectation to limit you. Awesome, isn't it?

How Do I Make the MerKaBa Permanent?

With daily practice the MerKaBa will become permanent on its own. I recommend you do it daily because each day you get a fresh start from the Universe. Each day you get to decide what you will make of your life. By choosing to do the MerKaBa daily, you give yourself the gift of a practice that leads to perfection, an open heart and stepping out of polarity. Not a bad investment for five minutes per day. Not to mention the fact that if you do it daily and then forget one day, your MerKaBa will still be actively running.

After my MerKaBa was permanent, my Higher Self informed me that I was supposed to keep doing it. Why would that be? Perhaps it is because I have such a big commitment to teach the MerKaBa. I do know that when I asked my Higher Self if my MerKaBa was permanent, I was told, *That is not the question for you, Maureen.* My Higher Self was aware that I would probably stop my daily practice if it were permanent. I then asked if I should keep doing it. *Yes.* Is it permanent? *Yes.* I continued to do the MerKaBa daily for more than eight years after that point. I still do the MerKaBa frequently.

Beyond Higher Self Communication— Feeling Body

Your feeling body is a higher-dimensional expression of your physical body. My first experience with my feeling body was when I was teaching an FOL class. I had a certain knowing that existed in my physical body, not my mental body or brain. I was being told very specific actions to take from another level, yet the mental instructions were also very clear to *not* think about it. I described this in detail in chapter 7.

We've all had experiences where we have known something at the body level. I've discovered that if you are having this kind of experience on a regular basis, you have found the way to experience new information through your heart, while completely bypassing conscious thought patterns. It is a direct link to fifth dimension and beyond to even higher dimensions. In the fifth dimension it is a dance—the mind participates but heart energy rules. It is the place of unconditional love.

Heart Knowing

The heart does not require a mental process to confirm a piece of knowledge. The knowledge that comes in is so perfect that it is not necessary to validate it any other way.

The mother who knows that her child is in trouble is one such example. Many people have known when a friend, partner, or spouse needed something. When caring for an aging or ill family member, sensing that the individual's death is imminent is another example.

Recently, I was getting ready to travel to a certain city for a workshop. When I went to bed the night before I fully expected to fall asleep right away, but I did not. Instead I lay awake feeling this great tension of excitement. I felt like a rookie football player who has signed his first multimillion-dollar contract! I was happy as could be and felt higher than a kite. Since I do not take drugs or drink anything but water and tea, it wasn't because of some mind-altering substance.

My heart knew my life was about to change, and it did. A number of magical and synchronistic events occurred during that trip. My anticipation and excitement were justified and my body confirmed it before I knew the details. The heart knows.

A Permanent MerKaBa

When your MerKaBa is permanent you always remember. Your Higher Self guides and directs you. You feel great love for everyone you meet. Life becomes compelling and heartwarming. Even difficult situations become manageable and joyful. Once your MerKaBa is permanent, you will always have an open and active connection to your heart.

10

Clearing Fear with Dolphins, Whales, and AroMandalas

What You Will Learn in This Chapter

- What is going on with cetacean energy?
- Fear and its use
- Dolphins and weather windows

Multidimensional Dolphin Adventures

A woman in a Caribbean-based dolphin swim workshop had a lame arm from a factory injury. Ilizabeth Fortune, a Flower of Life facilitator, and Drunvalo were leading this dolphin swim. When the wild dolphins were sighted near the boat, everyone jumped into the water, including the woman with the injured arm. Everyone was laughing and swimming with the dolphins. Their energy was euphoric!

When the dolphins left, everyone piled onto the boat and went back to their cabins for a nap. At dinner Drunvalo noticed the woman with the lame arm was using both of her arms freely. He pointed this out to her and she seemed surprised, "What are you talking about?" She didn't even remember that she'd had a lame arm when she got in the water! She literally jumped from one version of reality to another where that injury had never occurred. And she brought everyone else with her! You, too, can use this understanding to create alternate versions of reality that please you.

After learning the MerKaBa in 1994 I immediately went to a **rebirthing**◈ event where I undulated (the way a dolphin swims) the entire two hours I was "under the rebirthing trance." I now believe in one experience I was remembering a dolphin lifetime. I truly did not know I was doing that, and I could not seem to *not* do that. Maybe my dolphin friends joined me for healing and transforming. Fortuitously, later that year I was on two different dolphin swims getting my feet wet, so to speak.

That first dolphin swim was in 1994 with Drunvalo. I have been swimming with dolphins ever since. In 2000 I was given the go-ahead to offer the MerKaBa training and the advanced Flower of Life workshop along with a dolphin immersion experience. During each Dolphin Sacred Journey we have multiple swims with wild dolphins, and each year it is a unique and amazing adventure of love and light.

Dolphins Clear Fear

One year a woman named Sharon who was deathly afraid of the water joined us. I told her I was certified by the Red Cross with Level II of Lifeguard and Water Safety and had pulled a few people from the water, so she would be safe with me. Once when I was in my twenties, I saved a nun from drowning. Her convent was using our family swimming pool for a private swim. I was gazing out the window at our yard when my attention was drawn to the pool. I noticed there was a problem and was able to respond quickly. My mother always said I had earned my spot in heaven for pulling out that drowning nun!

Sharon was determined to get into the water. I noticed she was hanging on to her husband for dear life, even though she had a boogie board and was wearing a life jacket. I insisted that the next time she got in the water I would be her partner. I wanted to make sure her husband would not have to be her full-time caretaker. I took her wrist so I could keep her in my grasp. What happened next took me completely by surprise, as I was unexpectedly filled with fear. This was no ordinary fear. I am a fearless woman in or out of the water, and in that moment I experienced real terror.

In a flash I knew what it was like to be afraid of drowning. I quickly pulled the rest of this eerie energy from my swimming partner (Sharon) and grounded it through me, and then into the water directly into the center of Mother Earth. Otherwise I was sure I would have drowned. Sharon was quite startled and said, "It's gone! I'm not afraid of the water anymore! You cleared it!" I think I had a little help from the dolphins; they help us breathe deeply by releasing all fear that is in our fields. These energies can be like spider webs that can be pulled from the body. You'd be well advised to know how to ground and clear fear before attempting to pull this kind of energy from someone else.

Using Fear to Fuel Your Ascension Work

Your fears are keys to your own growth and understanding. They help you develop compassion for others by working with your own fears. Denying their existence no longer serves you. Please consider asking the Archangels to clear you of desires and patterns that no longer serve you, and to assist you in replacing them with desires, dreams, and patterns that *will* serve you. You can ask specific Angels to assist you. You'll find lots of information once you start to look to the Angels to assist you this way.

Over the years I have worked with supplemental tools to assist humans in processing these incoherent energies and emotions. You do not have to do it the long way anymore. The Universe has provided tools to help you shift quickly such as my AroMandalas-Orion Series essential oil blends discussed in detail later. Most of us tend to find our seat of security in the same place as fear, in the gut or solar plexus. While that is where you experience some emotions, if you allow yourself to open your heart you will find there are three key emotions—love, gratitude, and joy—that move through your heart. Science now knows the huge toroidal field that circulates around your heart is bigger than your whole body. This is where love resides. At an Earth/Sky/Heart Workshop of Drunvalo's that I attended, Lawrence, a mixed-race Black Indian, found that he was able to release the "guardedness" that he always felt around white people because now he was moving love through his heart.

Fear and Worry

What is the purpose of fear in the world? It was put there to slow our Ascension. Fear is a perversion of the past. Worry is a perversion of the future. Neither is real.

Who or what caused this? Initially Earth was the paradise of extraterrestrials. They did not want humanity to evolve too quickly because then Earth would no longer be their playground! These beings reprogrammed our DNA and created a way to limit certain human capacity. While they were at it they modified certain things, such as stepping up our sex drive. They also instilled fear in the consciousness.

How did they do that? They realized initiates in the mystery school were evolving quickly, and they began to teach these individuals how to use energy and amplify it. The mystery school students trusted their teachers. They thought they were being given real options for their benefit. In truth, the only real options anyone can have are the ones you give yourself.

A Rigged Test

In an ancient Egyptian mystery school run by lesser beings with outside agendas, initiates were sent down a long corridor with two doors at the end. One was dimly lit, the other was very bright. Of course most initiates chose the one with the bright light. Waiting behind that door were crocodiles, and they were eaten alive. But guess what? The darkened doorway had the same exact outcome! Both circumstances yielded a large amount of fear in the consciousness before the initiates died. Not all choices were like this, just enough to slow things down. This is how fear became amplified in the consciousness of humanity.

Now if you were fully connected to your Higher Self and had a MerKaBa up and running, you probably wouldn't be too inclined to take a rigged test. However, as an adept, with some spiritual mastery in a fearsome circumstance, you might find you had the ability to leave your body before any fear and physical pain were created, instead of taking the chance of having fear magnified by you, thus polluting the environment with your fear.

Once you face a fear head on, it loses its impact on you. What is it you fear? It usually is the unknown. If you have knowledge, even if it is incomplete information, it can lead you to an awareness of certain actions that remove you from the fray of activity. Full knowledge dissipates fear and provides you with an opportunity.

> Fear is a perversion of the past.
> Worry is a perversion of the future.
> Neither is real.

Survival Psychics

Some individuals are so filled with barriers against past hurts and experiences that left deep wounds that they are unable to let down their defenses. They have developed very powerful skills to protect themselves. These skills may include various forms of extrasensory, or beyond the senses, perception—telepathy (no-contact communication), clairsentience (perceiving things not normally perceptible), clairaudience (hearing things not present to the ear but having objective reality), clairalience (smelling), clairgustance (tasting), and clairvoyance (knowing) that access energy fields beyond the physical body. These survival skills can be developed enough to impersonate a real healer, with an open heart.

Having these abilities does not presume the individual is God-centered. You can usually sort this out as you observe their well-developed psychic skills, because they are not sending this awareness through the heart. Instead they are looping it (like fly fishing) from the solar plexus to the higher chakras. It affords them a form of protection since it lets them read fields and anticipate perceived danger. The disadvantage is that if you are used to getting information in this way, you might not bother with learning to open your heart. Opening your heart is key to your Ascension work.

Some abused individuals have taken the time to do their healing work. It is not easy going backward to gain a heart connection and then moving through it toward achieving mastery. Please consider taking advantage of the healing tools mentioned earlier.

Survival psychics are seriously wounded and seriously compromised. They have not engaged in spiritual work to open their hearts but seem to be able to sense things they have no real basis for knowing. They may even believe these abilities are *gifts,* but in reality, they are expressions of advanced survival skills they have developed to keep themselves safe. Some of these individuals are spiritually inclined, yet they lack the heart connection that would allow them to see and feel another's experience.

They unknowingly expend huge amounts of energy building barriers to the opportunity of really knowing and understanding their own fears. This is because if their fears were addressed and cleared, they would have to open their hearts the way everyone else on the planet does, which would be untenable by their current standards. I wrote about this struggle in *Reweaving the Fabric of Your Reality.* Please understand that I have great compassion for what they have been through and how very difficult life must be for them.

When these individuals use their specially developed skills to get information, they can be highly accurate. Remember that if you are one of those individuals, until you are able to express true love for yourself and others it will be challenging for you to move into your fifth-dimensional self. The emotion you create will always be operating at the ego level. The fifth-dimensional self realigns with the Higher Self. Your Higher Self will create an environment where safety is never an issue. If you are wealthy, money is no object. If you are fifth-dimensional, fear does not exist. Fear will block you from tapping into the profound abundance of the Universe that operates through the heart. You will always be operating from a sense of lack or limitation. This is based on experiences that were imprinted at the ego level.*

---

*There are many healers available to assist you with that process if you find you want to jump-start your healing. You might consider Emotional Freedom and Healing, craniosacral work, or NAET (Nambudripad's Allergy Elimination Technique) acupuncture.

Fear and Its Misuses

Fear can be something we develop on our own, or in certain cases it may be used by someone or some force that wishes to exercise control over us.

This quote from a newsletter of Patricia Cota-Robles, cofounder of the organization New Age Study of Humanity's Purpose, in 2006 gives a new slant on an old theme:

They informed us that if the *Truth* of what is occurring on Earth is not available to the newly-awakened souls, they will become pawns to the misinformation and disinformation being buffeted about by the forces of imbalance. These wayward souls are perpetuating fear-based thoughts of gloom and doom in a final attempt to maintain control and to terrorize Humanity. Their goal is to keep Humanity so overwhelmed and so focused on our fears that we won't be able to awaken effectively enough to fulfill our Divine Plans and our purpose and reason for being on Earth at this time. Their desire is to prevent the Earth and all her life from Ascending onto our next Spiral of Evolution. This is the spiral of the 5th Dimension, the spiral on which Humanity will co-create the limitless physical perfection of Heaven on Earth.[1]

Information dispels fear. This is why your Higher Self connection is so vital. When you have accurate information to follow due to your direct connection with God, you have nothing to fear. You will find that you are able to know what you need to know so perfectly that everything that you need to do, be, or know is effortless.

Fear of Shame

There are those who believe in integrity but "freeze up" when it comes to some personal issue connected to shame. It is important that you clear your shame so you can evolve and grow your own self-awareness to a place that allows true Higher Self to move through you. One of the easiest ways to do this is to use an essential oil blend. Effective almost instantaneously, AroMandalas-Orion Series Remembranz blend is able to clear shame because it bypasses everything and goes directly to the limbic system, where all core emotions reside in the physical. This enables the shame to be zeroed out like lightning conducted to the ground with a lightning rod. If you include the Intention disc from Vibranz, the fascia will rebound, resolving the tendency to reinjure with the same emotion.

Shame is a limiting belief that is rooted in the desire for victimhood. If you can convince yourself you are a victim of circumstances, you do not need to be responsible for your behavior or for what has happened to you. Shame is also a form of fear that drives individuals to behave in ways that are inconsistent with their stated beliefs. It is this inconsistency that causes the disconnect, making it difficult to connect with your innate wisdom. This is why clearing shame is so vital.

A woman I interacted with failed to keep her word—or even communicate about it—because even though she seemed to have high integrity she was embarrassed to admit she could not keep her word. Withholding this information is disrespectful. It's easy enough to admit *I forgot, I got tied up,* or what truthfully occurred to prevent keeping her word. In truth, she was ashamed of the information because it would mean she would have to stop being a victim and be accountable for her own actions. This person also did not notice that she had not expressed gratitude in this same circumstance because her primary goal was to keep herself in high regard. This was her normal. Her inability to feel or understand another's feelings prevented her from dropping her façade and loving herself.

Emotional Wounds

There are many ways to clear emotional wounds. It is important to recognize that the emotional wounds must be addressed, even if they have spontaneously healed or cleared. The ego clings to past wounds and hurts in an effort to protect the soul. When you become your fifth-dimensional self, there is nothing to hold on to since you are fully connected to God. Activating the MerKaBa, using tools, and specialized meditations will accelerate your effort.

The primary emotional wounds are helplessness, not belonging, resentment and frustration, anger and rage, disappointment, desperation, loss, feeling trapped, despair, terror, heartsickness, shame, unrequited longing, overwhelm, violation, and martyr/victim (male or female). There are AroMandalas-Orion Series essential oil blends to address each of them.

When I first worked with the essential oil blends that were channelled by Mary Magdalene and used to heal emotional wounds I wanted to know how they worked. How could they be any better than any other of the amazing blends from other companies? What I was told and shown in the Akashic Records, by others, as well as by my own Akashic Records guides, is that they came through me, and my vibration has to do with the blends. They work synergistically with the meditations, Intention disc, and other tools available on my website. Please check in for yourself if these will be helpful to you. How do they work? Emotions reside on the fascia. They create divots in the fascia that might not recover after the emotion is cleared. The oils clear the fascia. The Intention disc clears the incoherent energy of the fascia, making it recover its original shape like your activewear when it comes out of the dryer.

In a conversation in 2019 my business consultant asked, "What are you doing with the AroMandalas?" I answered that I felt I was not doing enough, I wasn't reaching an adequate number of the people who needed this simple solution to healing their emotional wounds. When she asked what I was willing to do about that, I laughed out loud and said, "I know what I will do; I will have a ceremony at the altar and ask Mary Magdalene about this!" My ceremony included asking the following from Mary Magdalene: *Is it in our highest and best good to take the AroMandalas to another level? If so, will you provide your blessing and assistance? I would be willing to show up, sell that part of the company, hire a marketing expert, whatever was put in front of me to move them into the next level of consciousness.* A few weeks later I had a very interesting experience.

I had purchased a violet laser from a company called Vibranz for clearing infections and fungus. This had been an ongoing problem for my lungs, and the laser definitely helped. At the next trade show where I was speaking, the same company was exhibiting and when I asked my Higher Self if there were any other tools that would help me clear the last 10 percent of the remaining fungus, I was directed to the Vibranz booth again. This time I was guided to ask to use the Frequency disc.

This is a deceptively simple piece of black marble or granite about the size of a drink coaster that is coded with human DNA frequencies. Unsure if I should purchase it, I asked if I could borrow one. The rep in the booth, Joe, offered to loan me the extra one he had in his backpack until the morning. Since I was done with my presentations for the day, I took the disc with me into the main hall to listen to another speaker. After about ninety minutes I could feel my body shifting upward, and my personal guide came in and told me, *You have just phased up.* By the time I returned to the Vibranz booth the following day the fungus had completely cleared.

Anyone who has dealt with a fungus infection of any kind knows how difficult it can be, and this fungus had settled into my lungs, causing all kinds of problems for almost three years! Joe's explanation of the metamorphosis is that the *Frequency* disc held open the portal for me to walk into my DNA frequency. I now understand that when we have ongoing health issues our body elemental can start to operate as if that were normal.* The body elemental has forgotten the ideal frequencies. Much as in a symbiotic relationship, the codependency—maintaining the status quo—becomes the operative frequency rather than holding on to the ideal frequency. The *Frequency* disc helped me to remember.

I returned to the booth healthy, happy, and excited to share my story of transformation. Joe suggested I share my story with the president of the company, who happened to be there that day, and my guides

---

*The body elemental is a type of engineer energy that works tirelessly for the physical human body. It is a gift of Mother Earth to the person and looks just like you, only it is smaller in size. It is your body elemental whose job it is help your physical body running in your earthly body. The physical body and the body elemental are paired, like headphones to your phone. They are joined so you can fit in on the earth. The earthly body needs an engineer to run all your systems, and your body elemental serves this purpose. More information as well as a guided meditation on interacting with your body elemental can be found on my website.

came in again and prompted me to ask him for help with the marketing of the AroMandalas, which I had in my tote bag. When I handed the oils to him he physically backed away at first, and then completely surprised me by saying that he had guidance coming in: *You need to work with this woman.* Thus the partnership of the Vibranz product with AroMandalas produced a potent opportunity for both companies. I was later informed that he had been told about the Intention disc having some kind of partner but he did not know what it was until he connected with the AroMandalas.

Weather Windows

One year we had strange weather for our dolphin swim, which was unusual because I have always experienced wonderful weather in Hawaii. Good weather follows me wherever I go. In fact, during the twelve years I lived in Wisconsin they had their mildest winters on record. The first year after I moved away was their worst winter in recorded history. New York City, during my first winter in my new home, experienced its mildest winter on record. In the early years I didn't realize I was influencing the weather in this way.

This Sacred Journey Dolphin Swim started with unusual weather. On the first morning of our scheduled boat trip we were greeted with an electrical storm. At breakfast we all looked at the grim weather, wondering if we would get into the water that day. Our boat captain, Veto, called and asked, "What kind of group do you have? Are they determined?" "I think determined would be a *mild* descriptor for this group," I responded enthusiastically. Veto said he would give it an hour or so and see what happened.

Shortly after breakfast we went directly into our meditation room and began a deep meditation petitioning Mother Earth to open up a weather window for our group to get into the water. Within two hours we were the only ones on the docks getting into our boat. A marvelous day was had by all and both the dolphins and whales came. It was pure magic.

The following day we encountered yet another electrical storm, completely different from the first! A new electrical bank was moving through the corridor off the Kona coast. This delay caused by the new storm sent the group into a meditation *before* breakfast, where we again asked for permission to get into the water with the cetaceans. We did this by creating an alternate reality and honoring the integrity of Mother Earth. This time our delay was only one hour!

I will admit it was shocking to me that we were having these storms and I certainly was not used to it. I checked with a few locals who informed me that these were the first and second electrical storms in Kona in seventeen years! Something was up! Jackie, one of the participants, started asking questions too.

Everyone who signs up for this dolphin swim is asked to do a daily prayer in advance of the trip on behalf all the participants and providers of service, including the elemental kingdom. "With all the work we did ahead of time, why did we have this terrible weather?" Jackie wondered. "Because we could make a difference," I mused.

My seminar is organized so we take a break from the sun and sea after two consecutive mornings and have only classroom time for the next day. Then it is back to the ocean for an early morning departure. The previous evening of our classroom-only day, after the two days of electrical storms, I had been on the phone with my mother, who also lived in Kona. She told me I probably would not be able to go out to sea with my group the next day because they were predicting high waves. Being on the boat with high surf is impossible, even if the weather is clear.

I mentioned my mother's prediction at dinner. Later that night, in their room, Jackie spoke with her daughter who was also on the trip. Jennifer encouraged her mom, a budding shaman, to go ahead and do a shamanic journey for this. A journey involves going into the alternate reality and working on the reality from that vantage point. Jackie checked in with her own guidance to see if it was appropriate to do a shamanic journey on the weather. In her tradition, once she received permission, she could connect with her personal power animal along with another animal that would be appropriate for the work she wanted to do. She called in a whale.

On her shamanic journey she asked the whale if it could hold back the high surf. The whale initially replied, *No, the energy is too big.* She suggested the whale could get help and the whale responded, *I do not know; we could try.* The whale put together a pod of six whales to help hold back the high surf in our location. All of this occurred without my conscious awareness.

The following morning when we arrived, the water was as calm as glass. I remember thinking as I looked at the tranquil sea that my mother is getting old and maybe she was confused! We had an amazing day. Dolphins came. Whales found us.

A dolphin circled Laura, another of our participants, that day and buzzed her with his sonar up and down her entire body. We all saw it. It was a young dolphin but not a baby. Later Laura revealed to us that she was pregnant.

In one of the dives I swam low (diving below the surface) with a colored scarf. One of the baby dolphins slipped away from its mom and tried to swim close to me. It truly was another magical day!

As we traveled at a leisurely pace back to the dock in our boat, I kept seeing the picture of a breaching whale in my mind's eye, and suddenly a dolphin jumped right next to the boat. Veto knew this was unusual, so we followed the dolphin into a quiet bay. There right in front of us was a female whale with her escort and baby. They played around for a while and once we had our cameras ready the male escort made a phenomenal breach. This was larger than any breach I have ever witnessed in my ten years of dolphin swims. Then as we watched from a distance the mother leisurely dove, giving us a full view of her tail for what seemed an endless display of her beauty. Our group yelled, cheered, and clapped in appreciation of this exquisite sight.

The wind had started to pick up by the time we got back to the dock. When we arrived at the hotel the palm trees were bent nearly in half from the super-strong wind. I had been planning on running an errand but decided there must be a really big storm behind all that wind and there was no way I was going out in that.

A few days later I asked my mom if she remembered the strange wind around noon on that Friday and she said, "Boy, do I ever. First of all, it came out of the wrong (opposite) direction. The wind never blows

Figure 10.1. Whale tail
(Photo by Andrea Holien, CC BY-SA)

from that direction. It blew and blew and then within a half an hour turned completely around (180 degrees) and blew in the other direction." As she spoke I was shown a slingshot. I was being exposed to how the whales had created a weather womb to hold back the weather for us.

The shaman in our group had secretly asked for a sign. That afternoon in class she pulled the card, "Answered prayer." I could tell from the look on her face that something was up and insisted she tell me. After that she revealed her journey work of the night before and that she had asked for a sign to verify if her shamanic journey was the reason we had experienced the calm waters. It was obvious that the answer was an enthusiastic yes.

I gave a radio interview about this trip on Dolphinville Radio, which you can find online.

Holographic Communication

Even though I have been with them many times, I really don't know much about dolphins. Nobody does! We do know that dolphins can communicate holographically. Anecdotal evidence supports this. There are many who see geometric shapes and other unexpected images around the dolphins. Swimmers say they experience holographic images, crystalline forms, diamond shapes, and more just popping into their minds after being with the dolphins.

Beyond being life's blueprint, DNA plays a powerful role in newly discovered communications between dolphins and humans, according to a team of cetacean (dolphin and whale) researchers at the Sirius Institute on the Big Island of Hawaii.[2] A study there showed these marine mammals receive and transmit sound signals capable of affecting the genetic double helix, and that using natural biotechnology, dolphins may heal humans swimming near them.

Fourteen years of multidisciplinary study at this arm of the Human-Dolphin Foundation indicate that the expression of DNA, traditionally considered the blueprint of life, can be changed by the sound and electromagnetic fields generated by dolphins. A startling report examines DNA's coiled design, vibrating action, and "electro-genetic" functions during bioacoustic interactions between dolphins and humans. The dolphin's acoustic and electromagnetic effects on the human body through DNA may best explain how remarkable healings, often reported by swimmers following dolphin contacts, have occurred.

Dolphins have larger brains than ours. Should their consciousness capacity be greater than the human brain? One would think so, yet it is difficult to anesthetize them for research, as they are conscious breathers and must have a part of their brains alert at all times. Thus they sleep with only one side of the brain resting at a time. When unconscious, they will stop breathing. This is also true of whales, who are also conscious breathers.

Have you ever wanted to swim with dolphins? You don't have to travel to them, although that would be ideal. They will come to you. Just ask them to come in your meditations or dreamtime. In time they will start to appear in your dreams. One woman's young daughter could not come on our trip with her mom. Within a week of this little girl asking daily, they came to her in the dreamtime!

When in the presence of dolphins we are co-creating information in a new language between us. My friend, Joan Ocean, a well-known dolphin communicator, founded the Dolphin Connection organization to explore dolphin communication and human consciousness. She told me they ask that we send out a tone, thought, or feeling, and they will return the tone, thought, or feeling. They are changing our reality here in a way we normally would not understand, a way that is outside the box. It is all about unconditional love.

They are moving us toward greater and greater awareness of group mind. Moving with one spirit takes us to the group mind, the next level of expression, where we can achieve perfection as we know it. This is fifth dimension. From there we may be able to move to higher and higher places of expression. Group mind is different from mass consciousness. Group mind is harmonious attention to the needs of all, whereas the term *mass consciousness* refers to the quality of sharing a belief about what is true, and then attempting to influence and control everyone else to promote and preserve this belief.

Dolphin vibrations increase our ability to hear. They (the dolphins) have a much broader range of pitch than humans and can hear seven times better than humans do. Their resonances with us activate broader frequencies in the human body. Your MerKaBa becomes more firmly a part of your reality by connection with the dolphins.

When you swim with dolphins, either in the water or in your dreamtime, you can rewrite your past and create a new present and future. This has come in handy on more than one occasion. Joan Ocean reports that the dolphins told her they are from Sirius and came into third-dimension Earth in the 1940s, stating, "We are here to come back in time and to redo our history and make it right."[3] Sounds like *Star Trek IV*! Think of the federal government's witness protection program and consider the possibility of bringing a whole history to life, as Joan and I believe. What is their proof? They tell Joan they left one continent without any history of the dolphins: Australia.

Those of you familiar with "the Bible code" may have heard that the reason it is "accurate" is because an ancient culture came back in time to "redo" their history. Although these same records state that the first five books of the Torah were *given* to Moses, ancient Sumerian records show the existence of this information before Moses presented it!* There is a similar story about the dolphins.

According to the dolphins that Joan is in contact with, our solar system is speeding up because we are moving toward another solar system that is at a higher frequency than ours. The dolphins tell her that at some point we are going to merge with that one and we all will be at a higher frequency. My guides have also told me there will be a new Earth for those who wish to stay behind and continue in the third dimension. I have known about this since 1994 and recently discovered that another author, Lynn Grabhorn, has written about this.[4]

History and Its Importance

Dolphins do not have or desire the capacity to write or keep records. If they are more evolved than we are, why would they choose this? A researcher I recently came across presents his teachings as Truth with a capital T, as if there is no other. This is an example of a recently "awakened" individual who has no sense of history or time and cannot comprehend why the saints or sages of old could have been given truth. It is nearly impossible for him to understand the history as we know it, since the timeline version of events he has tapped into is so new, there is no history behind it.

In fifth dimension where dolphins exist, the dolphins do not use beliefs as a way of determining behavior. They are unconcerned about what people believe or think. One dolphin's insights are different from another's, so they do not compare ideas or thoughts or come up with a consensus of opinion to determine a common reality. It is only

---

*If this traveling back in time story is not amazing enough, check out the Wingmakers website about an intergalactic mission that landed on Earth and time traveled backward to create a history.

in third dimension, where we rely on the intellect, that this is done. In the fifth dimension it is unimportant to believe in anything. Fifth-dimension beings choose their reality in every moment and enjoy what they have created in the moment. It's beautiful!

What Are
the Dolphins Doing?

My good friend Doug Hackett, who swims with dolphins almost daily in Hawaii and also works with Joan Ocean, tells the story of traveling with Joan to the Red Sea to do a dolphin swim with a tour company.

The local owners of the boat heard that Joan had done a special meditation the previous day with the dolphins suddenly appearing immediately after the meditation. The following day the owner decided to join them to see this magic lady for himself. Since not much was going on, they inquired if Joan wanted to do another meditation to call in the dolphins. She declined, so Doug held his own solo meditation to connect with the dolphins of the Red Sea to see if he could discern what was happening.

He asked them for their P.O.D. (plan of the day). He felt their energy and connected with them. When he asked them if they would like to swim with him, they responded, *Yes, but we are kind of busy keeping peace in the Middle East.* Just when you thought all they did was procreate, play, and enjoy life!

What about the Whales?

Drunvalo reports that whales go to the South Pole and get in a circle, nose-to-nose, and inhale for twelve hours. What are the whales doing? Tom Clarke, a former Navy Seal, saw this behavior. The second time he watched the video, during his second FOL workshop, he remembered synchronizing watches with other Navy Seals before a dive.

The whales explained to me that every year they go to the South Pole to synchronize with the magnetic field of the planet, so their internal navigation is oriented properly. Perhaps they are rebroadcast-ing a current version of the magnetic field for all the migrating animals. I was then shown that the whales act like cell phone towers. Just as human pilots must update their destination coordinates after six months, since the grids keep moving and changing, I believe the whales update everything else that relies on Earth's magnetic grids.

Working with Earth's Energy Systems

What You Will Learn in This Chapter

- What are ley lines and grid lines?
- What are implants and how do they interact with grids?
- What is gridwork and what impact do grids have on our lives?
- What are some of the specialized grids?

Ley Lines

Geopathic stress comes from a variety of sources. Geopathic lines can be deadly and are caused by the stress of the planet. I wrote about these lines extensively in *Reweaving the Fabric of Your Reality*.

Geopathic lines are 360–500 feet wide, reach five to six miles deep, and can extend like a sheet five to six miles above the earth. Underground water veins (sometimes called black water lines), ore deposits, and natural radiation from the earth contribute to these lines. Gamma rays from the sun and other rays flow into the earth's electro-magnetic field and feed these lines. Man-made energies such as electrical systems, microwave transmissions, cell-phone frequencies, and chemical and nuclear wastes are also feeding these lines.

There is another form of energy created by humans that flows into the emotional body of our planet. Human suffering, slavery, famine, genocide, dying solders in war zones, and fears of repression and loss have created unresolved emotional trauma that has literally been sucked into the body of our planet.

All these negative energies feed into a grid of energy lines that criss-cross our planet. Different doctors have identified two types of these lines. A German medical doctor named Ernst Hartmann identified "ley lines" that run north, south, east, and west and are fed by the electrical grids. These lines are known as Hartmann lines. Dr. Hartmann documented more than five thousand cases of cancer that were directly related to people sleeping on intersecting geopathic lines in his book *Krankheit als Standortproblem* (Disease as a problem of location).

These lines are one to two inches wide and six to twelve feet apart on a grid (like graph paper). You can check for them by dowsing. Cats like them and when they sit on the intersections, they convert the negative energy to positive energy. Cats generally choose cushy or warm spots to sit, so if your cat frequently sits on a spot that is neither cushy nor warm and sunny, it is very likely an intersection of energy grids being converted to positive chi. Thank you, felines everywhere!

These lines are considered to be channels of energy circulation that are aggravated by electromagnetic energy. To clear them, put a copper omega symbol where the intersections occur or simply create a program in your MerKaBa. You do this by saying, *The negative lines of force on the earth are completely filtered out by my MerKaBa.* A form of this program is found in the seven basic programs.

An American physician named Manfred Curry identified a group of lines that are commonly referred to as Curry lines. The Curry network is a diagonal grid to the Hartmann network. Its intensity is influenced by lunar cycles. There is a book with additional information on this written by a New Zealand airline pilot named Bruce Cathie.[1]

Precognitive Dreams and Visions of Dark Energies

My students have effectively employed this method to change the observed future and so can you. How do you change a fearful future event and stay out of fear? What could you do when you are reading, or clairvoyantly seeing, or connecting with terrible events that might happen? The MerKaBa is a manifestation field and you can co-create at will. I advise that you check in with your own guidance and ask, *Are these visions real? Do I need to do anything about it?* Very often the vision is being given to you so that you will take an action and because you *can* do something. Remember, we are co-creators!

You are not alone. Many of you have been given information so that you can help to clear the earth of these dark energies. I have a keen awareness that many individuals are helping to solve the negative manifestations of *those who would have us fail.* Please know that you do make a difference! A metaphor for this is imagining trying to break a band of sticks that have been tied together. If the sticks are banded together, it's impossible. Yet if the band is divided into smaller groups they can successfully be broken. We have strength in numbers.

Jumping Tracks

When you experience clairvoyantly, or hear of a "plot against the will of the people," take a moment to see a parallel version of the reality where the plot fails. See their equipment malfunction. See both versions (or tracks) coexist until the moment right before the so-called event occurs. See humanity jump to the version of the reality that is devoid of their mal-intent. See humanity on a track of the reality that is close enough to fool those of malicious intent and see them wondering why it did not work. See them wondering, *Why didn't this catastrophe occur? Why did this thing not happen?* Do this with peace in your heart.

See yourself and hundreds of your light friends (seen and unseen, Angelic and otherwise) smiling in happy victory, with a dark plan foiled again. See this visual, this movie-of-the-mind, every time you start to worry or get anxious that those who would be false might somehow succeed. They will *not* succeed. Your visions are versions of the future that you have the free will to change. Although we have free will to change these things, I still check in to determine my part. I never assume I know. I do this with a benign energy—looking for a preferred version of the reality—as opposed to a right or wrong version of the reality, which might set up a polarity version.

Every time you hear of a new plot to thwart the will of the people, you can be part of the action by creating the above scenario in your mind, which, by the way, is part of the quantum soup of the one mind of God. Run your movie-of-the-mind every time fear starts to move inside of you. Stay in your power. Stay gentle. Stay sweet and loving. Always check in with your Higher Self, to see if this is an action that is appropriate for you.

Begin with a Simple Statement of Purpose

You might state, *This far and no further.* You are creating energy systems for Mother Earth or humanity to use when so desired. Remember, we are in the free-will zone. Be clear that your energy gift is just that, a gift, exercising free will of all affected by this program. She decides if she will use it. She decides when. Allow yourself to reject what is happening from a vantage point of non-judgment. Simply recognize that the Universe is full of choices and your choice is something else. Do this peacefully, joyfully.

- Wait to act if you are feeling anger, judgment, or heavy emotion, as that (emotion) can be used against the light.
- Remember that a good martial arts master will use her opponent's energy and redirect her. Your opponent can and will use fear (your energy) against you, just as has been done for eons and eons. This time is different. You are prepared.
- Choose to stay in your joy.
- Clearly intend that their equipment and technology (software or otherwise) will not work when it is programmed against the Light. It malfunctions.
- Express your clear intent that any bad intention be turned upon its creator, causing confusion and error.
- See their equipment not working; see their bewilderment and smile.
- Be clear to avoid programming that is meant to deceive, manipulate, or defraud the reality you are creating. If you were to do so, you would be no different from them.

- Assuming your MerKaBa is up and running, you may wish to create important common regional programs, such as a program to decommission the energies of contrails or other subtle mind-control technologies.
- Always make sure your MerKaBa is active at all times. Remember to ask your Higher Self if you are required to keep doing the MerKaBa before releasing your practice. At some point the MerKaBa will be permanent but you may still be asked to continue the MerKaBa practice.

Gridworkers Union and Dissolving Fear of Lack

The Gridworkers Union is a group of volunteers who have learned how to work with grids and volunteer their time and energy to support the changes on the planet. Our Gridworkers Union has taken on some of these possible future events. This is not something everyone is called to do. If this does not interest you, skip this section.

I have been working with **implants**◈ from certain 100 percent God Light extraterrestrial beings who have placed devices in individuals, and in me, for the purpose of aiding mankind in its planetary Ascension. These devices need to come through the human at upper dimensional levels such as ninth dimension. Anchoring it into 3-D physical awareness requires the human to recognize this device and then release it at the appropriate time to the appropriate place (usually directed at the time of release). Each implant has a primary grid. Implants overlay grids and often are released into grids.

These devices become recognizable because when they show up the individual is usually in a lot of pain. They coexist on multiple dimensions and they ease the device into 3-D by anchoring it into the finer bodies at more evolved states (such as during meditation). The pain that occurs does not appear to be associated with an injury and is usually reconfirmed by checking in with guides or your Higher Self.

I have assisted in a number of such sessions and have been directed to receive assistance for my own devices when they need to be removed.

The following was submitted by one of our members who is working with the Lords of Light. She was one of our gridworkers who did not really believe what I was saying about implants and unexplained pain until it happened to her. She also does a beautiful job of explaining "switching tracks."

During last month's call I shared a vision that the Masters of Light had given me. This vision actually started with their showing me a black screen of space with a darker band that ran in a horizontal strip across the larger black screen. Within the darker horizontal band of black spaciousness were these softly shaped (not crisp) geometric solids that looked like they were carved out of soapstone or chalk. I instantly knew these shapes were seeds and as I saw the seeds the masters told me, This is not written, *and then they give me the vision. So I knew this vision had been seeded but was not yet written.*

This vision linked in with two other things: dreams of a warlike nature that I had been having, and a local event where a large incineration plant that supposedly produces electricity by burning chicken litter was almost a done deal for our town. This had come in before anyone saw what was happening. It was so odd that no one had been able to see this coming.

So I realized that these three things—the vision, dreams, and local occurrences with this incineration plant—are all a part of the same occurrence on local, national, global, universal, and galactic levels.

With Maureen's help I realized that the pulse I had noticed during the commissioner meetings regarding this incineration plant was there to keep people asleep (I kept noticing that the three hundred people who had come to this meeting to voice their opinions and concerns regarding this plant were struggling to stay alert and awake). I sat in the meeting and I watched them go in and out of alertness in a very even pattern during the entire meeting. I thought to myself that this was so odd but I did not know what it was. Then after I requested Maureen's assistance she directed me to her FOL website and the first thing I saw was the article about Hurricane Charlie and the ELF waves and I knew exactly what was going on during these meetings.

In chapter 6 I explained that the activated MerKaBa makes you immune to mass consciousness frequencies, which is why she could feel it and send the ELF waves but no one else could. The gridworker continued:

Maureen also directed me to her "Tools You Can Use" article on getting out of fear and specifically pointed out the rewriting tracks information. I immediately started using this tool and all of these wonderful and very comical things start unfolding before my eyes.

After asking for Maureen's help, it was phenomenal the level of help that instantly came from many levels. Thank you, Maureen.

The higher tracks of this same event always came in with a very pure white light emanating through the scenes. I also saw these golden particles that were like holographic wisps floating all around and in the higher visions as I rewrote the lower into the higher.

Eventually the golden wisps turned into beautiful golden cubes. I knew these golden cubes were the seeds for a very high version of the Divine Design unfolding here on all levels.

Many synchronicities started occurring very fast, many, many times daily—no lag time—confirming for me that this was the appropriate path. For example, a friend who has no idea about this work gave me a set of seven golden cubes and seven golden spheres; they are Alexandrite cubes that have been covered in gold. Another friend came to me and said, "While I was meditating today I heard that I should tell you about what I was seeing." Then she shared with me that she was flying through space that was made up of a very pure white light and she saw all of these golden cube shapes floating around her in this space of white light.

So many things have happened that I cannot share them all, but this is one last thing that is important regarding the **Dissolving Fear of Lack Grid**◈, which was created to assist humanity through upheaval and changes so that people do not create more fear.

I was reading one night and came across some information about a meditation room in the United Nations (UN), called "A Room of Quiet." The information described the room—a long narrow room with a black cube and a painting. I knew I had dreamed this room before even though I had never heard of it or seen it before. So I looked through my dream journals and I found a very detailed drawing of a room that I had drawn from a dream I had in 2005. I showed this to my husband and he said, "Let's look up UN meditation room images online and see." He did this and it was the exact room I had drawn from this dream. The details were the same, black cube, painting, and all.

A friend of mine who is also doing this work with the Gridworkers Union and I decided to participate in the monthly meditations hosted by the United Nations by meditating at the same time as these scheduled meditations in their meditation room. On Wednesday the eighth of April, we left another meeting early so we could sit in meditation at the scheduled time. This was a powerful and informative meditation.

A pure white light came in immediately. It was immense and easy to grasp. Then I was shown something very important. I saw that fear of lack as a vibration is being used to keep things down or to test us. I saw a mass of people representing people all over the world. I saw how fear of lack—if not supplied with an antidote—is being used to suppress people. I saw it keeps people in a state of chaotic panic and very separated from one another—the us vs. them survival mode. They showed me how this is being implemented now, and this is obvious to anyone who watches the news or has lost income.

Then I was shown the antidote or cure to this fear of lack play out before my eyes. I saw the same large mass of people that looked like an ocean of people. One by one the people started helping one another, assisting people around them. I witnessed people helping one another through simple acts of kindness or practical assistance where it was needed. This was done in a way that unites. There is no more *other* mentality. No more us vs. them. In helping one another the sea of people rippled into a state of unity. People knew they were not separate from one another.

This is the golden rule in action. We know our neighbor to be ourselves. There is no true separation. We are our brothers' and sisters' keepers. Wow! Since then I have been working with the Dissolving Fear of Lack Grid, the Easy Grid, and others.

My UN Assignment

Several months later I was called to do a meditation at the United Nations meditation room. It started with a conversation I had in Toronto with another teacher. She was telling me about a wedding she had attended in Mexico and how she and her husband had been called to conduct ceremony and activations while they were there. In response, I found myself announcing to her and myself that, "We are in a freefall for the future and all possible futures, including prophecy, and no longer are linked to this version of the reality!" The freefall is like skydiving.

In June of 2009 I was given an assignment by my guides related to this. The good news is that a parachute has been activated and there has since been a *new* and different future locked into place. The future is assured. Claim it!

I had been trying to schedule our ceremony at the United Nations meditation room for a few weeks, to no avail. Then all of a sudden everything easily fell into place. Leslie was over for dinner and we had a wonderful chat about what we would be doing at our meditation. She and I would go together.

I had been shown to approach this large stone altar, which was made of magnetite, and to treat it as if there were numerous drawers that could be pulled out laterally. I could see this at other dimensions. I was to pull out each drawer and replace parts of programming with different programming. This was also coming in from other dimensions. We were led to do toning in this room. For the most part there was no one else in the room. After the toning we sat in lotus and each of us left our bodies. I felt a huge column of light enter and I was gone in a flash. Leslie was able to maintain her focus at higher realms and could see other beings of light who were examining my work. She telepathed to them with concern, *Are you going to change it?* They responded by telling her, *That is not possible because Maureen did it.* They said it could not have been anyone else. Later, repeating this story to the woman who first directed our attention to this place, she said she knew this the moment she met me. In her meditation she had seen all that I described to her, including the freefall from predictions and prophecy to a new version of the future.

Update 2019: I was approached by someone who has worked at the UN for more than twenty years, while exhibiting at a trade show in New York, my current home. She said that she had been guided to come to this event, and that she would be shown with whom she needed to work. Her job was to ensure that I went back to the UN and did some specific work there. I intuitively knew that there was an upgrade required for the magnetite "altar." As we had for the activation in 2008, we struggled to find a good day to do this around both of our schedules. Then it just fell together. I was able to be the conduit for another layer of programing that was installed in the magnetite for the present cycle.

The Heart Grid

I encountered a family issue related to children being born with a hole in the heart. It is related to hatred of the mother through the male side of the lineage. I have been working actively to clear this at the cellular level, planetary-wide. I discovered this because of my own connection to this miasma. I was told to build two grids that week. The first one was for this program.

There is a precursor to this information. As I mentioned earlier, I have been working with implants from 100 percent God Light ETs who have placed devices in individuals for the purpose of aiding mankind in its planetary Ascension. These devices need to come through a human, so it is necessary for a human to recognize this device and then release it at the appropriate time. I have assisted in a number of such sessions.

A woman contacted me from Hawaii. She had heard of me through a conference speaker and had saved my information for several months. Now she was being directed to contact me about the pain in her knees. She thought she had injured her knees while swimming with the dolphins. It did not make sense to her since she did not know when or how it had occurred, yet she was in a lot of pain. Through an Akashic Records reading with me she was given very specific information that she had *not* taken an injury, but that the pain was actually caused by devices that were implanted into her body by ETs of the light. These devices were meant to be released into the atmosphere by her.

The record keepers asked her if she was willing to do psychic surgery for the purpose of releasing these devices into the atmosphere. She was familiar with this work and agreed to do this at the appropriate time, for which she would be guided.

I had already told her of the two blank grids that had been placed in the atmosphere for programming. I knew one would be used to heal the heart issues described above (hatred of the mother manifesting in the family lineage of a child born with a hole in the heart). The following is her story.

The First Device Is from the Left Knee—Mother's Love

It is the infusion of the mother's love. As humanity drinks in the pulsing, it will reverse the negative spiral to elevate the heart to a higher frequency of consciousness. This grid is an earth infusion completing the cycle of separation from the mother, providing Gaia and all her inhabitants with purity, innocence, and the ability to listen to and trust the heart wisdom.

Family lines, which in the past would have continued to be carriers of this genetic weakness or miasma due to hatred of our mother (universal mother), will be downloaded with layers of love transfusion as if to alter the blood—offering a window for vitality to spark healthy sperm and egg union. All mutations of the past resulting from hatred will be corrected and the will of the soul entering will be empowered to co-create a healthy, vital, loving heart chakra and system in which to operate. So be it.

During this time a member of our Gridworkers Union had a son who had expressed hatred toward his mother for the past fifteen years. He returned to her, reopening the door for love to be received and freely given. He told her, "I feel like a big weight has been lifted from me." His mom responded, "My heart is doing a happy dance." The hatred from the past was cleared.

Right Knee—Return of the Priestess to Earth

This device was placed in a sling or sleeve whirling with color and life like a living embryo, **Christed**◈ energy to assist with the holy union upon Earth. It would be birthed within the second grid as a crystalline light, such as we have not known upon Earth. This grid sets up a refined frequency to birth the internal balance of male and female in Christed union.

This sets up the new matrix all have been waiting for—the second coming—and it occurs within the divine human now awakening. Then two whole and holy individuals are magnetized to each other through the heart of Christ Consciousness, which has been birthed within them through this everlasting grid.

The grid itself grows exponentially as these inner and outer unions create the matrix for the stairway to Heaven on Earth, opening the way for higher-dimensional living for humanity's birthing of the crystalline ray. Masters of the Zeta Reticuli star system and Andromeda galaxy assist in bringing this creation into form.

More Device Info

Energetic imprints of each device are to overlay, as a gift of love, the other grids, for which they are not primary. They will offer the secondary support frequency required, which will be put and held in place by dolphins.

Prior to calling me, Joanna was guided to walk along the ocean at City of Refuge on the Big Island of Hawaii, a large picnic area by a grand bay that is quite remote and not usually frequented by visitors. Joanna walked to the far end of this bay and was prompted to return along the water's edge. When she was about halfway back, two whales appeared in the ocean moving with her in the same direction. They were active and breaching, staying visible the entire time, moving in the same direction. After this her discomfort and pain increased, eventually setting off a chain of events that caused Joanna to contact me. These two whales were the protectors of the Christed embryo until it was to be placed (that week) into the grid. They represented the matched Christed couple able to give birth to Christed creations on Earth. Activation occurred on February 19, 2008, the day before the full lunar eclipse.

I had been planning on doing this activation on the night of the eclipse and was preparing for it, but then I was told to go ahead and work with the tools on the night of preparation (the night before the eclipse). I went to bed holding the tools in either hand. My knees were supported by a pillow, which also supported my hands so that I could continue to hold both the tools. I then offered myself in service to the Legions of Light and waited . . . and finally fell asleep. In the middle of the night the tools started vibrating so strongly that I was awakened by it. I started laughing because I could feel the vibrations of the activation throughout my entire body! Even though I knew they were not moving in third dimension, the vibration was clear and strong coming in from higher realms. This all occurred around the time I would have been in Hawaii hosting a dolphin swim. It was as if I were still working with the cetaceans and dolphins through this experience. What an honor.

Later in that summer of 2008 some members of the Gridworkers Union and I were together in northern Georgia and were called to do some gridwork in the river. The whole process was preceded by my having a dream about a large group of people being held hostage. (Coincidentally my assistant Leslie, who is a member of the Gridworkers Union, had the same dream that night, even though she was in New York.)

The power went out while I was having this dream. I woke up before the dream, noted the time on the digital clock was around 4:30 a.m., then fell back asleep into this dream. Again I awoke, noted the clock was black (no power), and fell back asleep into the dream, as if I had not woken.

When I woke up I asked my Higher Self what was happening. I was told to do gridwork in the creek (behind the cabin) with Edward and Mark, two of the gridworkers, to clear fear.

Gridwork Key Elements

The three of us sat in a triangle formation on rocks in the creek with our feet in the water. We began with the MerKaBa. We then rotated our positions, changing seats clockwise three times. Each time we did additional energy work while holding various crystals. On the third change Edward, an amazing channel, was in the middle. He was guided to hold the ankh and together we activated this new grid. He felt three large electrical-type energy waves move through him into the water and earth. It was not painful for him, although he confirmed the energy jolts were substantial.

Retelling our story in a gridworkers meeting, another member confirmed that we were clearing Atlantean Fear Grids. This gridworker had a crystal from the John of God casa in Brazil, which holds strong, positive Atlantean energies. He reported that while Edward and I were sharing what had happened, his crystal became very active and he had the feeling of going back to the time Maureen, Edward, and Mark were doing the gridwork. It felt to him that the fear being released originated in the Atlantean Fear Grid. Due to this energy being released, people were less likely to resonate with the energies of fear.

Leslie remembered that astrologer Madeline Gerwick had predicted that individuals would feel this feeling of being held *hostage* shortly after this date. I realized that this is not the first time we have been called to energetically shift the energy on something before it would have occurred.

That same week, Lisa, another member of the Gridworkers Union, reported on an implant that she was guided to release into the water, and was also directed to connect this energy into the Easy Grid. This Easy Grid helps make the creating of positive change easier and less of a struggle, and is meant to reframe the it-will-be-difficult mindset, so common in our Western culture.

Lisa reported that she learned she had been carrying an implant in her right knee for a couple of weeks, but did not know why or when it was to be released. On a brief visit to a nearby lake she was guided to do the MerKaBa Meditation on the bank of the lake and to remove the implant during Breath 14. She was then guided to release the implant into a grid that had been brought to the attention of the group on our Peru trip.* Lisa got the sense that the implant was soaking in the

---

*In June 2007, Maureen led a Peru Sacred Journey to continue the tasks of the gridwork that had been started in Egypt the previous year.

experience of why and how change can be difficult, so that once in the grid, the appropriate antidote energy could become readily available, thereby reducing the obstacles and struggle that can often accompany positive change. One of the delightful antidotes in common usage today is the "easy" button from the Staples store commercials.

In June of 2008 a group traveling with me gave birth to the Sun Disk and it is now in place in Lake Titicaca, Peru, beaming to the planet so people can align with the will of God. Numerous groups around the planet were working on this project simultaneously, without conscious awareness of one another. This validated our own experience when these reports surfaced.

Specialized Grids

Just prior to this Peru Sacred Journey another member of our group had activated a proactive grid called the Sirian Carbon Sequestration Project grid. He has an amazing Sirian starseed friend, a microbiologist who has developed a process using microorganisms that could solve global warming if it were used at a large enough scale. The new grid will support his work.

Another member is working on the Antidote Mania and Depression Grid. She begins with the Angelic Gridwork Prayer. On an ongoing basis this grid antidotes mania and depression, as it is produced by humanity. At the same time she has been using the Remembranz AroMandalas-Orion Series essential oil blend to clear shame.

During this time of intense gridwork we found it was necessary for each of us to maintain spontaneity with our gridwork. I asked everyone to respond to the "call" of gridwork. One of our gridworkers describes her process:

I do an opening ceremony as best as I can remember it, calling in all the beings of light, Angels, and so on, and at the end of the opening ceremony, I state that it is my intention to do gridwork and I state on which grid I am choosing to work. From there I let it go. I used to remain in meditation and help with the work, but on Monday I was asked to do the gridwork at my job. They told me that I am their vehicle to take them anywhere they want to go. Or better yet, their bridge between heaven and earth. Just get us there (that is, build the connection), said the beings of light, and we will do the work. That is exactly what I did Monday and Tuesday and it definitely works. I built the bridge, so to speak, and went back to work (as a commercial electrician) until I was guided to do the closing ceremony.

Without a doubt I felt their presence while they were doing the gridwork and I could feel it in those around me more than I ever have. One thing I would like to add is that since I have been doing gridwork (I started about a month and a half ago) and I have worked solely on the Clearing Fear Grid, my own fears have dissipated or vaporized like clouds. To quote [the writer Rainer Maria] Rilke, "Our fears are like dragons guarding our most treasured possessions."

Another gridworker writes:

On Sunday I had a phone conversation with a friend who has an ex-boyfriend who was not handling his manic condition very well. She spoke about how she initially drew a tight boundary around herself and pushed him away one night when he came to her, clearly in a manic state (needing help), and she merely called his father and let him go on his way (unsupervised), rather than staying with him until his father came to pick him up. She left his family to be responsible for him rather than get involved, and spurned his attempts to get in contact with her after the incident. She was judging his manic behavior and distancing herself from it.

All of this information came pouring out of my friend yesterday, and as I spoke of my own experience with mania—that I do not like to be in the manic state and prefer to take medication that keeps me even and grounded, and that I accept my condition and know it is a part of my life and I have to control my symptoms always—her opinion of her ex-boyfriend began to expand and change. It was as if I were standing in for the antidote for mania (holding space for the grid) and giving her that information. People heal from this condition and they need others to be there for them. She started to consider emailing or speaking to him again, and offering support rather than non-compassion. She opened up the possibility that he is trying to reach out for help and understanding now, and she is beginning to listen to his pleas for connection to her.

It was a conversation that only confirms for me that the grid with the antidote for mania and depression is working. I have never had such an open conversation about mania with anyone else before, and I know what I was healing were not my emotions, but those of the planet. And the fact that my friend is opening up to her ex-boyfriend in a more compassionate way is tremendous. She is starting to accept her role in his healing process. I am so very grateful for this opportunity and the gridworkers.

We are most fortunate to have this information and for you to begin to understand that individuals are making a difference. So can you. If you are called to join with others, ask for the connection that is part of your purpose or contract so you can unite with your brothers and sisters in this work.

Creating Heaven on Earth

What You Will Learn in This Chapter

- What is heaven?
- The levels of dimensions
- What dimensions look like to our limited awareness
- How you will know you were there

What Is Heaven?

Look to the traditional faiths for descriptions of heaven. For most people heaven is a separate place from the earth where you become your perfected self. In heaven your interactions are perfect. You have to die to get there, although once there, existence is eternal. It is the place where God dwells.

Fifth dimension (5-D) is similar to what tradition calls heaven. Imagine your perfected self being fully connected to God. Consider the possibility that it could happen while you are still in your current body. Heaven on Earth could be described as achieving this state of connection and perfection while still living in the body. It is our ideal state right where we are. As we become our perfected selves we are also in the process of rewriting our history. Sometimes that may show up as forgetfulness. It is not that! Instead consider the possibility that you truly are rewriting your history. I call it *reverse déjà vu*.

Reverse déjà vu is when you are about to do something and you go blank. Wondering what in the world is wrong with you, you say, "What was I just going to do?" You did not forget. You are rewriting the reality. In that forgetting-like moment, your ego has completely disengaged from all the connections it normally maintains, which results in your *availability* to connect with another version of the reality. This new version is closer to perfection than the one before it. As you become more Higher Self–centered, and your ego merges with your Higher Self, these former "senior moments" can be redefined as "multidimensional moments." Moment by moment you are literally rewriting your most recent history and causing a domino-like effect on all of existence.

An activated MerKaBa leads to reverse déjà vu. It makes use of the recompression and expansion of the time-space continuum. Wait just a minute here!

Expansion and Contraction of the Universe

The Universe expands and contracts once every 250 millionths of a second, according to a teacher of one of my students. I like that. I also happen to think it might be true. Why not? It makes for lots of opportunity for change, does it not? Imagine that. No wonder we have the ability to co-create!

You have moved through more experiences and as you are opening up, you may be noticing things you did not notice previously. This is happening planet-wide as everyone has been given the opportunity to connect with new codes coming from higher dimensions. This gives us new information that previously was not available to us.

Each of us will find our own way, but at the same time, Source Codes have changed. This means that the "default pattern" that was here with mass consciousness has changed. Mass consciousness codes function like the autopilot setting that kicks in when the will does not make choices. Autopilot is the first version of everyone's reality. It is the basic data set that dictates behavior for those who do not exercise choice in any given moment.

Humanity's Reboot

There are data sets being co-created and broadcast to humanity in a way similar to radio waves. The mass consciousness data set has recently been upgraded by a few dedicated human souls. You can participate in that if you want. Clearly state your intention in your prayer work, and they (these volunteers) will actually find you. There are many groups on the planet doing this work. You can join them and should do so if it resonates with you. Some of this is identified as gridwork.

As of June 2009 our default patterns have been cleared from the mass consciousness data set. This means that the default "possibilities, probabilities, and prophecies" known from an alternate, earlier history of planet Earth have all been released and reformatted.

There is a new energy-opportunity and programming available to all who decide to participate. Deciding to participate is all that is required; a simple opt-in prayer will make the new energies more accessible to you. Old preferences, old beliefs, old pain and suffering all contribute to the rehash of old templates. Any time you get the opportunity to try something new within the bounds of old pain and suffering, grab it! You will be very glad you did, and you will be pleasantly surprised with the results. In real terms that means not reacting the way you used to. Instead, ask your Higher Self, *In this painful situation, what should I do?*

I recommend opting in every day until you feel these changes are permanent. Eventually everyone will participate anyway as their old records fade and cease to be available and therefore unusable. Anchoring these energies into your body will make it easier for all of mass consciousness to find their connection to the new energies, since they are now multiplied by *you*.

Sight and Vision

Many of you are noticing that your vision has expanded to include enhanced peripheral vision. When your awareness registers this, your ego wonders, *What is going on?* You are growing your awareness and expanding your vision. Why do you need to classify what is happening? Perhaps it is the ego trying to compartmentalize every-thing to keep it in its place.

Move into *wonder* instead and you will no longer have the need to know everything in terms of a relationship to everything else. Instead, you are able to view more than one relationship data set at a time. This is what experiencing multiple dimensions is all about. At this point you are start-ing to perceive fifth-dimensionally, yet your cerebral function, your mind, is not quite ready to accept this, so visuals creep into your peripheral vision and when you go for a direct validation . . . boom, it is gone! Soften your focus and allow your vision to show you what needs to be seen.

Orbs

I believe this is why our cameras are showing us visuals that most do not see with the naked eye. Some of you are starting to see (with the naked eye) the orbs that your digital photos have shown. What are they? I believe they are energies that have always been there and are now being photographed by people who are vibrating at higher dimensions than the third. The factor of their showing up is the consciousness of the photographer. In some cases the consciousness of the person being photographed has expanded to the point of influencing a larger field. Normally the camera registers where you are in the moment by the vis-ibility of these orbs (see figure 12.1). There is a factor of some darkness to capture them on the photo.

Dimensions

I was intensely curious about the dimensions. I thought that if I could carry a greater understanding about them, I could comprehend the strange things happening around me. This is exactly what has hap-pened. If I blindfold you and drive us to Disneyland you might have a vague idea where it is, or how far away it is, but if I tell you the name of the place we have just visited you can go there on your own. It is possible to recognize where you have been, which then enables you to return purposefully. Working inter-dimensionally gives you a greater understanding of life and its fullness that rewards you as the joyous mystery unfolds and is discovered.

Figure 12.1. Photo of Maureen with orbs
in the upper right and lower left of the photo

Asking for this information, I started with a blank template that listed each of the dimensions, leaving a space for the information. Essentially the following information came and filled in the blanks. Gradually, and then in one big download, I was given the rest of the information.

The dimensions are so vast that our ability to conceive of and comprehend them is limited by our perceptions. As we shift our perceptions from what is probable to what is possible, our vision, too, will expand to receive it. Even though I have attempted to outline the dimensions for you here, please understand that each of the dimensions has an expansive overtone series that provides for multiple variations of the dimensions. The multiples are almost limitless. This is more tangible in the 3-D world than in the higher realms.

First through Third Dimensions

First dimension is a point of self-awareness. It projects onto the screen of third dimension. From some vantage points it coexists with second and third dimensions. First dimension is a complete awareness of itself as the center of form. As a musical form it is the audible *hum* that is heard in certain kinds of deep meditation.

Second dimension is two separate but equal points connected by a line. This line extends in two directions—length and height, but not depth, sort of like a piece of paper. These two reference points are you. Both of them are you. This line is flat. Vincent, one of my students, asked his Higher (fifth-dimensional) Self to show him his first expression in matter. He saw a two-dimensional flat world that he experienced as "us."

The third dimension is a location that receives a projection beamed from the other dimensions around it. So like a multidimensional hologram that appears real, the third dimension is the playground (theater) for the projections of the other dimensions. Third gives us the ability to separate all the experiences into separate consecutive events.

In creation, thought produces outcome. So having a child might produce a full-grown new human. The baby being born and all the details of growing up and childhood would be absorbed into the finished idea. Therefore it is useful to look at life through the lens of steps that allow you to separate events and adventures.

We used to be at the base of third dimension. Most everyone reading this book will be at the upper overtone regions of third dimension, and very likely fourth and fifth dimensions. Exciting, is it not? You can tell by the way things happen. In third we learn to hurt and heal, to deal with matters working through the drama of good and evil. In the current "old" days, one would want to escape third dimension to go to heaven. Now you understand that you can create Heaven on Earth. It is from third dimension that you can and will open portals. It is in third dimension that you begin to see the potential to create Heaven on Earth. Be inspired to create Heaven on Earth. Creating Heaven on Earth allows for all the dimensions to coexist. The stage and lighting may change as one evolves to higher realms.

My First "Day of Heaven on Earth"

I accidentally learned the benefit of claiming a day of Heaven on Earth while traveling home on an overnight flight from the West Coast to Wisconsin. I was disembarking from the plane at 8 a.m. when I was addressed by a familiar United Airlines employee. She greeted me with, "How are you doing, Maureen?" Without thinking, I said, "Fine, considering this is my day from h***, since I have to be back here by noon to fly to the East Coast." I used to use that phrase—in the classroom—to provide a graphic description of a painfully intense day. I never had used it in my everyday language—until now. Horrified by what had just come out of my mouth, I self-corrected and offered, "But, I am having a day of Heaven on Earth because I'm flying with United." We both smiled and went about the day.

Upon my return home I could hear water running—but no faucets were on. Then I discovered about one inch of water on the floor of my basement laundry room, and looking up, I could see water spilling from an open section of the wall. I immediately shut off the water to the house and called my retired neighbor, Gene, who came over to help me assess the situation. We called the plumber and he said he would be there in thirty minutes. Gene said he would come back to watch the plumber so I could get ready for my next flight.

I immediately called United to request a change to fly the following day. They could not do it due to an oversold situation, but could offer me the later flight that night and would waive the customary change fee. I gratefully accepted their offer and began to do my errands and repack.

The plumber came on time and determined, as we suspected, there was probably a burst pipe between the walls. He thought the upstairs bathroom was the place to start—to cut a hole. I asked my Higher Self and was told, *No, downstairs bathroom.* (Handy, is it not?) The plumber wanted to know where. My Higher Self directed us to start in a specific spot in a particular wall. From that point we could see the problem and needed one more hole, nearby, to access the problem pipe. It was fixed in thirty minutes and the bill was only $150. Gene helped me set up fans to dry everything out and promised to come and check it the next day.

I was on my way home from my last errand, the bank, when I realized that I really needed only an extra hour. I could have caught my original flight! The phone was ringing as I walked in the door. It was United Airlines advising me that both of their feeder flights to Chicago were running about an hour late today. Because of this I would miss my connections to the East Coast. She asked me if there was any way I could catch the earlier flight, which was now leaving in about fifty minutes. Because my repacked bag was already in the car and I lived only fifteen minutes from the airport, the answer was an easy yes.

Sitting on the plane I pondered this unusual day asking, *What is going on?* My Higher Self informed me it was the statement "I am having a day of Heaven on Earth" that caused even a crazy day to turn out very well. Two other times when faced with similar intense days I decided to invoke this prayer. After that I figured I could ask for it every day. You can, too. Here's how: *I am asking for a day of Heaven on Earth for me and everyone I come into contact with and everyone with whom I am in contract.* Pretty simple. Pretty amazing results.

Fourth Dimension

The realms of big emotions, fantasy beings, and the elemental kingdom all come from the fourth dimension. It is the dominion of Sasquatch and gnomes, fairies, and elves. If you can see them you are fourth-dimensional in the moment and are seeing fourth-dimensionally.

The legendary stories of King Arthur and Camelot carry much of this fourth-dimensional energy. The 1983 historical fantasy novel *Mists of Avalon* by Marion Zimmer Bradley incorporates the principles that were practiced at that time. In this feminine perspective of the Arthurian legend of Camelot she describes Morgaine parting the mists. She also shows us the "accidental" walking into Avalon by Arthur and his future bride. How did they accidentally get there? Perhaps it was the synchronicity of their first meeting within the same location of Avalon, creating a portal that gave them this access. Understand, the mists served as a gateway to the alternate (fourth-dimensional) world where the fairies and other beings like Morgaine hung out. Their entrance to this "land" was hidden from anyone who didn't have the ability to slide between dimensions. In the recent fantasy series Harry Potter it is similar to attending Hogwart's school by running at the wall to enter a part of the train station no one else knows about.

Some of my personal experience with fourth dimension has been more prosaic. In 1994, after I had been teaching the MerKaBa, I noticed some of my stuff was disappearing. It wasn't the kinds of articles that interest teenagers, so I knew it was not my sons. I would put something away in a drawer and go back for it the next day and it was missing. As a pragmatist all I really wanted was my stuff to return. This is when I started asking my Higher Self, *Where did my stuff go?* You may remember from earlier in the book that the answer from my Higher Self was always the same, *It is in a higher dimension.* After a while even that answer was not enough. Half of the time I believed it. The other half of the time I was sure I was making all this up in my mind.

One day my son came home from school, threw his book bag on the floor, put something in it, and came into the kitchen to tell me a story. In the middle of his story he stopped, saying, "Here, I will show you what I'm talking about." He walked over to his book bag and reached in to get the item he had just placed in there, but it wasn't there. He turned to me with a shocked expression and said, "Mom, I just put it there!" and I said, "I know you did. I saw you do it."

Without even thinking, there in my own home with my son, I spoke out loud, "Oh, it is probably in a higher dimension; we will just ask for it to come back." Can you imagine what my sixteen-year-old son thought at this moment about his mother? I asked him to return to the kitchen and finish his story. By this time he had everything out of his book bag. He put everything back and came into the kitchen to finish the story. After it was finished we moved back into the living room where he reached into the top of his book bag and retrieved the missing item.

I was not surprised as it had happened so many times to me, but my son was flabbergasted. This was the first time I was sure I was not fabricating it. After that I told students in my classes to just ask for the missing item to come back from a higher dimension if your Higher Self tells you that. Do you recall the story of the missing cell phone in chapter 5? Now you know the basis for the mystery of the man finding his wife's cell phone under the seat in his truck.

After that I began teaching that there is only *one* question to ask, *What is going on?* (See chapter 4.) One day when something disappeared again, I inadvertently posed that question instead of my usual, *Where did my stuff go?* The Universe surprised me with the answer: *Maureen, you were in a higher dimension when you set it down.* Ladies and gentlemen, if I am losing my objects in a higher dimension because I was there, so are you.

You may have experienced an extremely emotion-filled moment and manifested your own miracles without realizing that this is normal for fourth dimension residents. For example, in a difficult separation and potential for divorce, and in an extremely distraught state a woman said with passion, "If I had an extra $2,000 (the fee the attorney she wanted to hire needed as the retainer) I would file for divorce tomorrow." The following day, she received a check from a concerned family member for $2,000. In a more positive example, another woman asked the Universe to help her find a medical intuitive. This woman lived in a pretty high fifth-dimensional state most of the time. The following week, while camping some hundred miles away from her home she made friends with a fellow camper who just happened to tell a story about her medical intuitive. Where did this woman live? In the first woman's hometown, yet she had not heard of her!

The key here is balance. It is easier to laugh, cry, and manifest from 4-D. It is also an arena of seduction, which means that on the downside, you can get caught in the quicksand of overly emotional realms. This explains why people tend to repeat themselves when they get emotional—the tendency to "go fourth" is reflected in this pattern of repetition. This pattern of repetition also explains the pull of addictions. Suffering begets more suffering because people want to validate their victim state. They usually look for another person to tell their story to, repeating and reigniting the wounds.*

The **astral plane** ◈ is found in the lower fourth dimension. I have

---

*I have written about this in more detail in *Reweaving the Fabric of Your Reality.*

never recommended that individuals go to the astral plane. The lower part of fourth dimension works like quicksand, making it difficult to pull yourself out of it. The astral plane is full of entities, demons, and other unsavory beings that can attach to you once you visit this realm. I consider it an undesirable part of fourth and recommend you aim to higher dimensions. Now that you have this roadmap there is no reason not to aim higher.

Recognizing Fourth-Dimensional Behavior

A way that consciousness seeks to maintain control is to elicit agreement. A group dynamic forms whenever a group of individuals join to commiserate or complain about something. These groups of individuals can be wallowing in emotional energy, which in turn exacerbates the situation. When you are changing how you are feeling about things, this downward energy can be dominant but it has nothing to stick to permanently. A person can be sympathetic or empathetic. If others in a group ask your opinion, your third-dimensional self might offer agreement. However, once you are expressing your fifth-dimensional self you have a detached and compassionate feeling toward this situation.

Fourth dimension is still polarity-based, so there is a high fourth and a low fourth. Low fourth can pull you into spirals of downward energy, such as crying jags or bouts of depression. On the other hand, the high ends of fourth are very close to fifth and the leap is easy. This is one of the biggest reasons why it is so useful as a bridge to fifth. Because the fourth-dimensional energy can vortex downward or spiral upward, the split between energies is more dramatic. Music here is highly emotional, either like the blues, which sing sadness, or hauntingly beautiful melodies that embrace joy. Heart-centered music, such as Mozart or harp compositions, will help you stay in your heart throughout realms so you can move easily into fifth dimension.

Fourth dimension is the environment that allows you to create very quickly. For example, imagine the spontaneity of driving by a car wash and immediately remembering you wanted to get the car washed and today there is no line and you have the time right now. The opportunity to co-create when you are in this state is significant. Because the fourth dimension still contains polarity, it can mean your dark thoughts will also quickly manifest. So there is merit to awareness that allows you to practice discernment. In this way you are in a place of conscious creation.

From fourth it is easier to get to fifth because you are closer to it. The intervals are like music intervals. There are whole steps between each of the notes of a major scale except 3 to 4 and 7 to 8, where they are half steps. In the same way it is easier to get to fourth dimension from third because it is so close. Once you are in fourth dimension you can easily move to fifth.

It is also useful to remember that fourth dimension still carries polarity, even though it appears magical to us from this perspective. The merit to knowing and understanding the fourth dimension is that you can recognize when you are expressing through it and then capitalize on it. Learn to recognize it so you can consciously choose to move into fifth. Consider fourth dimension a portal, a place to pass through, not a place to stay.

Moving to Fifth Dimension

How is this done? Allow yourself to slide into "non-polarity" or non-judgment when you feel yourself becoming emotional. Allow yourself to feel the feelings and then pull back just a little to move into your heart space, and voila—you'll be in fifth instantly! How do you know you are in fifth? You will act and feel as if you are in love—with everyone and everything! Nothing can touch you. You feel only love, joy, and compassion.

Fifth can be a place when you are in your joy about some wonderful thing that you have experienced or understood or discovered. According to bestselling author Zecharia Sitchin, the Sumerians had 244 sensories—faculties with which to experience reality—unlike our five senses of today. Your conscious choice to experience more of the emotion you are capable of is vested in your willingness to appreciate each and every moment and emotion as being valued. In this way your validated feelings will begin to sort and organize themselves into an understandable pattern that allows you to experience, recognize, and co-create from vaster states.

Becoming Fifth-Dimensional

There are many ways to experience fifth dimension. We are discovering more and more each day. One expression that I know for sure is fifth dimension is a place of fearlessness. When you are faced with a fearful situation and you feel no fear, you are fifth-dimensional in that moment. Forgetting is another way to experience fifth dimension. Yet another way is to lapse into old behavior issues and think you are having a relapse, but instead you are revisiting one of the versions of your past—while you integrate all of them into universal understanding. I now understand we are folding old timelines like a braid into one single thread.

Fifth-Dimensional Fearlessness

In the early years of traveling to present the FOL workshop I did not have a cell phone. One weekend my host told me when I arrived in Atlanta that she was really backed up at work and could I please take the MARTA (their mass transit train system) to her house, located on the other side of Atlanta from the airport. She would meet me there. Having lived in New York in my twenties, I figured I could handle it.

Her instructions were to call her once I was on the correct train. Even though I didn't have a cell phone, I agreed to this, thinking I could call her from the platform of the train. What I did not realize is there are no phones on the MARTA platforms like I remembered in New York. Since I could not call her I had to get on the train and figure out a way to call her. Otherwise I would be at my destination waiting for her. She knew it took twenty minutes to get to her stop on the direct train, and maybe thirty minutes if I had to transfer. She suggested I hop on the first train that came along, regardless of which one it was.

When the first train arrived (no transfers), I grabbed my luggage and boarded, followed by two individual women. Then a man about six feet four inches tall and weighing at least 250 pounds got on the car. One woman got off . . . and then the other, leaving me and this man as the only occupants of the car. I noticed this but thought nothing of it.

The doors closed and the train left the station. Immediately the large man came over to me demanding that I give him some money. I said, "No." "Give me some money!" he repeated. Again I refused. Then I thought that if he had a cell phone I would happily pay him to let me use it. So I asked him, "Do you have a cell phone?" "No!" he shouted. "I don't have a cell phone!" "Well then I am not going to give you any money." Can you imagine his confusion at this point?

Then he said again, "Give me some money." I responded, "I mean no disrespect, but I am having trouble hearing you," pointing to my three suitcases in tow. "I just got off a plane and my hearing's all plugged up. Are you asking me anything *different* from what you asked me a few seconds ago?" "Just give me some money," he demanded.

"Sorry, I do not do that." By then the train was in the next station and he moved toward the door. I said to him, "You might try sales, you are pretty persistent." I had absolutely no fear. This man may have been a panhandler and bully, but I felt no harm coming toward me. This is what is meant by being in a fearsome situation yet having no fear. That day I wasn't able to make my phone call but I knew I had been successful in a more challenging dynamic.

I act responsibly and pay attention to my surroundings. I never intentionally walk into a dangerous situation, I have been told to act quickly and change my plans on more than one occasion. Remember I was told by my Higher Self to go home immediately after my workshops on September 10, 2001. In the transit car example I *knew* there was nothing to fear, thus I felt no fear.

Changing History

As a fifth-dimensional being you will be able to recall all events without experiencing the pain of moments past. This means you can literally have a memory surface and then choose either to anchor to that or decide, *No, that does not serve me.* For example, when you retell the story of your "wound," if you find yourself getting worked up about it and expressing emotion you may be choosing the lower-dimensional version of it. The ego holds on to painful emotions and behaviors for self-validation. Not letting go of past hurt, wounds, and so on is a way of the ego staying in control. It keeps you locked in a version of the past that throws an anchor into that dimensional level. It is a form of masking your present situation. Masking keeps you out of the present and does not serve you. It also limits your Ascension work.

As you remember your past with new, softer memories, you are tapping into alternate versions of the past that carry the wisdom that being fifth-dimensional can bestow. This results in your telling your "story" with a sense of wonder and compassion. It is typical to have a sudden realization that there could be two versions of the same story!

As you reconnect with your Higher Self, the need to hang on to old, painful emotions will no longer be appealing. As these memories fade, your recall will be accessing them from the universal mind, or Akashic Records, which does not have the emotional charge carried by a person with body experiences.

Remember, emotions reside in the body on the fascia and there are many ways to remove them. Use your tools to expedite this process. Thus your memories will no longer be subject to the ego version, which allows great freedom to stay fifth-dimensional! Knowing this invites you to access (and have the ability to understand) the many versions of your reality and allows you to shift and let go of pain and suffering.

Freedom to Remove the Mask

Unmasking gives you the ability to see how fast change can move through you. The ego stacks layer upon layer of masks to maintain ego control. In reality you are capable of much more than your ego perceives you are. As you shift, change, and let go, you *unmask the limitations* you put there to keep you safe. In the same way that parents put their children to bed in a crib surrounded with rails to keep them safe, but remove the restraints as the child grows, as you "take off the mask" you will discover you can move through painful experiences very quickly.

Just as a snake sheds its skin when it is outgrown, so also we can choose to leave behind any aspect of ourselves that does not continue to serve us. We do not need our painful experiences to define us. We can choose how we define ourselves in each moment. When the pain of the past no longer pulls us, we discover how really free we are.

Three Steps Forward, Two Steps Back

In one instance a student who had cleared herself of a non-threatening mental illness contacted me. She had been well for quite some time but had recently been experiencing feelings of guilt and doubt about whether she really was healed.

Because of our connection, she called me when her regular support person was not available. When she heard my voice she almost instantly reconnected with her true essence in 5-D. Prior to that she had been experiencing connections to her past, like a reverse déjà vu. She observed herself in the previous expressions and then somehow slipped into one, like Alice in Wonderland going down the rabbit hole.

In her case there were several reality shifts in process. One version (or timeline), which we will call version three, contained the original template to this dysfunction and is now completely eliminated. Version four is still running and she occasionally visits it. It has some references to the former disease and still has a pull on her at the ego level. It is also reinforced by her family and their medical understanding of the reality. They feel the need to be witness to this and for them to be right. Her father, a psychiatrist, projects clinical behavior onto her based on his understanding of it. Her mother carries guilt about her daughter's suffering and worries that she could have done something to prevent this from occurring. Because she loved and respected her parents she allowed their versions of reality to overlay her own experience.

The version five timeline is the latest "clean" history—now running in her world. She has access to the memories of her illness but they are no longer dominant. Version five is fully accessible to her family members, who prefer version four; however for her it is a "living" fifth-dimensional field. Seen by her family, version four contains enough elements of version three to be recognizable to them. Viewed from her vantage point of version five, she sees the perfection in all of it.

She now has the ability to shift into those separately—which she did—so that the last part of her upgrade could be completed. She briefly panicked when she thought she was back in the old expression of version three, when she was there temporarily before it was completely eliminated. Version three was not completely eliminated until after the last bits of adjustments to her version four were completed. This upgrade needed to finish, so that when she accesses it in the future from version five, it will have no attraction to her.

In her case it was a *real* temporary location—which is why she mistook it for her current residence. She really was there—albeit temporarily. Imagine wearing your old raincoat while your new one is at the cleaners, because not wearing a raincoat was unthinkable. That is, until you access fifth dimension.

In fifth-dimensional expression no raincoat is required, which allows her to revisit these memories without attachment at the *ego* level. As a result she has presently anchored that part of herself in fifth dimension.

In a normal, unevolved human, the ego uses these "holding on" historical reference points to manage this system of information. As you move from ego, you resolve this issue and move to the universal perspective that embraces all of the versions of experience, and then choose to reside in the one that is most pleasing or useful in the moment.

Fifth Dimension— First Level of Non-Polarity

Fortunately, with an activated MerKaBa you will become fifth-dimensional! It is totally amazing and true. Seems pretty simple. Many actually are consistent enough with their practices to achieve this. You can, too. Remember to be aware of what you are eating, drinking, and smoking. If you are being pulled away from any particular substance, let that be the signal to change an old pattern. It is also the time to stop judging yourself no matter what your shortcomings are. Doing the MerKaBa—along with your Higher Self connection practices, which include claiming those *blows to the heart*—you stand a very good chance of becoming fifth-dimensional right where you are. In my opinion one of fastest ways to advance spiritually is to keep opening your heart through blows to the heart. (See chapter 2.)

Fifth dimension is akin to what the rest of the world might call heaven. It is where relationships, body type, size, age, and so on are all perfect. One time I was with my host the day after an amazing class filled with wonderful people and exceptional experiences. We were both extremely joyous. She lives on a hill in the countryside and we were sitting on the front porch watching the morning sunrise. The birds were singing like crazy. It sounded like we were in a jungle. We chatted softly with our hearts so open my host commented that the bird singing level was unlike anything she had ever experienced on her front porch before. She wondered what was happening. We both were told that we were in fifth dimension in that moment. A few minutes later when the conversation turned to more mundane things, including complaints and criticisms, the chirping and singing stopped. Listen and the birds will tell you when you are in fifth dimension.

Sixth Dimension—
The First Place You Start to Move
toward Group Structure

Sixth dimension is the place where we often go to during the dreamtime. It is a place that has structure and form if we desire it, but does not require it. It is the place of all templates for basic structures on Earth. For example, DNA, geometry, and light languages are structures that form the basis for developed expressions and experiences in third dimension. In sixth dimension you are so sated with individuality from fifth that you are ready to begin to express in groups. Yet the structure of group is still being refined.

This is the zone where you might begin to recognize other versions of you and recognize your work in someone else. You are already collaborating in sixth and bringing it forward to third. In order for a group to work together the members must create a form or template to support their joint efforts. Sixth is the realm of these master templates. You might use your MerKaBa to support creative endeavors as the basis of your group forms.

Seventh Dimension—
Moving to Group Expression

Seventh dimension is coming directly in from Source, yet it carries the material aspects of precision. The basis for group expression is found here. As such, this is the last place you can experience yourself as separate. As a member of a group your individuality expands to include group expression.

To understand this, imagine MADD (Mothers against Drunk Driving) can serve as an example of seventh dimension, in that it displays group expression. First the template of the organization is formed (sixth), and then the desired expression moves through the template (group). The MADD organization (group expression) succeeds in getting legislation passed and education into schools, and ultimately the organization saves lives.

Seventh is a place where you feel such sweet emotional connection with consciousness, as expressed through souls similar to yours, that manifestation in groups comes easily. Imagine a school of fish or flock of birds that is so connected that the individual members all move in unison.

Eighth Dimension—
Moving to Group Awareness

Eighth dimension is so vast that from this vantage point (third dimension) it is difficult to comprehend. You not only function in alignment with the group, you perceive yourself as the group. In eighth one cannot experience the self as separate, as found in seventh and below. Generally, when consciousness is focused here the third-dimensional self blanks out; the force of life becomes the collective collaborative whole. Although groups exist in this domain, the limitlessness of consciousness permeates. This is the arena where you are more "we" than "I."

Ninth Dimension—
Collective Consciousness

Ninth dimension experiences life inwardly focused. It represents the collective consciousness of planets, star systems, galaxies, and dimensions, yet awareness is inner-directed. As such, it holds the vastness of collective consciousness. It has no polarity (as with everything above fifth dimension) and as such is not agenda-driven like mass consciousness.

Napping During Meditation—
What Is Really Going on and Why

I have encountered many circumstances where individuals have apparently gone to sleep while in deep meditation. I used to wonder why they would do this. Of course, sometimes the body needs to be extremely still. Sleeping is more likely to make that happen easily.

I asked my guides about it and this is what I discovered: When a person is apparently sleeping but immediately wakes when the meditation is finished, she has been in other advanced dimensions (usually ninth and beyond) where there is nothing in common with the third-dimensional reality to make an association. Thus the mind blanks out and the body goes on holiday. It usually is a lovely respite because the "sleep" is tied to an evolved state, which produces endorphins and energies. Although not consciously understood, they usually can be felt within a short period of time and produce euphoria otherwise unattainable.

Twice while writing this my guides literally gave me this experience. Although I had not done this before—left my body while typing (and the typing stopped)—it was like falling asleep.

Upper Creation Realm—
Tenth through Twelfth Dimensions

Tenth dimension is where the beings of the basis for creation exist. Their energy is so vast it is really beyond our initial ability to understand. This is where the Divine Blueprint is formed. This is the source of the **Vedic system of the seven rays**◈ and the Hebrew **Elohim**◈. It is the source of the Great Central Sun energy as taught by the Ascended Masters. It is Source Code at its finest. It is where you will find the Source Code of the ten **seed groups of humanity**◈.

Eleventh Dimension

Eleventh dimension is a wonderful place of anticipation. It is the place where concept is more alive than form. It is an environment of the integrated awareness of the separated parts of God, held in a place of union and communion. The place of union is so ecstatic that it defies description.

We find the Akashic Records here. Remember, the Akashic Records are a living field that shifts and changes. Even though we use the word "records," which implies permanence, it is more of a living, breathing environment. Have you ever been to a wave pool at a water park? It is like that—contained but moving.

Eleventh is the region of the Archangels and of **Lord Metatron**◈, the Keepers, and mathematical codes that include the genetic codes for the expression of all the versions of the reality. Even these descriptors are finite; the energy here is so vibrant and kinetic it defies description. It also contains a quality of euphoria that would be akin to the moment before orgasm. Being connected to the eleventh dimension, for me personally, has changed my life dramatically. Once you have experienced this, you really are never the same being.

In certain environments while working in the Akashic Records I spend five to six hours a day in this zone. My close associates have commented to me that these extended periods of time in eleventh have changed my appearance dramatically, seeing more light emanating from me.

Twelfth Dimension

Twelfth dimension is the place of pure consciousness and light consciousness. It is the environment that is so connected to itself that there is no separation of any kind. It is, for some, the stopping point of creation.

Thirteenth Dimension

Thirteenth dimension appears to me as unity consciousness and a place for new beginnings. I have experienced this energy as the place where any thoughts of not-God would cause pain and are truly unthinkable. Love is the essence of all here, and even this description is insufficient.

Becoming Multidimensional

I keep forgetting things! What is going on? A multidimensional moment! One of the ways to experience multidimensionality is to completely go blank. Generally, when you forget what you saw or did in your meditation you have gone so high that there is no reference point. In conceptual terms it is like comparing a first-grader to a grandfather. It may be possible for the grandfather to connect with the child, but the child does not carry any understanding of what it is like to be a grandfather.

Another way the mind deals with the overload of changing the way you experience and understand the world around you is forgetfulness. You are about to do something, and then you realize you have forgotten what you were thinking about and you are afraid it might be serious. We addressed this earlier in the section on reverse déjà vu. These moments are a form of unhooking from the ego's holding-on mechanisms. Call it a multidimensional moment!

Why is this happening? This is a direct result of going fifth-dimensional. If you have a TV with a PiP feature (picture-in-picture), you can see more than one channel at a time. In my son's college dorm they had a bookcase that held four different TVs. They did not have the money for fancy equipment, but they accomplished the same thing. You are essentially viewing multiple screens the way these college kids did. You are starting to gain awareness of other dimensions but without the language or full mental capacity to understand how it works. You will simply forget where you were as you shifted from one dimension to another. And where you were could be fifth dimension or beyond that.

Initially the ego thinks it is losing control. This is normal. As your practice of the MerKaBa grows, your ego will be able to begin to trust your Higher Self's knowledge and this will get more settled. If you have not committed yet to the Higher Self practices found in chapters 4 and 5, now is a good time to start. Remember that the old life is dying and the new life is emerging. This is nothing to be anxious or concerned about.

Sleep and Lack of Ambition

The best news I have is that if you are finding yourself sleeping a lot more than you used to, you are probably going through an upgrade in consciousness. It is easier for your body to integrate the most evolved version of yourself that you can tolerate on this planet at this time when you are asleep than when you are awake. You find this drowsiness comes up and just knocks you down for the count. Your best choice is to sleep. And then, for heaven's sake, don't judge yourself. Losing your ambition is also related to this. Remember the discussion earlier about a multidimensional moment. Letting go of current motivations that are coming through the ego, which believes in some sort of rules of mass consciousness, is purposeful. If you are feeling this lack of ambition, you might be tempted to reprogram or upgrade your motivations. But sometimes it is easier to release your need to have motivations at all and simply *let go.*

Initially your fifth-dimensional self will appear as a singular, sweet self. If you have any emotional baggage it can reappear, as you are now able to hold on to more than one version of the reality. This can be quite disconcerting. Just remember if this happens to you to ask your Higher Self for the *most* evolved version of *you* to show up and manage this integration. Your Higher Self will allow your awareness to recognize that you can choose the expression or version of you that pleases you.

If you keep doing the MerKaBa these variations will settle down and the version of you and your history that works best for you will become dominant. The MerKaBa clears and balances every part of you. Keep your practice going through any crazy times and you will find it is easier to stay centered and in your heart through all of it.

Christ
Consciousness Grid

- Where did the grid come from?
- What does it do for us?
- What does it look like?
- What are we supposed to do with it?

If you ever see the Christ Consciousness Grid while stargazing on a dark night, you will be awestruck with the beauty and symmetry of it all.

The Christ Consciousness Grid is an etheric crystalline architectural structure of energy that envelops the earth and holds the energy of the Christ, or perfected human.* As such, it radiates and attracts the vibration of the most evolved possibility of human life on planet Earth.

---

*The word *Christ* comes from the Greek word *christos,* or anointed. The Christ Consciousness Grid refers to an energy in the hierarchy held by those who retained its self-mastery. In other words it radiates the energy of an ascended earth for all to move into resonance with it. It could just as easily have been named the Buddha consciousness grid or Mohammed consciousness grid.

Sharrel Boike's Earth Grid Image

Visionary artist and somatic psychotherapist Sharrel Boike created a grid rendering titled *Regaining Cosmic Integrity©* based on a vision of the earth poised in a starry sky that occurred while she was meditating. "I was just emerging from my own 'dark night of the soul' and was accustomed to nightmarish visions," she said. "It was most unusual for me to 'see' something so beautiful as the image you see here." Within her vision she "heard" the words: *"'I' becomes 'we,' must become 'we' to continue."* Boike didn't understand this until a day or two later when a book fell open in front of her to a Native American injunction: "You must bring your vision before the people." Although she had no artistic background, Boike was guided to create a triptych of three large light boxes for three Apollo space photographs of Earth. Superimposed over the images are polyhedron lines—first fragmented, then linked, and finally encircled by intersecting polyhedron lines of light.

Boike's use of the words "cosmic integrity" is significant; it is a fifth-dimensional expression evoking absolute integrity.

Figure 13.1. Sharrel Boike was guided to create this lightbox image, *Regaining Cosmic Integrity©*, based on a meditative vision of oneness.

What Is the Origin of the
Christ Consciousness Grid?

We know that the Christ Consciousness Grid comes from the Ascended Masters. Drunvalo tells us that the Ascended Masters built it for us and that it is a tool to assist mankind in its evolutionary process.

In volume I of *The Ancient Secret of the Flower of Life,* he reports that the Ascended Masters appealed to the galactic command for ideas to avoid humanity's destruction. I experienced this group as the Council of Light and I believe they are the same beings.

We were running out of time and needed a significant boost to achieve Ascension, otherwise there was a strong potential for self-destruction. Since we are in a free-will zone this was not an easy matter. Upon examining this crisis, the Council of Light created a plan to construct the Christ Consciousness Grid around the earth as a solution to help us avoid probable self-destruction.

I wanted to know more. I wanted to know *where* it originated. I wanted to know where the master plan blueprint for the grid was created. What was its Source Code? I kept thinking that it had to be very specific for the earth, otherwise it would not work. The answer I was given was deceptively simple. The Christ Consciousness Grid came from our future!

Initially, that answer was sufficient. If somewhere in our future the Christ Consciousness Grid had been built by humanity, because we were Christed ones, then it would be perfect for us. But then one day while working on *You Are the Genie in the Bottle*[1] material, the answer just floated into my awareness. What the Ascended Masters did was create a thread toward a possible future that allowed them to see the final result.

Much as we create in genie manifestation work, where we imagine beyond our desired outcome first and then create a thread back toward it, I believe the Ascended Masters executed a similar procedure and then followed the thread back to the outcome that showed them the version of the future where mankind had achieved Christ Consciousness.

In this location there was already in existence a Christ Consciousness Grid that we, humanity, had built. The Ascended Masters replicated this grid from our future and created it in the present timeframe as the Christ Consciousness Grid. This is exactly what we do to manifest in the genie system.

Imagine for a moment that there are many possible futures for evolution on our planet. Some have more energy—a greater likelihood of happening than others. With the help of the Ascended Masters we have magnetized the *one* possible future that *proves* we made it. In other words, of all the possible futures that could exist, the one that proves we made it to Christ Consciousness would produce a Christ Consciousness Grid. With this grid in place in the etheric realm, it is already magnetizing us toward that outcome.

With this grid in place it is far easier to lock into Christ Consciousness behavior, much like a GPS in your automobile locks onto your destination and no matter what turn you take, it constantly recalculates your next move based on your current position. In the same way, the Christ Consciousness Grid serves to assist planetary Ascension. Now we can understand the statement we have heard from many teachers that our "outcome is assured."

Every journey begins with movement away from or toward something. When you anchor the destination in your awareness, the remaining issues are what mode of transportation you will use and what route you will take. Thus the adventure becomes the *journey,* rather than the decision of where to go. All possible futures can exist. Some have more energy, a greater likelihood of happening, than others.

If you were a being of light at any level, and you wanted to ensure that the planetary Ascension occurred, wouldn't you pick out something that represented the planet's evolution—Christ Consciousness—and anchor it into the present? That is exactly what the Ascended Masters did. They pulled the blueprint of the Christ Consciousness Grid from a version of the future that says we made it—we arrived at our Christed expression. This way the future would be assured.

What Impact Does That Have on You?

It means that every action that is fifth-dimensional, or operating from a vantage point of unconditional love, will *resonate* with the Christ

Consciousness Grid, thus attracting more of the same energy to make it easier and easier to resonate for all of us at Christ Consciousness level. Every human action that is operating from unconditional love—the fifth dimension—is attracted to the Christ Consciousness Grid, and each perfected action serves to amplify it. This means that with the Christ Consciousness Grid in place, perfected human behavior is easier for all to express.

Power in the Form of the Christ Consciousness Grid

While on the Big Island of Hawaii on a dolphin swim, I helped my friend John Ammond build a physical replica of the Christ Consciousness Grid out of brass rods, using metal solder to connect the points. We were pretty excited about it. We then went to see the Kilauea Volcano lava flow with the Christ Consciousness Grid replica in tow. I had no idea what John had in mind.

We hiked into the area and got as close as we could to a moving lava flow, about three to five feet from us. He set it down on the ground directly in the path the flow would take. Since it was metal, we expected that as the lava moved closer it would melt or collapse the metal structure. What happens next is burned clearly in my mind. The lava moved into the space in front of it and then split into two streams around it—like a fork in a river. The lava diverted around it completely and did not affect it! We stayed for a few hours, expecting that eventually it would melt from the heat. By the time we left it was still fully intact, unaffected by the heat. It was an exciting moment for me—to recognize the sheer power of the geometric shape.

Can You See It?

Many individuals have seen the Christ Consciousness Grid. It is an energetic grid that sits above the earth about sixty miles and is described as a beautiful geometric pattern. Some people see its appearance similar to the Flower of Life pattern. When you are looking at it from the inside, with your energetic awareness, it resembles the Flower of Life symbol (see figure 13.2).

Figure 13.2. Flower of Life symbol

In reality it is a **stellated dodecahedron**. Its color is whitish with fairly broad lines. Those who have seen it are filled with a sense of gratitude and awe. It is best seen from locations with limited ambient light, such as Alaska, Hawaii, or the middle of the ocean. In truth you can see it from anywhere on a dark night, as long as you are in a place where the sky has not been artificially lit. A former Navy man, Daryl, used to see it at night from his perch on an airplane wing while sailing in the Pacific. He saw it all the time. Back then he didn't know what it was. Perhaps you have unknowingly seen it as well.

I first saw the grid while in Alaska for a workshop. I mentioned it in class the next day and discovered many of the residents in Fairbanks had seen it. One of the things I had been told by my guides that year was that my trip to Egypt was directly connected to my trip to Alaska. My guides showed me that I was building a link between Alaska and

Egypt and it was directly related to the Christ Consciousness Grid. I would be bringing energy from Alaska to Egypt for the purpose of stabilizing the grid in the Middle East.

One participant in my class had traveled from an area very near to Denali National Park and Preserve, midway between Anchorage and Fairbanks. She realized that my connection from Alaska to Egypt was extremely important and offered to ask her husband to bring us heart-shaped stones from their backyard, which was adjacent to this national preserve. She brought six heart-shaped stones to me.

Our group energized the stones with our own heart energy and energy from Alaska. The Alaskan participants gave permission to create a link to Egypt and the Middle East. I placed the stones in a special bag that would be used during the Egypt trip. I traveled from Fairbanks, then to New York, and then Egypt with a brief stopover in my home city. Each location in Egypt, from Aswan to Alexandria, was energized by the stones, with a culminating ceremony in Alexandria, where the Egyptian Society for Esoteric Knowledge accepted the last stones on behalf of the Middle East.

At the temple site of Abu Simbel I handed the bag of stones to a participant named Donna, who was selected because of a vision she had received some six months earlier about our trip. She was leading a special ceremony connecting the grids above Abu Simbel to the Alaskan counterpart. I had been guided that our group was to hold a special ceremony in Ramses Temple, while connecting it (the temple) with its *original* location on the physical earth.

When the Aswan Dam was built in Egypt, much of the surrounding area was flooded by the creation of Lake Nasser. All of the incredible structures of Abu Simbel were in the flood path, so they were eventually moved to their current location. Many other sacred sites were lost or flooded.

There are remnants of some of the Egyptian temples in museums around the world, because city after city agreed to dismantle and move these treasures in order to save this part of Egyptian heritage. In the case of Abu Simbel, the entire structure, including the four 65-foot statues of Ramses, were carefully cut, disassembled, reassembled, and relocated just a few feet from its original location, which is now under water.

The new location is on the same island in the Nile, but on higher ground. Care was taken to make sure that this temple is facing the direction it was originally facing. However, in order to maximize the mountain that is there, it is just a few degrees off. As a result, the sun enters the temple on October 23, one day later than the original date of the coronation of the King, for which it was designed. On this date the sun enters the open door of the temple, penetrates through the pitch black corridor of the hypostyle hall under eight pillars, each carved into a colossus of the king, and finally illuminates the seated statues at the back of the sanctuary.

It is important to note there was another individual who had intended to join our group, but at the last minute decided to wait until October 23 to be there. We met later that trip at our farewell party, where another tale of synchronicity occurred. Our connection called us to pass on the lineage of activation. It was imperative that she met me and connect with our energy, as it was needed for the final step of the activation of that temple, which would occur after our group departed on October 23. She was called to do that part.

On Ellie Crystal's website she told a story about a friend whose deceased father traveled with her in the ethers. Asking her what she saw, she answered, "Grids." He said, "That is correct. That is all there is."

Construction Issues

Ron Holt, former president of Flower of Life Research (now closed) and a self-proclaimed gridworker, reports there are sections of the Christ Consciousness Grid that were "blown open." He has been guided to work with the grid in healing these areas. On occasion he has asked other gridworkers to work with him in performing maintenance and repair. I have seen this in the Middle East as well. Patricia Diane Cota-Robles has also reported similar disruptions in the grid and a reflection on the opposite side of the planet expressing these "blows." It also makes sense that a calm area across the globe could support its energetic opposite.

If you are a gridworker you probably know it. You may have even seen the grid. Many of my students used to belong to the Gridworkers Union, a group of individuals who met monthly, by telephone, to share their work and encourage one another. If you find that you have a keen interest in this subject, you probably are partially responsible for the maintenance of one or more grids.

More Middle East Stress

Negativity in the Middle East has caused a huge amount of stress on this grid. Because of the fierce antipathy among many factions of the world religions focused in the Middle East, in 2007 my Sacred Journey group was called to place an energetic device in the atmosphere above Mt. Sinai. Later it was used to work with a peace grid designed to support harmonizing the three major world religions.

The Christ Consciousness Grid was activated in January of 2008, birthed with the move of Pluto into Capricorn. I was called into service to be involved in the birthing of this grid, and worked closely with the Ascended Masters and unseen helpers along with hundreds of others in programming and supporting the activation of this grid. It was not until after I saw everything go dark, from west to east in a type of power outage occurring within my field of vision, that I realized that mass consciousness had been disengaged from an old grid and the new one activated.

The MerKaBa field is similar to this, allowing individuals to personally acquire their own "**perfection suits**"◈. These sacred geometry fields are remarkable tools that support the evolution of creation and its return to God.

Maintaining Balance and Staying Connected

What You Will Learn in This Chapter

- Pulling it together
- Contracts with the Universe
- Multiple versions of the reality
- Misuses of emotional energy
- Messages from Sanat Kumara, Divine Feminine, and Archangel Michael

---

Are you wondering how this will all work? Maybe you are excited. Maybe you are scared. For sure there is change in the air. You, and hundreds before you, have felt the same way. It is my great pleasure to participate in assisting this process in reaching the highest potential of your own Ascension work. You are an amazing individual to have reached this pinnacle—toward the fulfillment of your destiny.

The Inner
Guru Is Your Higher Self

This is *your* time to achieve your fullest potential. The MerKaBa is one tool that activates your fifth-dimensional memories. You no longer have to rely on some other teacher or leader. The tools and practices I have been given to share with you, dear reader, will connect you with *your* inner guru, *your* Higher Self.

Time for Celebration

The new Earth is manifesting very quickly. The so-called "earth changes" are on a different timetable from what had been given previously. In August 2009, while I was in Japan, I was given a direct connection with Sanat Kumara. He appeared in numerous photographs like this one.

His signature is found in the ruby ray. It typically appears as two sharp rays at 90-degree angles, aimed toward the earth as shown in figure 14.1. All of the photos of this sunset taken over that entire afternoon (about an hour apart from first to last) contained this visual confirmation of his presence.

I was so intrigued by the presence of this energy in the photos that I asked my Japanese host if she had ever heard of Sanat Kumara. Her response was enthusiastic, so on that same trip we made a pilgrimage to Mt. Kurama near Kyoto, Japan—the location where, legend has it, Sanat Kumara's spaceship landed. There is a wonderful collection of shrines there, along with an ancient statue of Sanat Kumara. It was an amazing journey.

In the channeling of my own record keepers and Sanat Kumara, they identified me as a most ancient being of light. When I asked the purpose of my trip to Mt. Kurama, they said it was to anchor in the ancient memories that I had chosen to continue carrying as enlightenment to the world. We assembled the questions below to clarify some of the information.

We have reached the victory celebration. Although we have not gone through the graduation ceremony, enough has been accomplished to assure your outcome. The only remaining question is, how many of you will attend the party? The following section contains questions from my staff with answers from Sanat Kumara speaking for the Ascended Masters and channeled through me. I did not review or plan these questions in advance.

Figure 14.1. The signature of the Ascended Master Sanat Kumara typically appears as two sharp rays aimed toward the earth at right angles.

Earth Changes from
Mother Earth

Sanat Kumara steps forward to speak for the Ascended Masters:

"The first thing we wish to speak of is the earth changes. Mother Earth is waiting for mankind to catch up and make its Ascension so that when the earth goes through its changes, those who are ready will be waiting for Mother Earth. Destructive earth changes will not occur on the version of earth of the ascended humanity. The changes will not be noticeable to those who are on the ascending earth.

"We want you to understand that the earth and her people are no longer at risk. The sounding of the alarm is simply to ensure that everyone who wants to transform may do so and take advantage of this opportunity. Mother Earth will ascend. By announcing the opportunity in advance she gives the ability for many to join in the activity (much as a sale is advertised to give everyone the chance to participate).

"The earth is transforming. The earth is taking her time so that everyone who wants to evolve may do so. There is no rush; everything is in order.

"We are not suggesting that you avoid acting as you are compelled. What we are saying is that it no longer serves you to feel anxious about your ego demanding action. There is a definite timeline and all of the forces of heaven are supporting your success.

"You will not change things through rhetoric. You will only change things by accessing and using the new data."

Opening Your Heart

"Do the MerKaBa Meditation. Always seize the opportunity to accept a blow to the heart. Build a connection to your Higher Self by practicing your Higher Self connection. Increase the capacity of your pranic tube through your toning and chanting work. Look at every opportunity to expand your heart as a means of increasing your capacity to carry unconditional love. All this will lead the way to your Ascension."

What Key Elements
Are Primary in This Book?

The first key element is to focus on the opening of your heart. Part of this process is the emotional clearing work that will enable you to expand your heart's capacity to hold unconditional love. In each person, unconditional love is like a seed that can grow and expand.

The second key element is the activation and expansion of your Higher Self connection. Many of you already have a Higher Self connection, but the tools found in this book will ensure 100 percent accuracy.

Finally, above all else, integrity is required for these elements to work.

Misuses of Emotional Energy

Whether it's the water-cooler or Facebook or Twitter, you can find many examples of the slowdown of human progress toward Ascension by individuals investing their emotional energy in these things. During the Renaissance, mankind began to remember the knowledge that came from the grid or network of energy that was first formed in the ethers of planet Earth at that time. This cycle was moving individuals very quickly toward Ascension. However, at that time even the suggestion that the earth was not the center of the Universe was considered heresy and condemned by the Pope. Where did the Pope get his guidance? It came from the extraterrestrial known as Anu. Not only did Anu, through the Pope, arrest the development of the Renaissance, he also slowed to a crawl the high training that was offered in Egypt centuries earlier. At this time in history there are forces attempting slow down humanity's progress. This is the subject of many books. Our purpose here is to help you see that outside forces that you may think you should respect may have agendas that you do not understand or know about. Stay with the MerKaBa Meditation and you will be able to see those whose agendas are counter to humanity's Ascension into the light.

Every September in the United States there are big ceremonies to commemorate the 9/11 losses. It is a time when many individuals focus on their grief, and their losses are brought to light. You may have felt deep sadness and grief on these days as you channeled the massive energies of the American people. One year I was in another country across the globe and felt immense sadness on September 12. Only when I asked, *What is going on?* and tied my feelings to the date did I realize I was feeling it as Americans were feeling it, in real time (since I was twelve hours ahead on the clock). Only then did I know I was feeling this particular energy.

When you are experiencing deep energies like this, consider using emotional clearing techniques. This will enable you to move through this energy quickly. I wrote extensively about this in *Reweaving the Fabric of Your Reality*. My point here is to alert you to these deep-seated emotions, such as fear and grief, so you can decide to move through them. Decide that you are the maker of your destiny, not susceptible to some outside force that is throwing you a curveball through these intensely painful memories.

And always ask that your helpers be beings of 100 percent God Light.

Healing in the King's Chamber

There are many theories about the purpose of the King's Chamber inside the Great Pyramid. Although you may have been told it was an ancient Pharaoh's burial site, there has never been any evidence of anyone ever being buried there. No bodies have been found and there is no writing of prayers and spells on the walls—unlike the burial sites on the West Bank of Luxor and in the Valley of the Kings, which are covered with beautiful paintings and writing.

Duat is the Egyptian name given to the space between dimensions—the space one must cross to return home to God. Just as the Nile River separates the Valley of the Kings from the civilization on the other side, the duat (or Great Void) is said to exist between the Creator and creation. There is an unusual system of chambers and passages running throughout the Great Pyramid, and this may have represented ancient efforts to create a permanent duat.

The Egyptians believed the Nile also represented this duat, and thus associated crossing the Great Void with the crossing of the Nile.

I believe the King's Chamber may have been a healing sound chamber. The wavy granite walls above this chamber are open, with a texture reminiscent of the "sponge pyramids" found covering the walls of our contemporary sound studios. They are used to break up the standing wave ratio that would occur in any room, especially a **double square**◈. The double square shape will give maximum amplification (volume), while embodying the phi ratio in the 90-degree angle. However, the standing wave ratio will cause one pitch to be louder than all the rest. Try this sometime in your bathroom: sing low to high, sliding through pitches like a trombone or slide whistle. This breaking up of the standing wave ratio produces a normal balanced sound with which to "ride the sound wave" back home to God.

The portal of the sound aimed at the duat (the heavens) filled with three layers of granite—each with a roughhewn side toward the sky—supports this idea of the chamber being an amplifying sound chamber aimed at the heavens. I believe the purpose of the King's Chamber is a healing room where one rides the sound through the duat and reconnects with the Creator. In that special location with the Creator a new body part can be regenerated that will allow a person to be whole again. This could be true for all kinds of healing—physical, mental, and emotional. Many individuals have experienced sudden or spontaneous healings there. In all cases that I know of, the healings took place during sound ceremonies within the King's Chamber.

Toning in the King's Chamber can heal deep-seated wounds. This chamber was designed to concentrate electrons for resurrection. You can experience this energy for yourself through the use of my two-CD set *Sounds from the Great Pyramid: Toning in the King's Chamber,* also available as a download.

Survival Signals

Many individuals have developed gut reactions because of difficult situations they have endured throughout their lives. Those who have developed some sort of survival mechanism that tells them when something is not safe know how to react in similar circumstances. They can sense when a condition is not going well and know they need to get out of it. (See "Survival Psychics" in chapter 10.)

When you follow the Higher Self practice, and the exercise of asking the Higher Self yes/no questions, you will discover that this type of communication becomes clearer. These signals, once given a voice, will help you be proactive rather than reactive. This will have an impact on your future and quite possibly change your past.

You are a magical being and need to honor what you came to do. Even "late bloomers" can make a difference. Working for social change is important work, no matter what it is, and may be part of your Divine Plan. Any time you decide to join others and take a stand for what you believe in, you are making a change for the better. Even your physical ailments may improve!

> "A small body of determined spirits fired by an unquenchable faith in their mission can alter the course of history."
>
> MAHATMA GANDHI

Manifestation through the Heart

Remember that any of *your* emotions you experience through your heart will serve as rocket fuel for your manifestations. The unconditional love you move through your heart is key to manifesting. Learning to use emotions that you cycle through your heart is an ideal way to manifest.

In my *You are the Genie in the Bottle* workshop, I encourage participants to spend a certain amount of time on developing their heart energy and growing their awareness of their loving outlook. They learn how to expand the feeling of opening the heart. It is very valuable to choose emotions that you direct and move through your heart, so you are fully connected to your God essence. There are many spiritual practices that can help you, and many examples throughout this book. I encourage you to explore these and practice them until you actually feel different. Look for ways to support this inner growth and you will find them.

Sanat Kumara Speaks of Emotional Clearing

"Humanity is still hanging on to its emotions, thinking that is who they really are. People need to understand that their emotions are simply something they have manufactured that has enabled them to experience the reality more precisely. Feeling it is necessary, as emotion is an aspect of the polarity creation. Emotion has a life cycle and must be expressed. Once expressed, emotion zeros out and this neutral chi can no longer contaminate the earth.

"Emotion is energy, or chi, that has been imbued with feeling that must be expressed. Emotions are useful tools for experiencing the reality. However, when emotion was created it was not intended to cause so much pain and suffering. This pain and suffering have caused huge rifts in the etheric fabric of mankind and the earth. Much emotional baggage has been seeded in the earth. This is what is now being cleared. Many are being called to clear it. They are experiencing excessive emotion—thinking that they have not done their personal emotional clearing work. Actually, most of that is excess baggage you are clearing on behalf of your brothers and sisters, as well as yourself, in other lifetimes. Fortunately, it is not a difficult task; you do not have to go through a deeply emotional process for this to be resolved and cleared.

"Think of someone who has a big debt, who is given the chance to pay the debt at ten cents on the dollar. You are in the final upswing toward God. If you do not allow this to move through you, it will cause further pain. Do your part—feel pain and release it. We assure you, plenty of opportunity will be given to you to feel emotional pain and heal it. It does not require you to stay in pain. Acknowledge it, release it, and move on.

"You are not expected to do this alone. Always seek help. There is no reason to suffer or struggle alone. The experiences are noted and validated. This work is personal planetary Ascension work. You have the trainers, the cheerleaders, the caterer, the towels . . . but you still have to do your part."

Higher Self Connection

"The second key element of the book is the Higher Self connection. The Higher Self will give you everything you need and teach you everything you need to know. It will enable you to be where you need to be and help you to recognize what to do—even when to do it. Some of you will be called to move; some to stay. Some will be asked to sell everything; others will be called to donate to worthy causes. Some will be asked to build something new."

Ask Your Higher Self to Guide Your Every Decision

"Get in the habit of asking about everything consistently. Do not use your Higher Self to answer a question so that you can get permission to take a deliberate action. If you do that you are still using your ego to make a decision. Instead, seek to ask your Higher Self what the best course of action for you (and others) would be. In this way you will be merging your ego with your Higher Self. For example, if you are avoiding someone—and you know the person might be at an event you'd like to attend—do not ask your Higher Self if that person will be there. Instead, ask your Higher Self, Is it in my highest and best good to go to the event?"

Integrity

"Always act from a place of integrity. Do your best to be truthful. Do your best to be honest and sincere. Do not make little exceptions to the rules you have agreed to and then wonder why the Universe treats you like you are in lack! Do not allow a misunderstanding to exist by your default. Do not allow words to be spoken that lead someone in a different direction from what you know to be truthful. So if someone asks you, 'Were you at this place?' and you were, but do not want to admit it, tell the truth anyway. Do not say, 'Well I was kind of busy last night with a friend,' and push the question away.

"That would be a form of concealment that is no longer tolerated. Step into your power and speak your truth. When you deliberately try to trick someone so you will have more money, more power (as in a relationship), or whatever you believe is your right, you are telling us, the Universe, you do not trust that the Universe can take care of you. The ego is out there trying to make it happen for you. As long as you do these things, you are giving your

ego more power than your Higher Self. We say to you that the new way does not have room for an out-of-integrity response of any kind to any circumstance.

"If you find you are out of integrity, clean up your messes—like spilled milk. No big deal."

What should I do if I was out of integrity a long time ago?

"Stay in the moment. Do not worry about the past unless it is the immediate past. If the present moment is influenced by the immediate past, then you must speak the truth. You must stay in integrity. However, if your current situation is influenced by the distant past and this information has nothing to do with the present, then leave it alone. Yet, if you are in a discussion and the distant past does indeed have a bearing on the present, then you must speak the truth."

Why did Sanat Kumara come forward through Maureen at this time?

"Maureen's recent visit to Japan activated her memory of lifetimes being with Sanat Kumara."

I recognized Sanat Kumara the very first time I saw his image more than thirty years ago. You may have recognized him, too. His representation is found in the familiar painting from the Sistine Chapel of the bearded, long-white-haired man (God the father) reaching for the hand of man. William Blake's popular etching *The Ancient of Days,* another name for Sanat Kumara, can easily be found on the Internet.

Any remarks as to the accuracy and validity of the book?

"Maureen's information is mostly channeled. She is a highly accurate channel. Maureen does not like to be made special and seeks to avoid aggrandizing, so we will leave it at that. Her channeling is 100 percent accurate."

Is it possible to know who spoke through Maureen?

"It was mostly her Higher Self and Archangel Michael who provided the information that was given here. Much of what came through was the result of seekers like you who desired to learn. This created the space to hear and know. Additionally, Maureen has access to the dimension that had been closed for millions of years. She wrote of this in the first chapter.

"Her most significant information came through after that portal opened for her. This information had to be accessed by a human, not the Ascended Masters. She is not the only one who has access, but she is one of a select few."

Describe the role of humanity in regard to Mother Earth at this time.

"Humanity has always had a stewardship role toward Mother Earth that it has abused, but it is now coming back full circle."

What about the Higher Self?

"The inner guru is your Higher Self. Do your part so that you have clear communication with your Higher Self. That is, the Higher Self is of prime importance; everything else follows."

Regarding prediction and prophecy on the planet—like that of the Mayans and the meaning of their prophecy—can you comment on that?

"You are about to work on co-creating the new reality and the impact on prophecy will be substantial. Prophecy is meant to be wrong. People often overlook this. In order for prophecy to be successful it has to not happen. *Then it accomplished what was intended. Prophecy reveals a potential problem and points a spotlight on it. Mankind is given the opportunity to do something about it. Thus it reveals a problem, which then causes humanity and individuals to shift and change.*

"The Mayan prophecy did much to gather people. It opened their awareness to circumstances and gave them a working template. It invited people to identify what they needed to understand and got them to do something about it. Humanity needed to have something to work with since most were not aware of the problem. Many have been drawn to this knowledge and shifts have already occurred. Prophecy provides meaning so that the changes can be understood. If that had not been provided as a tool, it would cease to have meaning.

"Even prophecy itself is subject to interpretation. There are many ways to view and understand indigenous peoples' information."

Mass consciousness seems to place value on predictions based on scientific research, particularly that it has been observed that the earth shifts every 13,000 years and . . . (Sanat Kumara interrupts)

"We disagree. This is not a mass consciousness belief. Those who are using scientific knowledge to propel their own agendas are a small group. Science is useful when it helps consciousness shift and change. It is not useful when it fails to do so. Science is simply one way of interpreting the reality; it is not the only way, as indigenous people will tell you.

"It happens to be a common way of thinking on the planet right now, and when science provides information for the evolution of mankind that matches with spiritual teachings, then it is appropriate. Otherwise, it is not useful.

"There has been no real new knowledge (that is, discoveries) in science over the last fifty years. Much has been learned about details that were not known. However, the basic understanding in the quantum physics field has not changed. Science needs to catch up to the whole idea of how consciousness views the reality. Once this occurs, shifts and changes in spiritual thinking will occur as well. Although this process has begun, much more is needed.*

"Rather than using doom and gloom as a reason to change, look upon your own desire *to create change as the reason to change. Some will wake up one day and decide they will do something different. So can you. You do not need a crisis in order to change."*

What should we do if we find ourselves surrounded by persons filled with doom and gloom?

"Champion their rights to have those feelings. There is no need for resistance in the evolved soul. Evolved souls want their friends to be happy. If doom and gloom is their choice, they may have it. Give up the need to be right, the need to know, to feel above or superior to others.

"You are moving to a place where you are a perfected one. If they want doom and gloom that is their choice. They will find others who share that preference. If you do not wish for that there is no threat to you, as you will find evolved souls who want to share in what you desire."

**What I believe Sanat Kumara was referring to is the growth and expansion of manifestation teachings such as the film *The Secret* and others.

What if we are in fear and want to hoard? Should we just ignore our feelings?

"Fear is unnecessary. Go back to basics and make sure you are practicing the MerKaBa and developing your Higher Self connection. Then we ask that you check in with your Higher Self. We ask you to remember the changes that were predicted at the end of year 2000, called Y2K.

"Remember when you were asked to prepare for computers malfunctioning, stores shutting down, and all kinds of chaos? Many feared this. Maureen asked her Higher Self what she should do and was told, Nothing. She asked, Should I set aside water? *The answer was* no. I do not need to? *Again:* No. *Furthermore if your Higher Self tells you not to hoard water, it means the water will be provided for you. Do not manage your system with your ego or fear.*

"Do this from a point of surrender where you have joined with God, making God's will your will. In this way there is no conflict and you will always be guided to go where you need to go or be."

Is protection really needed? Do we need to seek protection daily?

"If you do not have a MerKaBa, then yes, you should seek protection. An activated MerKaBa does not require protection."

How should we call upon Archangel Michael for protection?

"Archangel Michael is the original sponsor of the MerKaBa on this planet. Not many know this.* Archangel Michael is here to provide protection if you need protection. However, understand that he had the wisdom to teach mankind the MerKaBa so they could become their fifth-dimensional selves and not need his protection. For people who do not know what to do, say:

'Archangel Michael, help me, help me, help me!

Help me clear my fear.

Do I need to be afraid? Do I need to do something?'

Maybe the fear is leading you to an important action."

Is there a way to seek out others who are like-minded?

"We encourage you to create study groups. Support one another in your soul's growth. Allow others to be who they need to be."

---

*In case you missed it, it was written about in the dedication and in chapter 1.

How can someone validate experiences when having thoughts like, *Am I making this up?* or, *This cannot be real.*

"The very act of the ego trying to validate experiences will negate them. We ask you to step back from trying to make things happen, including validating your experiences, and instead allow them to delight and surprise you. When an experience occurs you have a choice. You may consider the possibility that you are imagining things, or you could accept the possibility that you are not making it up and that it is real. We say do both. This way you offer no resistance to the reality or yourself.

"Then ask your Angels and guides to give you additional information about the experience. It may come in the form of synchronicity. It may come through understanding its purpose and meaning, and what is really happening. Often understanding grows through the Higher Self educating the individual. Each experience that is explained by the Higher Self provides a basis of understanding for the next experience. In this way the Higher Self shows the way."

How do multiple realities, alternate realities, and interdimensionality integrate with religious doctrine?

"Religious doctrine is invented by man. So, too, are multiple versions of realities. They are ways to understand consciousness in form. The body vibrates in agreement with what it needs. When it no longer needs the religious dogma, it will move on to other possibilities. As mass consciousness changes the ability to comprehend greater and greater expanses of awareness, it increases the likelihood of understanding multiple versions of the reality and letting go of the need for doctrine to dictate the reality."

Will past-life regression help us move toward Ascension?

"We are quite concerned about individuals seeking past-life regression information. There is a reason that many who seek do not receive past-life information. They then decide they must take a class and learn more. We say to you that their information is locked. Why would they have a past life locked from them? Our answer is that they have already completed their work on Earth and are back as helpers or way-showers. They do not need to open their records as their Ascension is already assured. They are not here to earn Ascension, as they are already complete. Instead, these way-showers can ask, 'What am I to do here?'

"There are people who will benefit from regression work. However, if your regression session turns up empty, count your blessings! Do not assume there is something wrong with you. Do not go into ego and reevaluate the situation. Decide to let go of your need to know and move on to the next moment. If you have gone to a reputable person and nothing comes up, it most likely means your records are locked. If you were to access them, it would be a disadvantage. It is like a trust fund—secure, but not available now."

What is the most benevolent outcome we can hold for Mother Earth as a vision in our consciousness?
"See the Garden of Paradise. Do not judge when a species dies. Do not judge when something in nature goes awry. See mankind as being part of the solution in ways that support co-creation of all.

"In each moment be guided by your Higher Self. If you walk down the street and are guided to pick up a piece of garbage, do it because you can. If you are led to a homeless person who asks for money, your Higher Self knows if it will be beneficial to give a gift at that time. Respond with your Higher Self accordingly. Change your own inner consciousness and all else will follow."

Is there a way to change the popular belief that our governments are secretive and self-serving?
"Pray that each and every government official worldwide will be guided by legions of Angels, his own Higher Self, and beings of light. Do this once a day."

This is the end of the channeled question-and-answer session.

Contracts with the Universe (Advanced Contracts)

In the polarity world of form you do not always tend to work in a spontaneous environment. The more you create in the reality, the more you will desire to create. Your *desire* to create is the inspiration to create bigger plans, ideas, and concepts. Fifth dimension is the world of infinite manifestation.

By contrast, in the three-dimensional world of form, manifestation takes time. You are the process. So part of the process of the contract is to examine all the aspects, subsets, and layers of the creation as it becomes manifest, rather than going right to the full expression. In the fifth-dimensional world of instant manifestation, if you wanted to have a son you would receive a completely grown son. You would miss all the fun of enjoying him as a baby, watching him evolve, participating in the process, and seeing him grow and become an adult man. Part of the pleasure that we give to ourselves (and God) in our creation work as co-creators is that we get to examine all the steps of the creation. This is very **fractal-like**◈.

Have you ever heard that a person's birth experience is just like her life experience? If she has a difficult time in the final hours of her birth, she could have a difficult time in her life when she gets close to completing something. I have seen this consistently. The approach we use to set things in motion at birth becomes a template and a form of a contract.

When we are ready for something new, this template supports us by giving us something familiar to relate to with our new experience. Of course, at the end of the day the template tends to be the messenger, and the content is the echo of the message. We use this methodology to create what we know—until we decide it is time to create something new and different. Thus we create familiar patterns that come into play through circumstances that unfold. We are in agreement as to what action might be taken. In other words, we agree to do new things in old and familiar ways until we are completely able to adopt new ways.

Default Template

Our default template shows us the way. We continue to behave in a certain way until we decide we would like to do something different. If we decide to change, we consciously look at an old situation while creating a *new* template. When we learn something new from a teacher, such as how to stop reacting to people and situations in a familiar negative way, we create our new template for staying in joy, and then we can select new and different experiences to use it more and more. This allows us to shift from our original construct so we break the pattern and create something new. Our contract, which was the original construct, encompasses a much larger picture. In most cases it is fractal-like, and, like a hologram, has larger and smaller versions of the same picture encoded in it.

There are also circumstances where you could deviate from that. When you deviate, what you get is variation on a theme. We find this in classical music. For example, think of Beethoven's Fifth (Symphony No. 5 in C Minor, Op. 67): "Ta ta ta TAAA." Even without annotated music you can *hear* that sound by reading my simple phonetic representation. This series of related notes repeats throughout the symphony featuring various instruments in a variety of tempos. The symphony helps us understand the pleasure of "working a theme" or "way of being." You no longer need to feel bad about doing the same thing over and over again with great variety.

Sacred Symmetry and Contracts

Because we are adding these variations, I believe that everything in creation is not an exact version of sacred geometry. If the manifestation is in perfect alignment with the original plan, then it is a perfect expression of sacred geometry; but if it is not, then it could be something different. This is the difference between a natural course and its variations. We have big contracts that we have agreed to and we do not worry about the details. We let the details take care of themselves.

We might set up smaller contracts as we go along. There are other contracts that we get into and later decide that we cannot proceed as we thought we could. As we examine them, we recognize that something has happened, some flaw or deviation. In the reality we might experience it as deciding not to do something we had signed up to do. It is no longer in our range of satisfying experiences and we do not want to proceed. In biology we would refer to it as a spontaneous permutation of the DNA or cell structures. Deciding you cannot proceed is akin to the nature metaphor where the plant aborts, or dies. When some kind of flaw occurs and adaptability fails we can choose a way out.

When we arrange our contracts we have circumstances in which we decide to partake. As we discover and explore circumstances, there are times when we decide we want to pursue a different path. We may decide to meet up further down the road in this direction. You might compare it to telling a hiking friend, "I will take this other route and meet you further along the path."

Other levels of contracts are the more spontaneous contracts that do not seem to fit the mold. Some of you will find your spontaneous contracts shift and evolve very quickly. As the world shifts and evolves, situations change and people need to change their contracts. Sometimes we volunteer to change contracts; sometimes we are conscripted to change contracts. I believe we are in a zone where our contracts are constantly being renegotiated. This is because we are in a cycle where we are evolving back to God. We are on the "in breath" of God. As we undo, clean up, and clear out so much of our history and the miscreation, what we are going to end up with provides many opportunities to change our contracts and take big, big leaps.

Why Do I Keep
Forgetting Important Things?

We covered this question earlier with reverse déjà vu. Yet many of my workshop participants ask this question. What you are forgetting is something that really does not serve you to know. You are allowing for the reformat of your version of the reality. The old templates are fading and the new ones are replacing them. These are dramatically different compared to those of the past.

In another kind of experience, you may think you are forgetting important things when in reality you are moving inter-dimensionally. The easy solution is to ask your Higher Self, *What is going on?* In that way you give yourself the opportunity to hear the whole story.

Right now, without your Higher Self connection providing information, your ego is reframing everything in terms of what it (or mass consciousness) wants you to believe. Ego deliberately takes experiences and puts them into a third-dimensional construct. The bottom line is you did indeed remember correctly, but your mind is trying to make your *memory* wrong, instead of accepting the multiple experiences of your reality. So open up to possibilities. The fastest way this can occur is to open up your heart, which will enable your Higher Self to communicate more clearly.

Ego wants to show the way and be in control. However, if you allow your Higher Self to show you what you need to know, you will be using the part of you that is already plugged into God. Your Higher Self consciousness provides the information instantly. It has the active ability to find answers, just as when you do a search on the Internet. Memory is an ego-based construct. Higher Self is *not* reliant on the past (memory) but the ever-present *now*. Seek to activate your Higher Self connection to know what you need to know, when you need to know it.

Multiple Versions of the Reality

There are three major components to these versions of the reality. There are multiple versions of planet Earth: The first version is the "crash and burn" version, the second one is an Ascension portal, and the third is a new polarity experiment in which you may request to participate.

Because we are using multiple versions of the reality, we can literally transform all of darkness into light. We no longer need to do it step-by-step, correcting each mistake. Instead, by creating from the highest and best choice of any set of possibilities in any given moment, we are experiencing multiple versions simultaneously, which are either God or not-God—one toward the light, one toward the dark. Although version two, the Ascension portal, technically contains version one within it, version one is not really recognized as part of version two's scenario. Because in version two, out of both versions being experienced, only version two is ultimately recorded.

Version One

Version one is the sacrificial lamb, as it is a duplicate (clone) of version two, but with a crash-and-burn outcome. Did you see the 2006 movie *The Prestige*? In a particularly stunning discovery, a magician uncovers a cloning machine. Then in his magic act he drops into a water tank and deliberately drowns himself while a clone of him appears behind a curtain a few seconds later. The movie is filled with macabre twists and turns but does an amazing job of presenting a facsimile of the possibility of being able to clone oneself immediately before dying, albeit in the film's case through special effects and technology. However, it does present an ethical issue (suicide) that I am not commenting on here since my worldview includes three worlds.

The implications are that although we know version one of the reality is set up to allow those who are intent upon destroying the world to have their way, it will not matter because there is another (true) version of the reality where that will not happen. By focusing on the most evolved version of the earth imaginable, you will ensure you will not be part of version one.

In version one, the crash-and-burn version, Earth will follow a course to destruction. It is an interesting scenario, which allows the free will of those determined to pursue greed and materialism to get what they created. Even if you are in this version (and that is *not* likely), you are probably not fully participating and your existence will become less and less real. If this feels like your current reality, choose to shift your focus to version two. There is likely a version of you already there, working its way through the Ascension energy.

We have already moved into version two. There is still some overlap from the crash-and-burn scenario, but we are well on our way to creating Heaven on Earth. Professional trance channel and prolific author Robert Shapiro echoes this sentiment in "ET Contact Update: A Heart-Opening Encounter" in the January 2020 issue of the *Sedona Journal of Emergence!*

Version Two

Version two is Earth and her Ascension. You are here. What I have been shown is that Mother Earth is taking her time making this Ascension. She wants as many individuals as possible to be able to become ascended beings in their three-dimensional bodies, so that when she becomes ascended, human beings are already there waiting for her.

At the end of this cycle version two becomes the beloved choice of mankind, which then allows Earth to make her Ascension gracefully, without massive harm or destruction to mankind. Version two is the Ascension portal where Mother Earth and all her inhabitants will move into a fifth-dimensional expression, and the great golden age that was predicted appears. We are already in the early stages of that.

Version Three

Once it became clear that Earth's experiment was successful, there was an immediate appeal to the Council of Light that requested the opportunity for a new Earth to continue the polarity experience, but to allow for a change in the rules. Version three is the version of Earth where there will be a *new* polarity game and the rules are different from the current rules. For instance, the elemental kingdom has appealed for (and won) the right to have a say in the way things work. In version three you will not be able to just cut down a tree; you will have to ask permission or have some sort of ceremony. Nature will be treated with greater reverence. Version three is a place where beings incarnate because they desire the polarity experience. However, compared to the version of Earth in which we are currently involved, beings in version three would not have the ability to go as deeply into pain and suffering. Those who are not yet ready to embody their full mastery will have the opportunity to evolve here.

Wild Walk-Ins

I believe that people are time traveling. I have been reminding students over and over that individuals are leapfrogging over themselves as **walk-ins**◈. This jumping ahead is easier than trying to learn everything! It is a much faster way of stepping away from polarity experience. The information I received from my guides is that when a person has a walk-in experience, the individual who leaves will go to school in the etheric realms and a more evolved version of the same being will move into that individual's place. Most walk-in experiences are higher versions of you. Who has a better right to walk-in to your body than you?

Other Versions of You

I believe that once a being becomes fifth-dimensional, any experience gained with the polarity and scarcity game loses its appeal. I prefer to bring in fifth-dimensional energies rather than stepping up the polarity party. We are changing the way we are experiencing life and not repeating the past.

In addition, I have seen multiple versions of the same people on the planet at the same time. If you are playing a game of chess, you are all the white pieces. You are the white rook and the white king, the white knight and the white pawns—twelve players in all. Many highly evolved beings have multiple versions of themselves here on the planet at this very moment.

Consider this passage from the book *Return of the Revolutionaries,* by practicing physician and reincarnation researcher Walter Semkiw:

> Perhaps the most dramatic example of Ahtun Re's abilities involves the case of Neale Donald Walsch, author of the *Conversations with God* series. When I asked Ahtun Re who Mr. Walsch had been in Revolutionary times, he told me that Mr. Walsch was a minister in Boston, a freemason, who was friends with Abigail Adams. Ahtun Re told me the minister's name was Reverend Walter. Though this minister is not featured in any history book that I know of, I was able to find Reverend William Walter through a genealogical society, and his facial features, personality traits, and interests matched those of Mr. Walsch. When this information was presented to Mr. Walsch, he resonated with it and agreed to be featured in my book as the reincarnation of Reverend William Walter.[1]

One of my clients approached Dr. Semkiw after his presentation in Seattle and told him that a teacher she knew (referring to me) said there is more than one version of a person in embodiment at a time. For example, that might mean that there is more than one Martha Washington. She asked if he had any comments on that.

He reported to her that indeed he felt that this idea was accurate, as he believed he had met another version of himself in Japan. After giving a lecture he was approached by a medical doctor from India. They each felt an instant familiarity with the other's work. Dr. Semkiw discovered this other doctor had been pursuing a similar but separate line of research. This was a line of research Dr. Semkiw previously followed, but had given it up as his current work took precedence. He has gone on to write several more books on his research into reincarnation.

In another dramatic example, two women with the same first name of Bonnie and last names beginning with the letter T wrote to me for Akashic Records readings in the same week. Later they both signed up for the same Flower of Life workshop in Atlanta. In class we discovered they had the same birthday and year. One woman was Caucasian and the other African American. They both wanted to sponsor me in Atlanta for a return class so we agreed to split it between them, and I would teach one class at each location. One of the women reported that a few months later she was on a flight to Mexico City. Looking across the aisle, she saw the other Bonnie at the opposite window. Interestingly, they were both in first-class seating.

There are significant souls who have come onto this planet and embodied in many bodies in order to be part of the consciousness shift. Thus, there really could be two of a famous person. If you were this masterful being, would you put all of your essence into *one* person expecting everything to work out? Hardly! Their place is purposeful and important, and so is yours. As these individuals shift and get into position, they may develop unique skills (or perhaps "remember them" is a more accurate phrase) and become highly specialized. They will often come together to create (remember) a modality or tool for humanity.

Occasionally a walk-in is the oversoul of the individual, in much the same way as the above circumstances we described. The oversoul is a more finely tuned essential energy that can anchor in more and more of the transformational energy that is part of our new Earth.

Bridge of Light

Volunteers from the Gridworkers Union worked with the Hathors to build a complex bridge of light on the planet to open a direct portal from Venus for the Hathors. This occurred around the time of the three summer eclipses of 2009. This group of gridworkers was asked to focus on one of four major areas on the earth, with each area carrying a specific energy type. With the group's participation, the Hathors then built a pyramid of light that is used as a portal or bridge between here and their home planet—Earth to Venus. Many of the individuals received significant messages, experiences, and tangible gifts as a direct result of this project. You can, too. I now understand the proof that this bridge is active in those pictures where Sanat Kumara's energy is present. Any photos you have taken with this striking appearance are an indication this energy is working with you.

Invite the Hathors into your world: Ask them to join you and assist you in becoming the most loving being possible. Then offer yourself in service to the Hathors by being their agent in the physical and moving their energy through you. You will be amazed at how this will improve your life.

Memo from the Divine Mother

In the summer of 2009, the planet was bathed in the energy of the balanced female for both men and women. There was a need for a new female energy on the planet. This new energy would replace all the misuses of the Divine Feminine.* Even my book editor—who is not prone to messages—was told in the shower, *The Divine Feminine wants to speak with Maureen!* He doubted it and asked his Higher Self if that message was real. She answered, *Yes.* (His Higher Self is a woman.)

When my boys were young I prayed daily for the mantle of the Divine Mother because I was so worried that I wouldn't do a good enough job as a single mom. Maybe I would have, but at that time I didn't want to take any chances. Earlier in this decade, after my own sons were grown, the permanent flame of the mantle of the Divine Mother had been bestowed upon me.

When my assistant relayed my editor's message to me, it was not a complete surprise; my Sacred Journey group had been working with these very same energies in Egypt. I had been told that this new energy would finally be installed into the reality by the end of September 2009. These energies would make it possible for all of humanity to embrace their femininity in a balanced way. Here is a note from my journal dated October 2, 2009:

---

*This topic is explored fully in my book *Waking Up in 5D*.

Last night I couldn't sleep. I was so excited, like a child before her first trip to the amusement park. One of the Egypt participants, Mark, who had been having pain in his shoulder, had asked if this pain was about the work we did at Isis Temple on Phylae Island, and I said it was. Mark could see the image and described it to me. I showed him the great winged disk [see figure 14.2] and his response was, "Yes, that is it!" He (Mark) said he was told in a channeling that when he released this device its purpose was to "anchor in the Divine Feminine for all of humanity." I began to realize that my excitement had to do with my soul's joy at these impending events. My guides came in to further clarify Mark's experience and said, This (Mark's message above) we say is true. Claim connection to this Divine Feminine energy.

Figure 14.2. The great winged sun disk is a symbol associated with divinity, royalty, and power. It is said to confer protection against evil.

Here is the rest of her message, delivered through me while I was in Egypt:

"We are here for you. Give yourself permission to be the Divine Feminine in action daily.

"Take time daily to scribe your thoughts. Invite the true Divine Feminine to speak through you daily.

"Do it like this:

"I ask that the Divine Feminine speak through me this day. I ask permission for the Divine Feminine to reside here, in the physical, in my body. Let all aspects of the Divine Feminine be anchored here in my body so that I am expressing the fullness of the Divine Feminine through me this day.

"Do this prayer daily. Do it three times in a row, spoken out loud. Conclude with:

"I ask this for myself and for all of humanity.

"Your work with the Divine Feminine was to anchor this very energy into the physical, which you have done.

"Your ceremony at Phylae in the Temple of Isis is significant. You anchored into this reality the great winged disk that represents balance of both male and female. Mark (Egypt participant) carried this device into the physical, as he was a priestess in the sacred temple here in Egypt. He volunteered for this job because of his connection here. You anchored the energy into this crystal with your work earlier.* He threw it into the water after the removal and launched the device (winged disk) spreading this energy to the entire planet through the river Nile.

"Everywhere on the planet the role of the Divine Feminine is changing. Your job is to anchor in this energy through your prayer."

I asked, *Should this message go out to the world?*
The Divine Feminine responded,

"Yes, in the Beyond the Flower of Life *book. This message must be treated with utmost respect.*

"Earlier we came through you when you asked about the Sacred Sex Magic of Isis. The time has come for this magic to be reinitiated on the planet. When you were asked, we spoke through you to explain that the Divine Feminine is to initiate women into sacred sex. They are to learn this and then teach it to their beloved partners. Male impotence on Earth represents the dysfunction of males on the planet who have been emasculated by women and then expected to perform in bed."

I asked, "What is to be done?"

---

*Maureen had been given a crystal that had been mined in the Arctic Circle for the purpose of serving the highest good. She connected it to her alpha and omega crystal and her other crystals that carry special programming for the planet. This crystal was given to Mark before the ceremony in Isis Temple so that he would have it to throw into the Nile at the conclusion of the ceremony.

"Men and women everywhere must learn to embody the Divine Feminine. Only then will this torture stop."

Michael's Message on Light and Dark

While in Paris following my sister's funeral, I came up from the Paris Metro heading to Notre Dame and saw a magnificent mural of Archangel Michael wielding his mighty sword, artfully assembled into the tiled wall. It was more than twelve feet tall. You may recall that he is the sponsor of this book and of the MerKaBa.

At that moment in the Metro Archangel Michael showed me the balance of light and dark. It was a huge "aha" moment for me. What he explained is that we no longer have to see an equal amount of darkness as holding the balance for the light. He went on to provide an example: All we need is the equivalent of a homeopathic dose of darkness. That small amount will be able to maintain balance with the light, and allow the light to permeate our reality.

I leave you with this wonderful message of hope for yourself and for our planet.

Notes

1. History of the MerKaBa and Important Notes for Your Practice

1. "The Divine Throne-Chariot," The Dead Sea Scroll Collection, The Gnostic Society Library (online).
2. James Breasted, *The Dawn of Consciousness* (CreateSpace Independent Publishing Platform, 2017), 71.
3. Maureen J. St. Germain, *Waking Up in 5D: A Practical Guide to Multidimensional Transformation* (Rochester, Vt.: Bear & Company, 2017).

2. New Tools for Learning and Practicing Unconditional Love

1. Hiroshi Motoyama, *Karma and Reincarnation* (London: Judy Piatkus Publishers, 1992), 52.
2. Tony Stubbs, *An Ascension Handbook: Channeled Material by Serapis* (Lithia Springs, Ga.: World Tree Press, 2009), 93.
3. Susan Sheppard, illustrations by Toni Taylor, *The Phoenix Cards: Reading and Interpreting Past-Life Influences with the Phoenix Deck* (Rochester, Vt.: Destiny Books, 1990).

3. Toning, Chants, and Exercises to Open Your Heart

1. Wayne Dyer, *Getting in the Gap: Making Conscious Contact with God through Meditation* (Carlsbad, Calif.: Hay House, Inc., 2014).
2. Tom Kenyon and Virginia Essene, *The Hathor Material* (Santa Clara, Calif.: S E E Pub, 1996), 126–29.
3. Kenyon and Essene, *Hathor Material,* 126.
4. Mark L. Prophet and Elizabeth Clare Prophet, *The Masters and Their Retreats* (Gardiner, Mont.: Summit University Press, 2003), 158.

5. Kenyon and Essene, *Hathor Material,* 127.

6. Kenyon and Essene, *Hathor Material,* 127.

7. J. J. Hurtak, *The Book of Knowledge: The Keys of Enoch* (Lowell, Mass.: Academy of Future Science, 2009).

8. Robert Gass, *Chanting: Discovering Spirit in Sound* (Portland, Ore.: Broadway Books, 1999).

9. Phil Catalfo, "Kirtan 101: Can You Say 'Om Namah Shivaya'?" *Yoga Journal* (online), August 28, 2007.

4. Initiating Contact
with Your Higher Self

1. Maureen St. Germain, *Reweaving the Fabric of Your Reality: Self-Study Guide for Personal Transformation* (Alpharetta, Ga.: Phoenix Rising Publishing, 2006).

8. Surrogate MerKaBas:
Both Useful and Destructive

1. Jonathan Cott, *The Search for Omm Sety: A True Story of Eternal Love— and One Woman's Voyage through the Ages* (New York: Grand Central Publishing, 1989), 271.

10. Clearing Fear with Dolphins,
Whales, and AroMandalas

1. Patricia Cota-Robles, "An Opportunity to Help," Era of Peace Newsletter, 2006.

2. Leonard G. Horowitz, *DNA: Pirates of the Sacred Spiral* (Epub: Tetrahedron/Elsevier, 2004).

3. Joan Ocean, *Dolphins into the Future* (Kealakekua, Hawaii: Dolphin Connection, 1997).

4. Lynn Grabhorn, *Dear God, What's Happening to Us?: Halting Eons of Manipulation* (Charlottesville, Va.: Hampton Roads, 2003).

11. Working with Earth's Energy Systems

1. Bruce Cathie, *The Energy Grid: Harmonic 695: The Pulse of the Universe [The Investigation into the World Energy Grid]* (Kempton, Ill.: Adventures Unlimited Press, 1997).

13. Christ Consciousness Grid

1. Maureen J. St. Germain, *Be a Genie: Create Love, Success, and Happiness* (New York, N.Y.: Rising Phoenix Publishing, 2013).

14. Maintaining Balance
and Staying Connected

1. Walter Semkiw, *Return of the Revolutionaries: The Case for Reincarnation and Soul Groups Reunited* (Charlottesville, Va.: Hampton Roads, 2003).

Glossary

Akashic Records: *Akasha* means sky in Sanskrit. The term *Akashic Records* was popularized by Madame Blavatsky, founder of the theosophy movement, as well as Edgar Cayce, American seer and mystic. When Cayce was asked, in a trance, where his information was coming from, he channeled that it came from the Book of Life (referred to in the Old Testament) and later explained the Book of Life as the same as the Akashic Records. In *Opening the Akashic Records,* Maureen St. Germain channels this message from the Keepers of the Gates of Akasha:

> *"The idea of Akash or Akasha is often used to refer to anything unusual in the vast domain of the universe. The actual Akashic Records are a vibratory location that stores possible futures, probable futures, the present, and the past. The availability of information in the Akashic Records is to assist humans in their return home to God. It is to help you acquaint yourself with the bigger picture of life among the planetary systems."*

ankh: A device shaped like a cross with a loop for the top. It has multiple spiritual contexts and was used by Ancient Egyptians in spiritual ceremony.

Ascension: The ritual whereby the soul reunites with the spirit of Source, creating the perfected human. This is the first attempt for humans to ascend without death.

astral plane: The astral plane is a vibrational part of the lower fourth dimension. Fourth dimension is a polarity plane of existence where energies vortex upward (high fourth) or downward (lower fourth) It is a plane of seduction and challenging to move away from. Because the astral plane has been muddied by impure human thoughts and feelings, the term astral is often used in a negative context to refer to that which is impure.

Bhagavad Gita: A highly regarded Hindu spiritual text telling the story of Arjuna and Lord Krishna. It is part of the larger epic the Mahabharata.

bhajan: Sacred music from India where the songs are sung in unison, saying sacred prayers.

Christed: A person earns this title (like one might earn the title of *general* in the military) by self-mastery through the seven rays and balance through the threefold flame of the heart (Love, Wisdom, and Power) along with achieving mastery of the four lower bodies, becoming a master like the Christ, Buddhas, or Muhammad.

cosmic latticework: A network of energy lines forming a grid around the planet. The Christ Consciousness Grid is a well-known cosmic latticework.

Dissolving Fear of Lack Grid: A grid that was created by the gridworkers to assist humanity through upheaval and changes so that people do not create more fear.

double square: This is two squares side by side, and has been used to define the space within the King's Chamber of the Great Pyramid.

elemental: A fourth-dimensional being or energy that may interact with third dimension. Elementals do not have free will and may operate in individuals, such as the body elemental; take the form of large energies, such as the elementals of earth, air, fire, or water; or operate singularly as in the elementals of fire (salamanders), earth (gnomes, elves, fairies), air (sylphs), and water (undines).

elemental kingdom: The seen and unseen forces that animate the flowers, plants, trees, soil, sand, rocks, stones, crystals. Although humans also have a body elemental, it is not quite the same, and you may work with your body elemental in a very personal way. Your body elemental is equivalent to an engineer, running the autonomous systems, and does not have free will. See also **elemental** above.

Elohim: Creation Beings who came out of Source (God). They are the builders of form mentioned in the first verse of the Bible, also referred to as the morning stars. They hold the highest concentration and vibration of light that we can comprehend. They oversee the four elements of earth, air, fire, and water.

fifth-dimensional: A category of vibration without polarity. It is the equivalent of what traditional religions call heavenly.

fractal-like: Fractals are a term invented by mathematician Benoit Mandelbrot, who created the term referring to the resulting images created from massive iterations of fractions representing irrational numbers. Fractal images have a quality of appearing self-referencing, even though they come from irrational (not resolvable) numbers.

implants: Specifically refers to alien implants that may be positive and/or negative in influence.

Lord Metatron: Overseer of the Angelic realm, he burst forth from God, yet is not God. He sits at the right hand of God, and stands between creation and the void.

perfection suit: A term I created to help you understand that your Ascended Master body will be the equivalent of perfection.

pranic tube: An eighteen inch or wider cylinder-like tube that resembles a florescent light bulb, running from above your crown chakra (about five inches above your head) to five inches below your feet.

rebirthing: A specialized healing modality created by Leonard Orr to facilitate out-of-body spiritual experiences that advance the consciousness of the individual.

seed groups of humanity: According to esoteric tradition, there are seven primary seed groups, known as the seven root races. The earliest root races achieved Ascension before the fall of Adam and Eve. It was during the fourth root race that incarnated on Lemuria that the perversions of free will occurred.

Seichim Reiki: A modified form of Reiki that utilizes a high vibrational energy and heals on a deeper level.

star-tetrahedron: Two tetrahedrons nested midway to produce a six-pointed three-dimensional figure.

stellated dodecahedron: A regular polyhedron with twelve pentagonal faces, which have an elevated point in the center connected to the intersection of each edge. Each face looks like the Chrysler symbol.

toroidal/torus: A torus vortex is an expression of dynamic life force whether in climate, ocean currents, chemistry, or many other vitally charged energy forms. Its shape can have many variations depending on the medium in which it exists. For example, a smoke ring in air or a bubble ring in water both form the toroidal shape of a donut. And yet an apple, pinecone, or barrel cactus are torus forms but are more overtly spherical.

Plants and trees can display the same energy flow process, yet exhibit a wide variety of shapes and sizes. Hurricanes, tornadoes, magnetic fields around planets and stars, and whole galaxies themselves can be toroidal energy systems. Since the study of sacred geometry has observed this dynamic shape to be a consistent flow form in the quantum realm, we can postulate that atomic structures and systems are also made of the same dynamic form. Physicists who witness this energy form indicate that, for the most part, its influence is not in the visible realm.

undines: Commonly referring to the elementals of water. See **elemental** above.

Vedic system of the seven rays: An organizing system of wisdom, law, and thought initially taught in the Western world by theosophy and later by the "I Am" movement. It is defined by color, as well as Ascended Masters, and location (i.e., Mt. Shasta).

Violet Flame: The seventh-ray energy of transmutation and forgiveness, established by the Ascended Master St. Germain, to assist humanity on their return path to Source.

walk-ins: Individual souls who have desired death or had near-death experiences and trade places with another soul willing to take on the physical body position in order to continue a mission. A walk-in is always by agreement.

Index

Page numbers in *italic type* refer to illustrations.